# Self-Determination in the Post-9/11 Era

I0127916

This book discusses the increasing tendency in certain government quarters to incorporate struggles by peoples for their self-determination into the wider anti-terrorist agenda of the post-9/11 era. This tendency distorts the laws of armed conflict and of peace alike. As inter-state anti-terrorist co-operation becomes more extensive, the transaction costs of international peace and security between states increase. Modes of domestic state governance are left increasingly to the vagaries of inter-state non-interference in the domestic affairs of each other. The 'war on terror' and an increasingly strict, domestic state law-and-order approach to silence political opponents increases the dangers for civilians, eliminates rights and generates suspect communities. At the same time, public institutions and private corporations are harnessed into the mechanics of a broad project of prevention and control.

Distinctively, the book considers the impact of the recent 'war on terror' on the politics of the self-determination of peoples. It draws together issues related to governmental forceful action, an increasing intolerance towards non-state violent acts, the content of international and regional codifications, expansions in state discretion, the encroachment of surveillance powers and the interaction and overlap between intelligence and law enforcement agencies.

*Self-Determination in the Post-9/11 Era* will be of interest to students and scholars of public international law, criminology, comparative criminal justice, terrorism and national security, politics, international relations, human rights, governance and public policy.

**Elizabeth Chadwick** is Reader in War Law at Nottingham Trent University, UK.

# Routledge Research in International Law

Available:

**International Law and the Third World**
Reshaping Justice
*Richard Falk, Balakrishnan Rajagopal and Jacqueline Stevens (eds)*

**International Legal Theory**
Essays and Engagements, 1966–2006
*Nicholas Onuf*

**The Problem of Enforcement in International Law**
Countermeasures, the Non-Injured State and the Idea of
International Community
*Elena Katselli Proukaki*

**International Economic Actors and Human Rights**
*Adam McBeth*

**The Law of Consular Access**
A Documentary Guide
*John Quigley, William J. Aceves and Adele Shank*

**State Accountability under International Law**
Holding States Accountable for a Breach of Jus Cogens Norms
*Lisa Yarwood*

**International Organisations and the Idea of Autonomy**
Institutional Independence in the International Legal Order
*Nigel D. White and Richard Collins (eds)*

**Self-Determination in the Post-9/11 Era**
*Elizabeth Chadwick*

Forthcoming titles in this series include:

**The Law on the Use of Force**
A Feminist Analysis
*Gina Heathcote*

**International Law in a Multipolar World**
*Matthew Happold (ed.)*

**International Law, Regulation and Resistance**
Critical Spaces
*Zoe Pearson*

**Participants in the International Legal System**
Multiple Perspectives on Non-State Actors in International Law
*Jean d'Aspremont*

**Sovereignty and Jurisdiction in the Airspace and Outer Space**
Legal Criteria for Spatial Delimitation
*Gbenga Oduntan*

**The ICJ and the Development of International Law**
The Lasting Impact of the Corfu Channel Case
*Karine Bannelier, Théodore Christakis and Sarah Heathcote (eds)*

# Self-Determination in the Post-9/11 Era

Elizabeth Chadwick

Routledge
Taylor & Francis Group

LONDON AND NEW YORK

First published 2011
by Routledge
2 Park Square, Milton Park, Abingdon, Oxon OX14 4RN

Simultaneously published in the USA and Canada
by Routledge
711 Third Avenue, New York, NY 10017

*Routledge is an imprint of the Taylor & Francis Group, an informa business*

First issued in paperback 2013

*British Library Cataloguing in Publication Data*
A catalogue record for this book is available from the British Library

*Library of Congress Cataloguing in Publication Data*
Chadwick, E. (Elizabeth)
  Self-determination in the post-9/11 era / Elizabeth Chadwick.
    p. cm.
  Includes index.
  ISBN 978-0-415-55004-8
  1. Self-determination, National.   2. Terrorism–Prevention–Law and
legislation.   I. Title.
  KZ1269.C48 2011
  341.6–dc22

                                                        2010043823

ISBN13: 978-0-415-55004-8 (hbk)
ISBN13: 978-0-203-81839-8 (ebk)
ISBN13: 978-0-415-85978-3 (pbk)
Typeset in 10/12pt Garamond
by Graphicraft Limited, Hong Kong

'Your gracious lordship, I'm your man-at-arms
Appointed to stand sentry by the hat.
I caught this man here in the very act,
Failing to show the hat all due respect.
When I arrested him, as you had ordered,
The people tried to set him free by force.'

(Freisshardt, *William Tell*, Act III, Scene 3)

# Contents

# Preface and acknowledgements

This monograph concerns the contemporary position occupied in the world today by the principle of the self-determination of peoples. For many decades, self-determination has served as a social and political platform from which peoples and groups could seek to alter and improve the conditions of their daily lives and to challenge the structures of state governance. In the contemporary era, however, the struggle to achieve self-determination has become somewhat more complicated. The end of the Cold War effectively transformed the direction of many longstanding liberation struggles, while the slow encroachment of a post-9/11 anti-terrorist environment, in which the downing of four hijacked passenger airliners on the East Coast of the USA by Al Qaeda terrorist hijackers in 2001 has become emblematic, has helped to alter the scope of many individual human rights entitlements. As inter-state anti-terrorist co-operation becomes more extensive, it seems an opportune time to re-assess the impact of that co-operation on the politics of self-determination.

Having said that, it remains the case that current events are notoriously difficult to get right, in terms of selection and interpretation; one should normally await the passage of time and historical study and debate. However, the processes of societal change are all around us and never more so than during a revolutionary epoch such as the post-9/11 decade has been, in the sense of a period of time in which system change – peaceful or otherwise – has been achieved rapidly. In turn, as the transaction costs of international peace and security between states increase, modes of domestic state governance are left increasingly to the vagaries of inter-state non-interference in the domestic affairs of each other. The rapid restructuring of many social relations over the past decade thus highlights a continuing human need to secure those individual and group rights entitlements that have been left out in the cold for far too long, such as that of self-determination.

This is a simple enough proposition, but one that is contested increasingly within the vice-grip of an anti-terrorist focused approach to sovereign state rights, inasmuch as the domestic populations of entire states are being placed under the control of the special services. Strong sovereign rights generally mean that the outside world will hesitate to intervene should a state utilise excessive force against one or other sector of its own population, and the terrorist atrocities of 9/11 have only increased the scope for governments to put pressure on their domestic populations within many frameworks of ordinary life, e.g., immigration and financial matters. As more members of human networks come to experience the threat of punishment, not so much for actual violations of the law, but instead, for appearing to move towards committing a crime, it is worth recalling that 'law' alone has never been able to prevent a people from rising up against injustice, inequality and discrimination.

In that *rights* to self-determination, and to struggle for it, are likely to remain the creatures of both circumstance and opportunity, my task has been one of selection, in order to attempt to air the breadth of debate surrounding contemporary self-determination exercises. A primary emphasis is placed on the efforts being made in certain government quarters to block the politics of self-determination by integrating those politics pre-emptively within the broad post-9/11 anti-terrorist agenda. Thanks are most certainly due to my LLM students over many years, whose lively debates and international perspectives in my taught modules (on international terrorism and aggression and war crimes) have informed many aspects of this work. My thanks are also due to Nottingham Trent University for its excellent library facilities. Special thanks are due to Emeritus Professor S.R. Giles for his many constructive comments and observations, to Mr. Michael Pitt for his excellent proof-reading skills, and to my other friends and relatives, whose patience has been most appreciated. All errors are, of course, mine.

E.C., 31 August 2010

Final note: Subsequent to this monograph going to press, the following developments are of importance. Hundreds of thousands of diplomatic and military documents and cables have been published by Wikileaks. Tunisia and Egypt have experienced revolutionary upheaval involving acts of violence between government forces against the resident populations.

# List of abbreviations

*Organisations*

| | |
|---|---|
| ASEAN | Association of South East Asian Nations |
| BSEC | Black Sea Economic Co-operation |
| CIS | Commonwealth of Independent States |
| ECHR | European Convention of Human Rights |
| ECtHR | European Court of Human Rights |
| EU | European Union |
| ETA | Euskadi Ta Askatasuna (armed Basque nationalist and separatist organisation founded in 1959) |
| FATF | Financial Action Task Force on Money Laundering |
| ICC | International Criminal Court |
| ICCPR | International Covenant on Civil and Political Rights |
| ICJ | International Court of Justice |
| ICRC | International Committee of the Red Cross |
| ILA | International Law Association |
| IRA | Irish Republican Army |
| KLA | Kosovo Liberation Army |
| NATO | North Atlantic Treaty Organisation |
| OAS | Organisation of American States |
| OAU/AU | Organisation of African Unity/African Union |
| OECD | Organisation for Economic Co-operation and Development |
| OIC | Organisation of Islamic Conference |
| OPEC | Organisation of Petroleum Exporting Countries |
| PFLP | Popular Front for the Liberation of Palestine |
| PLO | Palestinian Liberation Organisation |
| RAF | Rote Armee Fraktion or Baader Meinhof |

| | |
|---|---|
| RUSI | Royal United Services Institute for Defence and Security Studies |
| UKHL | United Kingdom House of Lords |
| UNGA | United Nations General Assembly |
| UNODC | United Nations Office on Drugs and Crime |
| UNSC | United Nations Security Council |
| UNSecGen'l | United Nations Secretary General |
| USC | United States Code |
| USCS | United States Consolidated Statutes |

## Journals

| | |
|---|---|
| A.J.I.C.L. | African Journal of International and Comparative Law |
| A.J.I.L. | American Journal of International Law |
| Ann.Surv.Int'l.&Comp.L. | Annual Survey of International and Comparative Law |
| B.F.S.P. | British Foreign and State Papers |
| Br.J.Crim. | British Journal of Criminology |
| Buff.H.R.L.R. | Buffalo Human Rights Law Review |
| Cm. or Cmnd. | Command Paper (dependent on year issued) |
| Colum.J.Transnat'l.L. | Columbia Journal of Transnational Law |
| Comp.Law. | Company Lawyer |
| Crim.L.F. | Criminal Law Forum |
| Crim.L.R. | Criminal Law Review |
| C.T.S. | Consolidated Treaty Series |
| E.H.R.L.R. | European Human Rights Law Review |
| E.J.I.L. | European Journal of International Law |
| H.J.R.L. | Hague Journal on the Rule of Law |
| H.R.L.R. | Human Rights Law Review |
| ICJ Rep. | International Court of Justice Reports |
| I.C.L.Q. | International and Comparative Law Quarterly |
| I.L.M. | International Legal Materials |
| Int.J.Const.L. | International Journal of Constitutional Law |
| Int.Rel. | International Relations |
| I.R.R.C. | International Review of the Red Cross |
| J.Con.&Sec.L. | Journal of Conflict and Security Law |
| J.Fin.Cr. | Journal of Financial Crisis |
| J.Int'l.Banking.L.&Reg. | Journal of International Banking Law and Regulation |
| J.Int'l.Crim.J. | Journal of International Criminal Justice |
| J.MoneyLaund.Contr. | Journal of Money Laundering Control |
| J.Ref.St. | Journal of Refugee Studies |

| | |
|---|---|
| L.N.O.J. | League of Nations Official Journal |
| L.o.N. | League of Nations |
| L.Q.R. | Law Quarterly Review |
| Leid.J.I.L. | Leiden Journal of International Law |
| L.R.B. | London Review of Books |
| Max Planck U.N.Yb. | Max Planck Yearbook of United Nations Law |
| Mel.U.L.R. | Melbourne University Law Review |
| Minn.J.Int.L. | Minnesota Journal of International Law |
| M.R.G. International | Minority Rights Group International |
| Nottm.L.J. | Nottingham Law Journal |
| O.HallL.J. | Osgoode Hall Law Journal |
| Oxf.J.L.Stud. | Oxford Journal of Legal Studies |
| P.L. | Public Law |
| R.Hell.deDr.I. | Revue Hellenique de Droit International |
| UKTS | United Kingdom Treaty Series |
| U.N.O.J. | United Nations Official Journal |
| UNTS | United Nations Treaty Series |
| Vir.J.I.L. | Virginia Journal of International Law |
| YaleJ.Int.L. | Yale Journal of International Law |

# A quick guide to the operation of international law

Public international law contains the rules that operate to regulate state conduct. Readers who are less familiar with the mechanics of public international law should note first that there is no such thing as an 'international government'. The United Nations has no governing powers, as such. Only the UN Security Council holds 'enforcement' powers, but these powers must be exercised in accordance with the procedures outlined in Charter Chapter VII, entitled 'Action with Respect to Threats to the Peace, Breaches of the Peace, and Acts of Aggression'. At its most fundamental level, the state obligations found in public international law are grounded in the consent of states. Consent implies a high degree of political willingness between and among states to co-operate with one another. The legal source materials of public international law include treaties, international custom and general legal principles. International judicial decisions and legal commentary are based on these source materials.

The Statute of the International Court of Justice is annexed to the UN Charter and provides for the legal competence of the Court in contentious cases as follows:

> *Article 34(1):*
> Only states may be parties in cases before the Court.

> *Article 59(1):*
> The decision of the Court has no binding force except between the parties and in respect of that particular case.

As for advisory opinions on points of law, the Statute of the Court provides as follows:

> *Article 65(1):*
> The Court may give an advisory opinion on any legal question at the request of whatever body may be authorised by or in accordance with the UN Charter to make such a request.

The hierarchy of international legal source materials consulted and applied by the Court, is as follows:

> *Article 38:*
> 1. The Court, whose function is to decide in accordance with international law such disputes as are submitted to it, shall apply:
>
>     a. international conventions, whether general or particular, establishing rules expressly recognised by the contesting states;
>     b. international custom, as evidence of a general practice accepted as law;
>     c. the general principles of law recognised by civilised nations;
>     d. subject to the provisions of Article 59, judicial decisions and the teachings of the most highly qualified publicists of the various nations, as subsidiary means for the determination of rules of law.
>
> 2. This provision shall not prejudice the power of the Court to decide a case *ex aequo et bono*, if the parties agree therefore.

As recognised in ICJ Statute Article 38(1)(a) (just examined), states that have bound themselves voluntarily through treaty have expressed their willingness to comply with the terms of that treaty as a matter of international treaty obligation. Thus, the 1969 Vienna Convention on the Law of Treaties provides, in pertinent part, as follows:

> *Article 18:*
> A State is obliged to refrain from acts which would defeat the object and purpose of a treaty when:
>
> (a) it has signed the treaty . . . , until it shall have made its intention clear not to become a party to the treaty; or
> (b) it has expressed its consent to be bound by the treaty, pending the entry into force of the treaty.
>
> *Article 27:*
> A party may not invoke the provisions of its internal law as justification for its failure to perform a treaty.

The rule indicated in Vienna Convention Article 27 has its origin in the *Alabama Claims Arbitration* of 1872. In that arbitration, the view was promulgated that it was no defence to a breach of international law to rely on an 'insufficiency' in domestic state legal provision. Such insufficiency is often caused by states themselves, which fail to implement treaty obligations, where required, into domestic rules.

International customary law consists of a more informal set of rules, evidence for which is created by consistency in state practice, coupled with *opinio juris* in support of that consistency. International custom may strengthen over time sufficiently to be made express in treaty form. In contrast, treaty rules that contain 'new' law may only 'crystallise' into customary international law once states follow those rules as a matter of general obligation. Accordingly, the 1969 Vienna Convention provides as follows:

*Article 38:*
Nothing in Articles 34 to 37 precludes a rule set forth in a treaty from becoming binding upon a third state as a customary rule of international law, recognised as such.

The content of international customary law is thus somewhat less certain, e.g., regarding certain aspects of human rights law. For example, the existence of a right of peoples to their self-determination is memorialised in various international legal instruments, the most important of which is the 1945 UN Charter, but to the extent that substantive rights of self-determination rights are acknowledged in customary international law only, the legal force of those rights may remain more indeterminate.

In turn, while some international obligations need to be implemented domestically for those obligations to take effect, the localised substance of those international obligations can vary between states. Moreover, states also exhibit their mutual agreement (or not) by what they choose to do in terms of domestic state governance. Accordingly, the specific rights entitlements that a people may choose to claim when seeking their rights of self-determination can be somewhat vague in terms of legal enforceability and, as the search for a global approach to self-determination rights entitlements continues, the merits of one or other claim to possess such rights themselves can be a subject of deep controversy. What little consensus has been achieved to date is based principally on strict international guidelines, such as are found in the anti-colonialist agenda or domestic state constitutional provisions designed to ensure rights and freedoms. Demands for self-determination can also be satisfied by formulating regional or federal territorial accommodations. Most controversial of all, however, is when force is utilised to achieve, or to block, a claim to self-determination, at which point third states may react to the disturbance of the wider peace in many ways, e.g., a refusal to recognise the statehood of a new territorial entity.

It must nonetheless be kept in mind that the force brought to bear by 'law' alone to sway events at the international level can be somewhat rare. Other factors, such as local culture, tradition, politics, alliance structure, economics, etc., can prove much more persuasive when the time arrives to alter an existing status quo. Accordingly, the discussion that follows is intended to illuminate the post-9/11 status and operation of the principle of the self-determination of peoples within such alternative issue areas as international terrorism, the use of force and the contemporary meanings attributed to such common terms as 'war' and 'peace'.

# Part 1

Government is not reason; it is not eloquent; it is force. Like fire, it is a dangerous servant and a fearful master.

(attributed to George Washington)

# 1 Introduction

Struggles for self-determination have a history of defeat. Nonetheless, as a social, political and/or economic phenomenon, self-determination is continuously re-invented, whether in a new guise or country. Yet more chapters will no doubt be added to the chronology. The adding of new dimensions to the scope of self-determination means that the decade since the 9/11 terrorist attacks of 11 September 2001 offers a unique perspective from which to look back and evaluate the politics and practice surrounding self-determination and terrorism alike. This is so for many reasons. First, there exists much historic evidence for the triumph of political power over social principle. Second, modern states are the result of prior territorial conquests, so the recent legislative explosion in the breadth and scope of new 'anti-terrorist' criminal prohibitions serves not only to widen any existing gap between democratic accountability and administrative arrangement; the overly broad approach adopted for post-9/11 anti-terrorist arrangements has also greatly hampered social spontaneity. Third, the new anti-terrorist laws and policies adopted since 9/11 have resurrected the old conflation of terrorist acts with liberation tools.

Many more reasons certainly exist that justify a new look at self-determination, but it remains the case that, while one non-state entity may be viewed as heroic when struggling to attain greater rights entitlements, another such group will be regarded as 'terrorist' for employing similar tactics. This is why many of the new anti-terror laws have effected a marvellous levelling device through which to neutralise various liberationist causes, by means of the mechanics of domestic criminal law structures and procedures. The recent show of international solidarity to prevent acts of international terrorism thus not only permits governments to penetrate more deeply into the routines of individual daily life; it has facilitated a more generalised criminal law approach to the various forms and modalities of participatory activity. For example, a government can more easily suppress spontaneous or organised shows of popular antipathy to one or other state policy; such justifications as 'national security' or 'safeguarding public safety' easily transform public protest into behaviour that is contrary to law and good order.

Therefore, a prohibitory 'anti-terror' net has slowly been extended to cover not only those persons agitating against the state itself, but also those persons who collectively pursue progressive policies such as greener energy policies, animal welfare or an end to financial impunity. A brief background to contemporary notions of self-determination is now outlined, after which more recent political – and legal – contexts in the modern phenomenon of self-determination are aired. This is done in order to introduce what is intended to be a fresh look at the ultimate danger posed by self-determination in the contemporary era, to wit, the more often one or other form of self-determination is attained by a people, the more dangerous the principle is to certain states.

## A context of history

It is a truism that competing notions of nationhood can survive the steady pace of state territorial consolidation.[1] Yet, governments typically respond to group demands for greater autonomy with overwhelming counter-demonstrations of coercive, centralising tactics and tendencies. The very assertion of an entitlement to self-determination thus creates wider uncertainty due to an underlying 'change' agenda. There are, of course, many advantages in limiting certain state sovereign rights, particularly in the context of the strong connection to be found between respect for the rule of law and economic prosperity.[2] By the outbreak of the Second World War, for example, a concept of self-determination had certainly emerged, yet it was one which remained confined within a twin-track approach: one track for those state boundaries that survived the First World War; and, for those that did not, a new accommodation for minorities protections was negotiated for application within the boundaries of the new successor states. The former group of states largely carried on as it had done previously, while the latter was required to sign Minority Rights Treaties as a pre-condition to membership in the League of Nations.[3]

In thus institutionalising in the new states an early, limited form of collective, international control over their use of sovereign powers, the League hoped to spread a 'civilising standard' of sorts. As central purposes of the League were to ensure the peace through the collective use of force and to guarantee the integrity of existing state territorial borders,[4] it was hoped

1  Lenin attributes this to the 'historico-economic conditions of the national movements' and the capture of larger markets for commodity consumption. V.I. Lenin, 'The Right of Nations to Self-Determination', in *Lenin's Collected Works, Vol. 22* (Moscow: Progress Publishers, 1972, first published 1914), pp. 393, 396.
2  See, e.g., G. Skapska, 'The Rule of Law, Economic Transformation and Corruption After the Fall of the Berlin Wall' [2009] 284 *H.J.R.L.* 1 (this point attributed to Max Weber).
3  League of Nations Covenant (as amended) [1919] 225 C.T.S. 195.
4  The League Covenant has been characterised as 'primarily a military compact'. D.J. Hill, 'Permanent Court of International Justice' [1920] 14 *A.J.I.L.* 387.

that social cohesion within the new states would benefit from strong, protective rights laws that could bind the ruler and the ruled alike – a necessary precondition not only for social peace, but also one deemed in some quarters to be required for 'rational' economic action. Indeed, this ethos was reflected as long ago as US President Woodrow Wilson's Fourteen Points speech of 8 January 1918, in which the benefits to be gained from 'peace without victory', free trade, democracy and self-determination, were interconnected. Nonetheless, a test of the early Wilsonian approach to self-determination would be somewhat thwarted by the League of Nations itself, in the famous Aaland Islands dispute of 1920.

The Aaland Islands dispute arose from the historic legacies of the First World War. Sweden, forced to cede both the Aalands and Finland to Imperialist Russia in 1809, was asked by the Aalanders to annex their islands. The Aalanders had requested secession from Finland after the Finnish parliament proclaimed its own independence from Russia in 1917 on the basis of Finnish national self-determination. The Aalanders, too, wished to manage their own exercise in self-determination. Civil war in Finland left Sweden referring the matter to the League of Nations. The case was handed to the International Commission of Jurists, which based its responses largely on territorial grounds.[5] First, the Commission found no independent right to secede in positive international law and discouraged territorial secession in any event as anarchy could otherwise ensue. As for rights of national self-determination, the islanders fared no better; in representing less than 10 per cent of the Swedish population in Finland, they did not qualify. A subsequent opinion by a League Commission of Inquiry modified these findings, however, and secured the islanders' international right to a referendum on separation should Finland go on to breach the Aalanders' cultural rights.[6]

In contrast to the US President's position on the economic benefits of good governance, however, Comrade Lenin on the opposite side of the economic spectrum was attributing the denial of national rights of political self-determination to the demands of capitalism. The very economic interests of capitalism depended on the acquisition of new markets from which to source and sell industrialised commodities, he posited. In turn, as markets were captured, subject peoples would find themselves exploited, and oppressed, whether in imperialist–territorial contexts, or merely in terms of economic subjugation. Accordingly, once notions of social welfare or

5 The islands are separated from Sweden by deep water, but joined to the Finnish archipelago. Japanese interests in the Pacific meant that Finland received important support from Japan in the matter.
6 Decision of the Council of the League of Nations on the Aaland Islands Including Sweden's Protest [Sept. 1921] L.N.O.J. 697. See also C.G. Fenwick, 'National Security and International Arbitration' [1924] 18 *A.J.I.L.* 777; Editorial Comment, Eagleton, 'Forces Which Will Shape the Rebuilding of International Law' [1942] 36 *A.J.I.L.* 640.

tribalism were debilitated by the all-powerful capitalist bureaucratic managers, nations and nationhood would fracture, leaving only international class consciousness to take their place. Lenin thus argued that questions of economic dependency must remain of secondary importance to 'the question of the *political* self-determination of nations and their independence as states. . . . Even Russia', he wrote in 1914, 'is entirely dependent economically on the power of the imperialist finance capital.'[7]

The principle of the self-determination of peoples thus remained somewhat indeterminate during an inter-war period characterised by political and economic competition between capitalist, corporatist and communist systems of government. The linkages between the rule of law and economic prosperity, which had once appeared so obvious, suddenly seemed less so, particularly in those states in which national self-determination had in fact been subsumed by the rather less well-understood politics of class struggle. By 1941, the year US President F.D. Roosevelt returned to Wilson's theme and urged support for his 'four freedoms' (of speech and expression, of worship, from want and from fear), the international community had experienced a decade of economic depression. This President's vision for a post-war world order, configured alongside that of British Prime Minister W. Churchill and contained in the Atlantic Charter of August 1941,[8] places both indirect and direct emphases on the moral and political bases of self-determination.

The emphasis on self-determination in the Atlantic Charter was indirect, in that the leaders sought no aggrandisement, 'territorial or other'; it was direct in assurances that future territorial change would accord with the wishes of the peoples concerned (a principle of political redistribution). Further Charter assurances included the right of all peoples to choose their form of government, and to re-acquire their sovereign rights and self-government if forcibly deprived of them. While such a post-war vision was no doubt helpful in encouraging a greater number of colonials to enlist or otherwise help in defeating the enemy, Laing notes that:[9]

> [T]he wide-ranging concerns which the Allies viewed through the prism of the Atlantic Charter should not disguise the fact that the matrix within which they were working and the vital essence of the Atlantic Charter was comprehensive and universal human rights. This was due to the realisation of the Allies that the war was about one thing, the rights of individuals and reciprocally, the absolute need to reduce the preoccupation with the evils of state sovereignty, racism and nationalism which had spawned Fascism, Nazism and anti-semitism in Europe and anti-Europeanism and economic expansionism in East Asia.

7 V.I. Lenin, supra note 1, p. 396.
8 Text provided in the Appendix.
9 E.A. Laing, 'The Norm of Self-Determination, 1941–1991' [1993] 22 *Int.Rel.* 209, at 255.

By 1945 the United Nations had determined to pursue the Atlantic Charter agenda. The means with which to address such 'evils' as are indicated above required the principle focus to be placed on ensuring the future peace. This in turn required the maintenance of a workable balance between state sovereignty, territorial integrity and political independence; any guidance needed within this triangular structure of existing constraints could then be sought from the more inspirational theme of equal rights and self-determination. However, it could only really be agreed via this post-war political settlement to negotiate at some future point regarding specific details. Further, in order to use the UN Charter in a new era of wildly competing political and economic agendas, the ideals incorporated in the Atlantic Charter had to be made much more conditional, and contextualised, such that what had been hoped would constitute new, and significant, human rights and guarantees needed to be downplayed.

It is thus hardly surprising that the first reference to self-determination, as found in the non-binding preamble to the UN Charter, is indirect: '[w]e the Peoples of the United Nations'. The first binding reference is found in Charter Article 1(2), but self-determination is not characterised as an independent right; it has instead become a facilitator for achieving one of the Organisation's fundamental purposes. Article 1(2) looks '[t]o develop friendly relations among nations based on respect for the principles of equal rights and self-determination of peoples'.[10] This conditionality indicates not only that the future friendliness of inter-state relations is not taken for granted. It also made it easier for certain early commentators to argue that this reference to self-determination, taken as a whole, was intended merely to reaffirm the sovereign equality of states, i.e., that only states are deemed to possess equal and self-determining rights.[11] The Charter phraseology is then reconditioned again in Chapter IX Article 55, in the context of inter-national, economic and social co-operation, 'with a view to the creation of conditions of stability and well-being which are necessary for peaceful and friendly relations among nations'.

In other fundamental UN principles, such as the non-use of force by states against the political independence and territorial integrity of other states (Charter Article 2(4)) and the non-interference by states in the domestic affairs of each other (Article 2(7)), the future circularity of the 'self-determination of peoples' is ensured. The underlying parameters of the Charter right then create a central paradox, which produces competing theories of self-determination. On the one hand, if made strictly applic-able to states, 'equal rights and self-determination' attribute only a formal,

---

10 Neither 'peoples' nor 'nations' is defined by the Charter, but it is arguable they are used interchangeably.

11 Sources cited by E.A. Laing, supra note 9, p. 217 n. 36. Contrast UNGA Resolutions 545 (VI) of 5 February 1952, 637 (VII) of 20 December 1952, 1514 (XV) of 14 December 1960, 2105 (XX) of 20 December 1965, and 2625 (XXV) of 24 October 1970.

external quality to highly unequal states in terms of power and influence. However, this creates a greater potential for internal differentiation, as states are left to manage their own affairs. If, on the other hand, self-determination applies to peoples and/or nations, international human rights operate to recognise the formal, individual equality of individuals within each state, which permits less differentiation between peoples. This paradox, mirrored throughout the fundamental inequalities in international organisation, is discussed in subsequent chapters.

For present purposes, what is noteworthy is the innovative attempt made in the UN Charter to place a rights agenda central to the Organisation's future, as the attribution of rights sidesteps the traditional prohibition of non-interference found today in Charter Article 2(7).[12] The core weakness in this plan resides of course in national frameworks for human rights implementation. Thus, even though respect for human rights is made a matter of Charter obligation, these rights imply new limits to certain sovereign state powers. However, should a government choose to ignore or disregard human rights, the enforcement and further development of those rights must rely on self-interested individuals who are sufficiently willing or able to challenge their own governments. In a Hohfeldian sense, this rather converts any correlation between legal rights and duties into the politics of 'powers' and 'disabilities', as is now briefly introduced.

## A political context

This introductory chapter thus points from the start to the many defeats of self-determination. As very few peoples have succeeded in acquiring rights of self-determination *without* the consent of their state and/or of the broader international community, and fewer still have attained complete independence, either *de facto* or *de jure*, through the use of force and/or secessionist tactics,[13] what should be kept uppermost in mind is that many peoples who struggle for greater rights of self-determination do not necessarily reject the notion of the state. Group frustrations are often focused more on the achievement of better governance and/or simply the means to oppose the way in which the state is currently organised and administered. Contrariwise, government stonewalling of a rights-based self-determination agenda can itself provoke rebellion. It is thus perhaps not so remarkable that a traditional and anarchic international society of state administrative

---

12  E.A. Laing, supra note 9, p. 222, quoting Brownlie in 1973: 'self-determination [is] a legal principle, and UN organs do not permit Article 2(7) to impede discretion and decision when the principle is in issue' (citation omitted).

13  See S. Talmon, 'The Responsibility of Outside Powers for Acts of Secessionist Entities' [2009] 58(3) *I.C.L.Q.* 493; S. Mancini, 'Symposium: Rethinking the Boundaries of Democratic Secession: Liberalism, Nationalism, and the Right of Minorities to Self-determination' [2008] 6 *Int.J.Const.L.* 553.

units built on the bloodshed and power politics of centuries should retain its core political flexibilities in approach to the control of domestic populations.

Certainly, the vicissitudes of the modern age have not alone created the need to protect the governed against their government.[14] The early League focus on minority protections survives[15] and the term 'self-determination' itself has long conveyed a central message of protection. The term's internal semantics mean simply that there exists a practical desire of the 'self' to 'determine' its own freedom of action beyond the control of others, as opposed to the determination of that self by a government or other authority. When claimed by a similarly minded group, self-determination can exert a unifying spirit within the group itself to change some aspect of the *status quo*, and/or to be respected for what it is. This perspective then implies the likely existence of some inequality in domestic state organisation, as highlighted earlier in the paradox of competing theories of state self-determination. In other words, if nothing internally is amiss, there is no need to make a claim for self-determination.

Accordingly, ascertaining 'which' peoples are 'entitled' to assert rights of self-determination in the contemporary era is not so much about identifying certain privileged groups; instead, it is the opposite. What is conveyed by use of the phrase is a quest to secure those human conditions and linkages deemed necessary to sustain mutual survival, and life itself, within an economically challenged, political hierarchy controlled by state administrative units. As noted earlier, the modern notion of the self-determination of peoples has long occupied the politically insecure ground between international sovereign state rights and domestic 'human' rights of individuals, such as they may be.[16] Therefore, not only is the self-determination of peoples distinguishable from sovereign state rights in that a claim to sovereign territory is not required for the former; positive international law in any event guarantees no hard rights 'entitlements' to (undefined) peoples. The assertion that entitlements exist must instead be intended to denote one or other political, economic, and/or socio-cultural necessity.

So long as 'rights' to self-determination in general are not justiciable in state domestic courts, a self-determination wish-list will remain just that. The existence of such a list proves that individuals seek a stake in their own future and claim rights at least to a degree of autonomous life, which might include a right to live on historic lands and control natural resources

---

14 See, e.g., M. Sterio, 'On the Right to External Self-determination: "Selfistans", Secession, and the Great Powers' Rule' [2010] 19 *Minn.J.Int.L.* 137.

15 See, e.g., P. Thornberry, 'Self-determination, Minorities, Human Rights: A Review of International Instruments' [1989] 38(4) *I.C.L.Q.* 867. See also the innovative work performed by the Minority Rights Group International accessed at www.minorityrights.org.

16 See, e.g., Office of the High Commissioner for Human Rights, General Comment No. 12: The right to self-determination of peoples (Art. 1, ICCPR): 21st Session, 13/03/84, para. 3 (many state reports 'completely ignore Article 1').

or a right to prevent government arbitrariness or discrimination. At a stretch, a right to complete independence may arise. However, permitting rights protests against one government can prove dangerous to all governments, so it is more helpful to look to the mechanics and operation of the *enforcement* of individual rights when seeking reasons to explain or justify the flattening legal effects of certain anti-terrorist arrangements. For example, suspicion of a 'common enemy within' can be constructed via the abuse of certain enforcement mechanisms, such as discriminatory 'stop and search' practices. The rationales for intentionally excluding entire communities or individuals by legal means are well documented and can be particularly useful to governments, as depicted in theoretical works by theorists such as Agambon in his study of *homo sacer*.[17]

Accordingly, individuals who demonstrate openly within state territorial borders for or on behalf of legitimate public concerns can be silenced by domestic 'anti-terror' laws much more easily than those who pursue indiscriminate violence, because legitimate protesters are present and available for arrest. An international checkmate against states affording outside support or assistance to an oppressed people exists as the maintenance of global order in the UN era is premised, after all, on the non-use of inter-state force *and* the non-interference in the internal affairs of other states. In combination, these factors can leave many peoples with little hope or future expectation. It is also unsurprising that a Charter drafted by states for states says nothing about lawful limits to internal state powers when the time arrives to regulate their civic organisation or use of force. There is thus no attempt made in the Charter to conform or rebalance the internal domestic power structures of 'self-determining' states, e.g., from dictatorship to democratic accountability, from centralised to regional governance and/or from strict majority rule to a proportional and anti-discriminatory representation of specific nations, groups or individuals.

Moreover, as the Charter references to equal rights and self-determination are conditional, the strength of those principles cannot be compared to the strong(er) rules for maintaining international peace and security and against the use of inter-state armed force (particularly once nuclear weaponry had been invented). This relative ranking in importance not only helps those governments that choose to strip certain self-help measures and revolutionary tools from their subjugated or oppressed populations. It is equally unsurprising that states retain full sovereign control over their domestic affairs, including the implementation and enforcement of international obligations such as human rights. The mere fact that human rights are designed and intended to be enjoyed at an individual level as against the state provides

---

17 See, e.g., G. Agambon, *Homo Sacer: Sovereign Power and Bare Life* (trans. Daniel Heller-Roazen) (Stanford: Stanford University Press, 1998). See also C. Aradau and R. Van Munster, 'Exceptionalism and the "War on Terror": Criminology meets International Relations' [2009] 49(5) *Br.J.Crim.* 686.

but weak insurance cover against the greater value of those rights to states that can substitute notions of individual rights for the more destabilising ideas of peoples' or national self-determination. Every trade unionist knows the greater strength that comes in numbers; similarly, personal value from rights can arise only by the collective assertion of those rights.

Therefore, the notional entitlement of a 'people' (rather than a 'nation') to self-determination was highly restrictive from the beginning of UN practice. The conservative view holds that such a 'right' is admitted only in relation to former colonial or other non-self-governing territories. More liberal views tend to contemplate, at an outer stretch, that a struggling people can justify seeking to reacquire a formerly independent existence and that they might have an entitlement to do so, but this may be so only when their claims attract sufficient international support. Even then, any claim to territory is rigidly confined by the legal doctrine of *uti possidetis juris*,[18] such that only borders attributable territorially to a colonial or pre-existing, ascertainable administrative unit are admitted.[19] Either way, the attempt to confine the right of self-determination within this doctrine means not only that the dead hand of colonialism, etc., lingers on,[20] but further, that the refusal to evaluate the many injustices that peoples and/or minorities suffer under, whether from colonialism, conquest, oppression, etc., can only be seen for what it is: a politics of convenience for states.

The great resistance reserved for territorial secession without state consent ignores the most liberal approach of all, which is found in recent theories of so-called 'remedial' self-determination. Remedial self-determination posits that a people today might:

> [A]ccrue the right to some form of self-determination if it can demonstrate that it has been subjected to harsh oppression, that it has a relatively weak central government, that some type of international administration of its region has already taken place, and that it has garnered the support of the most sovereign states on our planet, the so-called Great Powers.[21]

---

18 Meaning effectively that, on independence, former administrative boundaries constitute the recognised future international boundaries, regardless of linguistic, ethnic and/or cultural differences of the inhabitants.

19 Contrast the Aaland Islands dispute, supra note 6, and the unsuccessful attempt of the Bosnian Serbs to argue their right to self-determination within the mid-1990s borders of Bosnia-Herzegovina. 'Conference on Yugoslavia, Arbitration Commission Opinions 1–10 on Questions arising from the Dissolution of Yugoslavia [11 January and 4 July 1992], Opinions 2 and 3', reprinted in [1992] 31 I.L.M. 1488, 1497–8, and 1499–1500, respectively.

20 For a spirited attack on *uti possidetis*, see G. Abraham, '"Lines upon Maps": Africa and the Sanctity of African Borders' [2007] 15(1) *A.J.I.C.L.* p. 61.

21 M. Sterio, supra note 14, p. 176 (comparing the cases of East Timor, Chechnya, Kosovo, and Georgia). See also M. Weller, *Escaping the Self-Determination Trap* (Leiden: Martinus Nijhoff Publishers, 2008), pp. 59–69, and 139–43.

While one might prefer to see the connector 'or' rather than 'and' in this quotation, the achievement of those peoples who have in fact gained greater accommodations with their governments since 1946 should not be diminished. System alteration has been effected, for example, in successful claims for enhanced forms of self-governance, regionalisation, federalisation, conditional or deferred self-determination and so on.[22] This choice in approach nonetheless leaves failed attempts at oppositional politics, including uses of armed force or other violence, to await description variously as 'terrorism'. 'Self-determination' may thus remain the rhetorical device of choice through which to assert an alternative agenda, but the enduring disregard of state internal organisation runs the risk of transforming what many view as a natural 'right' of self-determination into a matter of forcible self-help. Therefore, the gap which persists between contemporaneously-promoted doctrines of 'lawful' parameters to self-determination and the actual pursuit of the principle merely reinforces the mutuality of difference between equal, sovereign states.

The assertion just made also points more to the core theory of state self-determination made in terms of equal sovereign rights, rather than as rights attributable instead to peoples. Therefore, for so long as doctrinal competition in orientation persists in fact as to the true subject of the right, self-determination must remain little more than the poor relation of an isolating, individually focused human rights paradigm.[23] This then implies that the answers to certain questions, such as 'which' peoples may exercise self-determination and 'which' rights constitute their entitlement, continue to rest on preferred contexts in state interpretation. Factor in the recent 'war' on international terrorism and the increase in governmental anti-terrorist activity and any indicative ilk of actor can be officially targeted through funding sources, networks and alliances. Accordingly, the issue is not, and never has been, whether or not one or other tribunal or judicial body should or can discover a rule that is adequate to 'entitle' a people, nation or similarly minded group, to their self-determination, as is now briefly introduced.

## A legal context

The many competing territorial, political and economic experiments in play during the distinctive contexts of Cold War bipolarity, the more fractured

---

22  For discussion of the various types of compromise put into play, see generally M. Weller, supra note 21.
23  See, e.g., A. Asthana, T. Helm, and R. Syal, 'Britain Scraps Report on Human Rights Abuses', *The Observer*, 22 August 2010, p. 1 (Foreign Office Annual Report on Human Rights downgraded to protect trade relationships).

post-Cold War era, the 'anti-terrorist' post-9/11 decade and the international financial crisis beginning in 2007–2008 would make it seem foolhardy to opine that the rule of law alone – international or otherwise – can ever succeed in binding the ruler and the ruled alike. Rulers – whoever they may be or wherever found – make and enforce their rules. Just as market traders can only build competing models for 'guaranteeing' their own favoured notions of market foreseeability and predictability, the law, too, can only proffer selective guidance for 'rational' action. This means the rule of law cannot be enforced without consideration being paid to the special interests reflected in specific legal prohibitions. A neutral, 'rational' approach to the substitution of oppression by greater autonomous rights entitlements can hardly be imagined, much less attempted, within individualised and currently static territorial borders.

Having said that, international law can and often does establish appropriate parameters to expectations of social behaviour, such that the laws of armed conflict, for example, are viewed increasingly as relevant in certain civil war situations.[24] However understandable it may be that armed struggles for self-determination easily blur the dominant political labelling processes, international unity on any issue can and does fracture when pressing problems arise closer to home, as has been seen in the recent controversies surrounding Kosovo's declaration of independence[25] and Georgia's armed conflict with the Russian Federation over South Ossetian self-determination.[26] Similarly, certain post-9/11 consolidations in political power within individual states over subject populations have generated political frictions between states at many points. Nonetheless, as governments come under increasing exhortation to incorporate and/or be mindful of minimum human rights considerations when adopting new anti-terror measures, one positive benefit has been a renewed international focus on certain struggles for rights of self-determination.

24 E.g., those situations indicated in Article 8(2)(d) and (f), Rome Statute of the International Criminal Court (ICC), Doc. A/CONF.183/9 of 17 July 1998, in force 1 July 2002. See also Articles 12(1) and (3), 13(a), 17, and 25(4), and Chapter 3, infra.

25 Full text: 'Kosovo declaration', 17 February 2008, news.bbc.co.uk/1/hi/world/europe/ 7249677.stm. An earlier declaration was issued in July 1990. See 'Request for an advisory opinion of the ICJ on whether the unilateral declaration of independence of Kosovo is in accordance with international law', UNGA Resolution 63/3 of 8 October 2008, UN Doc. A/RES/63/3, Agenda item 71; *Accordance with International Law of the Unilateral Declaration of Independence in Respect of Kosovo (Advisory Opinion)* [22 July 2010] ICJ, General List No. 141.

26 E.g., 'Report, Independent International Fact-Finding Mission on the Conflict in Georgia, Vol. 1', September 2009. The Mission was established by Council Decision 2008/901/ CFSP, 2 December 2008, concerning an independent international fact-finding mission on the conflict in Georgia. U.N.O.J. [3/12/2008] L 323/66.

Thus, while some liberation causes endure miserably, such as that caused by occupation of Palestinian territory,[27] the contemporary list of 'peoples' still utilising force to claim rights of self-determination under such themes as fighting 'oppression' or 'hegemony', etc., shows little sign in modern conditions of being shortened. As terms such as 'lawful police action', 'terrorism' and 'armed conflict' come to be employed in an increasingly misleading way, what becomes apparent is that certain legal categories that generally should entail highly differentiated consequences have started to indicate a circularity and integration in underlying political technique. It is at this point that some working distinctions are useful. First, peacetime law and laws of war are highly different in approach. Second, peacetime law incorporates the fundamental right to life. Third, international laws of armed conflict incorporate a fundamental distinction between lawful and unlawful military objectives, e.g., between combatants (who may be attacked and killed) and uninvolved civilians (who may not).

Unfortunately, frameworks of national security distort the parameters of laws of peace and of war. This is why the relaxed practice of employing the rhetoric of war when politically describing the use of armed force against criminal 'terrorists' is astonishing. Moreover, states increasingly justify such uses of force on grounds of rights of 'self-defence' – a term normally reserved for contexts of force used between states.[28] It can thus be seen that the aftermath of the 9/11 atrocity has proved highly convenient for certain states that have chosen to pass off their more draconian domestic laws as fully sanctioned by international law. Not even on the basis of dedicated anti-terror instruments have states previously sourced a blanket rationale for depicting local measures as being automatically in full compliance with international law. However, to do so in contexts of global anti-terrorist action implies a more-or-less unlimited choice in governmental decision making in relation to what *it* considers an unlawful use of force and effectively seizes control of UN Security Council primary responsibilities under Charter Chapter VII.[29]

---

27  See, e.g., Report of the United Nations Fact-Finding Mission on the Gaza Conflict, 'Human Rights in Palestine and Other Occupied Arab Territories (Late Submission)', Human Rights Council, UNGA Doc. A/HRC/12/48 (25 September 2009), www2.ohchr.org/english/bodies/hrcouncil/docs/12session/A-HRC-12-48.pdf.

28  See *Legal Consequences of the Construction of a Wall in the Occupied Palestinian Territory (Advisory Opinion)* [2004] ICJ Rep. paras. 138–41, www.icj-cij.org. See also UN Charter Article 51; UNGA Resolution 3314 (XXIX), of 1974; Assembly of State Parties, Review Conference Resolution 6, 'Crime of Aggression', Annex I, Article 2 [adopted by consensus 11 June 2010]. Contrast 'The Chatham House Principles of International Law on the Use of Force in Self-Defence' [2006] 55 *I.C.L.Q.* 963, at pp. 969–71.

29  Cf. Special Report, Chassay, 'Lethally Accurate', *The Guardian*, 24 March 2009, p. 18 (former Israeli spokesman states 'if you do something for long enough, the world will accept it').

Another theme expanded on in subsequent chapters is the difficulty in orientation that exists between the different standards of peacetime and wartime 'necessity' and 'proportionality'. While it may well be the case that, as noted by the UN Secretary General in May 2006:

> [T]errorism in all its forms and manifestations, committed by whomever, wherever and for whatever purposes, is unacceptable and can never be justified,[30]

the law cannot, neither does it try to place the same or similar limits on all users of armed violence. It is for this reason that international law can attempt to regulate outer limits to the use of armed force in times of war,[31] but in times of peace this is much more difficult, if only due to the variations in interpretation of human rights standards.[32] The Secretary General's conclusion (given in the quotation) should, of course, cause little surprise, in that it is premised on a more generalised shift in international frustration at non-state violence and the aftermath of the 9/11 terrorist attacks, but it is the position of this discussion that the legal and political attitudes being adopted towards terrorism in the contemporary era facilitate an automatic criminality for many non-state actors, including those peoples who seek their self-determination.

It should also be recalled at this point that the original promotion of self-determination in 1945 – to restore former colonial lands – constituted one means to liberate international trade. In contrast, modern attempts to freeze state territorial borders are utilised to discourage inter-state wars and non-state violent actors alike, regardless of whether the latter are involved in a legitimate struggle for self-determination, or 'terrorism'. Not only does this rigidity erase many former limits on state power to use force domestically. The blanket condemnation of all 'unauthorised' violence also involves turning a non-interfering, blind eye to 'authorised' violence within states, encourages government impunity and damages the rule of law. It also assumes that the basic human need to protect oneself is conditioned by a prerequisite of state consent. This unprecedented attack on the right of resistance, under the putative aegis of international law, constitutes an

---

30  Sec. Gen. Kofi Annan, 'Address of 2 May 2006 to the UNGA on the launch of Uniting against Terrorism: Recommendations for a global counter-terrorism strategy', www.un.org/News/ossg/sg/stories/statments_search_full.asp?statID=23. See also Joint Committee on Human Rights, Counter-Terrorism Policy and Human Rights: Terrorism Bill and Related Matters (2005–6 HL75, HC 561), para. 176.

31  With perhaps the notable exception of nuclear weaponry. *Legality of the Threat or Use of Nuclear Weapons Case (Advisory Opinion)* [1996] ICJ Rep. 916.

32  An exception being in certain regional human rights legal regimes. See, e.g., W. Abresch, 'A Human Rights Law of Internal Armed Conflict: The ECtHR in Chechnya' [2005] 16 *E.J.I.L.* 741.

equally unprecedented attempt to outlaw revolution, assuming the latter term is taken to mean simply the achievement of fundamental change – accomplished peacefully or otherwise – to one or other state structure, power or organisation, within a fairly short period of time.

The anti-terror agenda of the post-9/11 era thus certainly poses new challenges, as revolution cannot be forbidden. Chapters on self-determination will continue to be added to the chronology and new dimensions to the scope of the principle. The renewed global focus on international terrorism in a less well-anchored post-Cold War environment, the mandatory contexts of international action to promote the criminalisation of all acts of non-state violence, and the efforts to eliminate non-standard and non-transparent funding sources, simply pose new obstacles to peoples struggling to improve their conditions of life. The decade after September 2001 thus affords a unique opportunity to reflect on the meaning of self-determination.

The discussion that follows is divided as follows. Part 1 continues with a short overview of the approach adopted in Chapter 2. The largely structural legal foundations for modern uses of armed force in struggles for self-determination are outlined in Part 2. Part 3 then examines concrete examples of state action attributable to a global anti-terror co-operation adversely impacting self-determination.

# 2 Perspectives on self-determination in the post-9/11 era

## Introduction

It is necessary to outline the perspectives adopted in this book, in order to create a framework in which to consider the ongoing viability of struggles for rights to self-determination by peoples. Specifically, this framework is oriented primarily within the context of the aftermath of the atrocious Al Qaeda terrorist attacks on New York, Washington, DC, and Pennsylvania of 11 September 2001, or '9/11' as the date is more commonly known. In turn, those events and that date have had a huge significance on the issue of struggles for self-determination. The subsequent importance placed on a broad, universal approach to deterring violent Islamic extremists is capable of extension to the self-determination struggles of many radical separatist groups. Where this has, in fact, occurred, it has been at the expense of international restraints, such as those imposed on states by international laws of armed conflict, human rights laws and obligations to settle disputes peacefully in general.[1]

Nonetheless, in a nod to *realpolitik* it must first be noted that the term 'self-determination' conveys a great deal of baggage. Struggles for self-determination that exhibit varying levels of violence may overstep many international limits on the use of force in an armed conflict, as well as domestic peacetime laws. Liberation struggles are also controversial because the political preoccupation of 1945 to find means to end colonialism is no longer so pressing. However, even though the vast majority of former mandates or other non-self-governing territories have been afforded an opportunity to emerge from colonialism,[2] little true international 'peace' has, in

---

1 See, e.g., the US action taken in the Redesignation of Foreign Terrorist Organizations Act, 68 Fed. Reg. 56,860, 56,861 (2 October 2003).
2 Only 16 or so non-self-governing territories await a successful conclusion. See 'The Second International Decade for the Eradication of Colonialism', set to end in 2010. UN Press Release, 'Secretary General Calls for Renewed Commitment', UN Special Committee on Decolonisation, 1st Meeting (PM), 27 February 2009, www.un.org/News/Press/docs/2009/gacol3183.doc.htm.

fact, resulted due to that fact alone. In that new conflicts in which rights of self-determination are claimed continue to unfold, the perspectives adopted in this discussion on non-standard contexts for self-determination are as follows.

## Approach

The preliminary issue concerns the lawful use of armed force. Any government may decide to respond to demands for greater self-determination by opening political negotiations, but it is more likely that that government will react instead with centralising tactics and reactionary coercion, in order to contain and/or repress that people into obedience. However, should civil unrest or rioting result and threaten to become a high intensity domestic armed conflict, only the military can normally regain control of domestic order. Therefore, as soldiers are acting under orders, military operations should be regulated under laws of armed conflict,[3] including certain rules that continue after the end of hostilities, while soldiers act under orders. This issue is important because the lawful limits for regulating official uses of force differ according to whether the military or the police is called on. If the former, international laws of armed conflict should apply; if the latter, laws of peace. Either way, the government is prohibited from ordering the outright murder of its civilian opponents.

Second, self-determination involves the power of ideas, while acts of terrorism constitute but one means for expressing ideas. Rules of armed conflict are thus crucial to forceful struggles for self-determination inasmuch as those struggles are often waged violently in pursuit of a people's ideas. Moreover, the application of rules of armed conflict reflects self-discipline, and the existence of limits on force, in view of the known consequences of wanton destruction. Self-discipline and limits are thus a rational way to proceed when in pursuit of ideas, as to do so is fundamental to progress, economic stability and cultural life. In that the governed often need protection against their government, the post-1945 principles and ideas of equal human rights and the self-determination of peoples ensure a form of double protection against a state's monopoly over the use of force. In turn, this monopoly over force is equally rational for the protection of individuals and groups and thus warrants their support within limits.

Third, it is instructive to consider the approach to peoples, in the context of self-determination, which has been adopted by the International Committee of the Red Cross (ICRC). The ICRC identifies a relevant 'people' by its 'common sentiment of forming a people, a political will to

---

3 This is one conclusion in the ILA Use of Force Committee, 'Final Report (Draft) on the Meaning of Armed Conflict in International Law', submitted at the ILA Annual Conference, The Hague, 15–20 August 2010, at p. 31, www.ila-hq.org.

live together as such', as well as by such means as 'a common language, common culture or ethnic ties'.[4] This viewpoint is very open ended and pays little attention to narrow personal criteria or the issue of territory. Instead, for the ICRC, self-determination involves the existence of a discrete community of people who share certain human values. These values and ideas could be put to use in states in a positive manner to reshape or alter an existing allocation of rights entitlements. By the same token, states in the post-1945 era prefer to maintain a status quo and to admit a 'right' to self-determination only in respect of a limited class of peoples, e.g., those inhabiting former colonies, due to the wider dangers of territorial secession.

Fourth, states have for some time been deeply divided about the forceful means and methods adopted by certain liberation groups. By integrating struggles for self-determination into increasingly broad terrorist categories, governments find it easier to prosecute their means and methods through domestic criminal laws than they would in accordance with international laws of armed conflict. Accordingly, while individual and group rights should be capable of imposing counter-constraints on governments which over-utilise their domestic criminal laws for penal reasons, the relative strength between government and civil society can prevent this. A state that prefers to characterise liberation acts quasi-automatically as terrorist offences can influence other states also to extend the outer limits of their own sovereign entitlements to use force when faced with internal disorder. The frequent use of official force to bolster the right to rule thus sheds light on theoretical disagreement regarding the true subject of rights of self-determination, i.e., states or peoples.

Fifth, the post-9/11 environment in particular has made it much more *attractive* to governments to re-designate many more violent actors as 'terrorist' opponents. This makes it relevant also to consider whether it is even tenable under present circumstances to attempt to differentiate between 'freedom fighters' and 'terrorists'. For example, support for a multifaceted group having – if only in part – a terrorist agenda attracts lawful censure, as terrorist acts involve indiscriminate death and damage. That is why such acts are condemned both in laws of armed conflict and those of peace. However, armed conflicts by their very nature cause death and harm to the innocent. In order to maintain a rational dividing line between the two legal frameworks (war and peace), *only* laws of armed conflict permit civilian collateral damage, if an important military objective is at stake *and* the armed forces act proportionately for reasons of military necessity. This fact makes it doubly unfortunate that military force is utilised in a 'terrorist' situation which is itself dangerous for civilians.

---

4 Y. Sandoz, C. Swinarski and B. Zimmermann, *Commentary on the Additional Protocols of 8 June 1977* (Geneva: Martinus Nijhoff Publishers, 1987), p. 52.

A sixth point is that system change can be sought and accomplished domestically through peaceful means as easily as through violent ones and many recent political and economic 'revolutionary' accommodations have, in fact, been effected worldwide without undue loss of life, as has been made crystal clear during the post-Cold War era. Nonetheless, and similar to a 'canary-in-the-mine', the politics of self-determination have long had an uncanny knack of signalling certain emerging themes in international life. As the political rhetoric used to condemn terrorism starts to include liberation struggles, the long-held view of certain states, that self-determination is merely a recruiting ground for 'terrorists', makes any surviving distinction between the two a point of deep international friction between states themselves.[5] For example, disunity persists at UN level, as arguments continue to be aired to exempt legitimate liberation wars from ongoing efforts to formulate a 'universal' definition of terrorism in a draft Comprehensive Terrorism Convention.[6]

Expense to governments makes a seventh issue. All governments must tax their populations,[7] even though states having centralised economies may find it somewhat easier to raise the requisite monies. Once a government chooses to redefine certain groups as 'terrorist', broadly defined, the re-characterisation justifies the adoption of more coercive action, e.g., to supply security personnel and equipment, surveillance capacity and so on. If 'protective' security planners are positively encouraged to speculate about more and more 'terrorist' enemies, and to factor in wilder probabilities, official cost estimates can spiral. In turn, increased demands for coercive action can be good for business, as they provide new opportunities to mix public and private provision in a highly profitable way. Therefore, when viewed through the lens of a state's right to rule, the financial attractions to governments of conflating the respective definitional scopes of self-determination and terrorism are evident.

This raises an eighth point. Certain states have sought to *generate* an extremely broad category of 'terrorist' opponent, which they then promote heavily elsewhere. Peer pressure, and the onerous obligations imposed by the UN Security Council on all states,[8] to pursue international terrorism exacerbate another problem: the economic disparity between the first and

---

5  M. Hmoud, 'Negotiating the Draft Comprehensive Convention on International Terrorism: Major Bones of Contention' [2006] 4 *J.Int'l.Crim.J.* 1031.

6  See 'Background, etc., Draft comprehensive convention on international terrorism', accessed at Inventory of International Non-proliferation Organizations and Regimes, Center for Non-proliferation Studies (last updated 27 May 2009), regarding which several delegations continue to emphasise the distinction between acts of terrorism and the exercise of the right to self-determination, http://cns.miis.edu/inventory/pdfs/intlterr.pdf.

7  R.E. Backhouse, *The Penguin History of Economics* (London: Penguin, 2002), p. 283.

8  L.M.H. Martinez, 'The Legislative Role of the Security Council In Its Fight Against Terrorism: Legal, Political and Practical Limits' [2008] 57(2) *I.C.L.Q.* 333.

third worlds. New international obligations to reduce bank secrecy,[9] and to prevent money laundering and the financing of terrorism, can distort the financial traditions of many peoples, as easily as it does those of some states.[10] Less wealthy states are held to the same (or similar) standards of enforcement obligation, but should the necessary infrastructure be lacking, poorer states can find themselves under suspicion, e.g., that their territories are usable as 'terrorist' havens. It thus appears not only that dominant states are seeking to integrate struggles for self-determination within an anti-terrorist agenda; they are also seeking to entrench structural economic inequality more completely.

As a ninth and final point, the lawful limits of rights to self-determination have yet to be fixed definitively,[11] terrorist havens can infect local struggles for self-determination ideologically, and modern communications facilitate connections between many criminals, terrorists and/or revolutionaries alike. For as long as the UN Charter speaks only of a *principle* of self-determination, *rights* of self-determination must remain creatures of their circumstances. This indeterminacy practically invites certain dominant states to seize the new opportunities afforded by 9/11 to strengthen an already existing framework of inter-state co-operation, such as quasi-automatic extradition arrangements, in order to entrap an ever larger variety of people and institutions.[12] Therefore, not only have new formats of state solidarity appeared since 9/11; there also appears to be a new willingness by states to accept the extra-territorial reach of one another's criminal laws, despite wide variations in practice.

In short, self-determination is at a dangerous crossroads in the aftermath of 9/11. While the focus of this book might have been directed towards the post-Cold War era to highlight the steady increase in strength of the principle of self-determination in customary international law, a post-9/11 overlay demands an alternative viewpoint. A post-Westphalian legacy, the dead hand of which lingers on, mandates that *only* states possess equal

---

9 UNSC Resolution 1373 (28 September 2001), UN Doc. S/RES/1373 (2001); Documents regarding the Counter-Terrorism Committee, www.un.org/Docs/SC/Committees/1373. See also O. Elagab, 'Control of Terrorist Funds and the Banking System' [2006] 21(1) *J.Int'l.Banking.L.&Reg.* 38.

10 See, e.g., R. Bosworth-Davies, 'The Influence of Christian Model Ideology in the Development of Anti-Money Laundering Compliance in the West and Its Impact, Post 9-11, Upon the South Asian Market: An Independent Evaluation of a Modern Phenomenon' [2008] 11(2) *J.MoneyLaund.Contr.* 179.

11 Even the ICJ avoided this question in *Accordance with International Law of the Unilateral Declaration of Independence in Respect of Kosovo (Advisory Opinion)* [22 July 2010] ICJ, General List No. 141. Cf. the 1988 Rome Treaty on Maritime Navigation, Preamble, which 'affirm[s] further that matters not regulated by this convention continue to be governed by the rules and principles of general international law'.

12 See, e.g., the UK's Landsbanki Freezing Order 2008, No. 2668.

rights.[13] In turn, the manner in which that rule is expressed within states varies greatly and can be used on *national* security grounds to designate unpopular persons as criminals and to curtail individual rights, such as those of expression or association.[14] The post-9/11 construction of a strong anti-terror paradigm thus simply contributes another platform from which states can oppose self-determination. On this basis, revolution remains available, as is now introduced.

## The role of force

As previously discussed, the reconstruction of international relations after the Second World War included, among other things, both direct and indirect references to 'peoples' being *entitled* to determine their system of governance for themselves. As for whom those 'peoples' might be, the vague principle hinted at in the UN Charter – of the equal rights and self-determination of peoples – promised little of a concrete approach for adoption in subsequent practice. Accordingly, the conservative state attitude adopted early in the post-1945 era regarding the decolonisation agenda could never have contemplated what was to become a demanding agenda in which disparate peoples could also seek additional rights. Contrariwise, the very vagueness of the principle helped to inaugurate a new international ethos which has succeeded rather well in deterring outright expansionist urges between states,[15] even as it facilitated more covert forms of interference in the domestic affairs of each other.[16]

It is thus a telling point that UN Charter Articles 1(2) and 2(4) express a collective and immediate desire to encourage peaceful and, in the future, friendly inter-state relations. Obviously, global society at the time was exhausted by war, yet already was divided ideologically. No doubt all were fearful of nuclear developments yet to come. In that the relevant prohibitions on the use of inter-state force could not rest merely on ideals, the Security Council was given primary responsibility to maintain international peace and security and provision was made for collective action in Chapters VI and VII of the Charter.[17] States also were placed under a fundamental international obligation to keep the peace internally. Admittedly,

---

13  The Peace of Westphalia ended the Thirty Years' War (1618–48) in Europe. The Westphalian settlement marked the beginning of the modern system of nation-states.

14  See also R. Schabl and P. Beaumont, 'Israelis Rebel over Bid to Gag Boycott Debate', *The Observer*, 11 July 2010, p. 13 (500 Israeli academics face criminalisation for opposing Gaza Strip blockade).

15  And, is today considered to be *jus cogens*. *Military and Paramilitary Activities in and against Nicaragua (Nicaragua v. United States of America) (Merits)* [1986] ICJ Rep. p. 14, para. 190.

16  See, e.g., Q. Wright, 'Subversive Intervention' [1960] 54 *A.J.I.L.* 521.

17  UN Charter Article 24.

nothing is intimated about the precise limits on their uses of force, per se, particularly once such matters fail to be regulated by other international instruments[18] and/or within the scope of Charter Article 2(7) regarding non-interference.

The very existence of Charter Article 2(7) communicates that governments should possess the means to quell domestic disruption and that consequential damage inflicted against a population will rarely be of concern to the wider community, unless it disrupts the wider peace.[19] An inventory of institutional resources available to governments reveals the military, the police, the judiciary and so on. Article 2(7) thus makes it highly controversial to question the *lawful* limits of individual state uses of force domestically and what rules there may be are typically ignored. Therefore, on the premise that states alone are bound directly by the UN Charter, and assuming Charter provisions do not (and cannot) in fact go far enough to maintain peace and security *within* states, it becomes arguable that there is no immutable prohibition in international law of revolution – a view that has the advantage of encompassing the many complexities of historic conquest, population transfers, imperialist condescension and so on.[20]

In any event, the international community as a whole often lacks the political willingness to involve itself collectively in local disputes – particularly those that involve the wider contradictions which arise between state and human rights when the time arrives to use force. The composition of the UN Security Council itself reflects the tensions over individual human rights, as its permanent members each have different conceptions. Individual governments are thus left for the most part to contain their own revolutionary upheavals and, regardless of whether or not a struggle for self-determination by a people in such contexts can ever resemble a 'classic' revolution, non-state actors continue to revolt despite, or perhaps because of, the development and growth of new human rights expectations since 1945.

Accordingly, there has only been war of some sort, and continuous planning for war, ever since 1945. Today, regardless of whether or not a 'war' remains of the kind once sourced in the bipolar rivalry of the Cold War, or more recently might be attributable to private and state corporate interests vying to develop new markets and exploit natural resources in

18 See Chapter 3.
19 E.g., UNSC draft resolution on unrest in Burma, Doc. S/2007/14, was vetoed by China, Russia, and South Africa for concerning a domestic question posing no threat to regional peace and security, UN Doc. S/PV.5619, 12 January 2007. See C. Focarelli, 'The Responsibility to Protect Doctrine and Humanitarian Intervention: Too Many Ambiguities for a Working Doctrine' [2008] *J.Con.&Sec.L.* 191, 208–9.
20 See, e.g., P. Harris, 'Destitute Tribe Wins Rich Slice of the Hamptons', *The Observer*, 11 July 2010, p. 12 (New York Shinnecock tribe reacquires control of historic lands).

foreign lands, there are apparent three principle types of 'revolutionary' struggle for self-determination: anti-imperialist, secessionist and/or religious/ ethnic.[21] For example, the secessionist wars waged in the former territory of Yugoslavia throughout the 1990s were viewed in certain quarters as wars of self-determination, even though that term was deemed officially to be irrelevant in that particular context.[22] Equally, the rhetoric of self-determination has been utilised in certain religious extremist struggles which began to attract wider notice at roughly the same time. It could be argued in this vein that a spillover effect, from extremism into separatist warfare, lies but a step away.[23]

A successful revolutionary/self-determination agenda of whatever ilk can thus be premised on a variety of grounds, particularly should peaceful, constitutional procedures not exist through which to achieve change, or where they exist, be stonewalled by entrenched interests. The use of police or military force to restore and/or maintain the status quo is thus but one tool of government control. Nonetheless, while the use of official force may not be regulated *in* law, it is invariably *privileged* by law. This reality in effect raises the status of the armed forces above the rest of society. As noted by Best:

> Except in cases where an armed force or a coalition of armed forces succeeds in totally militarising society, or where a 'war-minded' ideology possesses a whole society to the extent that every citizen is as much a soldier as any other, there are bound to remain differences and distinctions between the armed forces on the one hand, and the societies from which they spring on the other.[24]

He adds: '[a]nd yet, while there are differences and distinctions, there must also be relationships and interactions'.[25] It is thus a matter of logic that political power rests ultimately on the possession of superior force, even as the sharing of kinship ties between the military and the rest of the population must in some respects temper domestic uses of official force.

---

21 E.g., the ongoing 'Troubles' in Northern Ireland, despite the political settlement contained in the 'Good Friday Agreement' of 1998.

22 See the 'EC Declaration on Yugoslavia and Guidelines on the Recognition of New States in Eastern Europe and in the Soviet Union', reprinted in [1992] 31 I.L.M. 1485, and 'Conference on Yugoslavia, Arbitration Commission, on Questions arising from the Dissolution of Yugoslavia [11 January and 4 July 1992], Opinions 2 and 3', reprinted *ibid.*, at 1488, 1497–8, and 1499–1500, respectively.

23 See Chapter 6.

24 G. Best, 'Editor's Preface', in *War and Society in Revolutionary Europe 1770–1870* (Stroud: Sutton Publishing Ltd, 1998), p. 9.

25 *Ibid.*

In terms of structure, the armed forces arise through state military traditions. Many states, for example, still require compulsory conscription,[26] so that many people will be instructed in handling weaponry. In turn, the military's strength is only as good as the instruction and training it is provided, particularly on such matters as discipline, cohesion and loyalty. The heavy reliance placed during the last century on mechanised and technological means also ensures that military expertise and know-how can be diffused throughout the surrounding communities, which helps to foster not only a deeper civilian–military accommodation (both direct and indirect), but also broader employment opportunities. The mutual military–civilian co-operation that results then may encourage a population to adopt similar modes of behaviour in their daily lives.

Compulsory military training has, in turn, one main drawback: it constructs a good civilian capacity to utilise force, as military discipline is imitated throughout the population at large. The sheer availability of forceful means highlights only the fact that the use of those means constitutes the centre of importance. For example, greater opportunities are available for irregular fighters to adopt civilian anonymity when targeting militarily weak points in towns and populated areas.[27] A widespread knowledge of weapons handling can be put to oppositional use, particularly in those states in which the possession and use of personal weaponry is positively permitted.[28] The availability of forceful means then alters the focus somewhat more than might otherwise have been thought from the *fact* of those means to the central importance of loyalty to one or other *idea* of government. In other words, and to misquote John Locke, the authority and might that stand behind rule cannot alone protect that rule or make it 'just'.[29]

Crucially, governments that must rely domestically on their official monopoly over the use of domestic armed force make more contestable the monopoly itself, in that it generates only a relative equivalence in mutual fear between the governed and their governors, at which point the wide availability of weaponry ensures a greater willingness by all concerned to resort to forceful means. This is what makes the absence of effective procedures so dangerous, particularly should one or other faction among the governed seek to alter and reorient existing institutions, the better to accommodate their interests. As good order does not normally arise

---

26 Of 180 states surveyed in a 1998 report by War Registers International, some form of conscription existed in 95, 59 of which did not recognise a right of conscientious objection. Statistic cited in *Sepet, et ano v. SOS for the Home Department* [2003] UKHL 15, at para. 18 (per Lord Bingham).

27 A.P.V. Rogers, 'Zero-casualty Warfare' [March 2000] 837 *I.R.R.C.* 165.

28 See, e.g., P. Herby, 'Arms Availability and the Situation of Civilians in Armed Conflict' [Sept. 1990] 835 *I.R.R.C.* 669.

29 See J. Locke, *Two Treatises of Government* (first published London: Awnsham Churchill, 1690).

from mere control or the propagandistic euphemism found in nationalist or liberal rhetoric, for example, the juxtaposition just outlined, between facts and ideas, places a primary emphasis instead on the importance of consent by a majority of the governed to the manner in which law and order are actually maintained.

The mutuality of fear which arises between the governed and a government the public do not like then breathes renewed life into the idea of self-determination, which subsequently rationalises social and political upheaval. Assuming therefore for purposes of argument that the idea of self-determination is asserted by persons and/or groups who seek change in their conditions of daily life, the characterisation of violent acts perpetrated by governments and non-state entities alike boils down to the power of labels, whether employed to depict localised and/or sporadic uprisings, 'terrorism' or the central platforms built to sustain or oppose the weight of 'revolutionary' struggle for self-determination.

## Conclusion

The UN Charter era has succeeded well in deterring inter-state armed aggression and in encouraging the peaceful settlement of inter-state disputes. This is but a preliminary, if practical step towards achieving the overarching aim of the Charter agenda to build peace and international friendly relations, both between states themselves and between states and their peoples. However, as peoples and individuals are not made the subjects of international law, they can rely only on the strength of inter-state obligations to convince their governments to put substance into equal human rights and self-determination. In turn, many states do not always support inter-state compliance obligations, even though only states enjoy equality, *inter se*, in terms of their respective sovereign entitlements, in regards to each other.

There is also the Charter matter of maintaining international security between states, which leaves to individual states many options when choosing mechanisms to ensure their own domestic security arrangements, even though 'peace' *and* 'security' are rather more complicated than their maintenance between states alone. The integration of struggles for self-determination into the global anti-terrorist agenda thus makes it arguable that states shoehorn anti-terrorist laws into the politics of mutual state survival as a matter of sovereign convenience, as, unfortunately, what has been omitted in the Charter era is the innovative use made during the League of Nations era of international law as the primary legal yardstick for international and domestic questions alike.[30] There is instead only Charter

---

30  L. Gross, 'The Charter of the United Nations and the Lodge Reservations' [1947] 41 *A.J.I.L.* 531, 538–44.

Article 103, which makes the UN Charter, in all its indeterminacy, the supreme treaty.

The recent alacrity of certain states to utilise military force against 'terrorists' is thus particularly alarming, as alternative formats to organising social life do, in fact, exist. Inasmuch as this alacrity helps to construct a 'new class of outlaw' – one deemed to have forfeited both its civil and combatant rights[31] – it signals an intensifying willingness by states mutually to halt further progress towards human rights and humanitarian restraints and to reverse much of the progress achieved so far. The challenging (albeit obvious) solution to the conundrums of peace, security and law is to assume instead that the future cannot be dominated by one or other system of governance or source of power, particularly if the latter is to be grounded only in the use of superior force.

In order to discuss these and related issues, Part 2 introduces the political, etc., agenda behind adopting international and regional instruments to deal with 'terrorists' (however defined), which is a term assumed throughout to extend to struggles for self-determination. Chapters 3 and 4 adopt a structured approach to war and peace and their respective frameworks of applicable law. Specifically, the use of official force to counter 'unlawful' violence is highlighted within the different variants of war and peace, first, by illustrating the legal standards that should apply when governments utilise military force, and, second, by indicating the dangers of conflation between those legal standards should states prefer instead to combine only the flexibilities of each.

Part 3 is, in turn, devoted to practical examples of inter-state anti-terrorist co-operation in which struggles for self-determination are re-characterised as mere 'terrorism'. Chapter 5 reviews the conventional instruments in force at the international and regional levels, while Chapter 6 concentrates primarily on the influence exerted by the practices adopted by the Permanent Member States of the UN Security Council in their own domestic arrangements over the rest of the international community. It is concluded that, inasmuch as states generally are able to utilise a vast range of means and methods having few international obligations attached, doctrinal consistency in international law regarding the use of force could be lost unless practical opportunities are taken rather closer to home, e.g., to foster domestically the means to generate human consent rather than coercion, which alone is capable of making wars of self-determination a matter of history.

---

31 Book Review, Sedley, 'Enemies of All Mankind', *L.R.B.*, 24 June 2010, p. 33.

# Part 2

In framing a government which is to be administered by men over men, the great difficulty lies in this: you must first enable the government to control the governed; and in the next place oblige it to control itself.

(James Madison, *Federalist Papers*, No. 51)

# 3    The role of laws of warfare

## Introduction

This chapter is intended to provide a general background to laws of armed conflict, inasmuch as those laws may be applied to struggles for self-determination. For this purpose, it must first be pointed out that a contemporary confusion in distinction between 'lawful' and 'unlawful' uses of force generally has been encouraged by the many new technological devices and tactical landscapes of recent years. Even as peoples gained their territorial independence from states in the early decolonisation process, the longstanding equivalence in mutual fear between certain governments and their populations ensures a tendency to resort to armed force to maintain order. The prioritisation of state security over the development of that state's own peoples thus reflects a government run not so much on trustee or caretaker lines, but instead, as a rent seeker claiming an entitlement to prohibit specific modalities of life within that society.[1]

The normalisation of domestic violence by a government is a hallmark of an oppressive state. In turn, modern developments in laws of armed conflict reflect the fact of raw power, even as those laws constitute an attempt to temper that power. For this reason, laws of armed conflict are applicable in violent struggles for self-determination only on a conditional basis: as a minimum, intense and/or prolonged exchange of armed force between a government and an organised liberation group should first be in evidence for this body of laws to apply.[2] However, even below this minimum scope and intensity, some states take the view that laws of armed conflict should always be the primary consideration among the armed forces as a matter of policy, as this body of law reinforces military self-discipline, tempers the use of armed force and restrains members of the military in their treatment of the enemy and civilians alike.

1 For expansion of this argument, see M. Duffield, 'Global Civil War: the Non-Insured, International Containment and Post-Interventionary Society' [2008] 21 *J.Ref.St.* 145.
2 The relevance of laws of armed conflict to insurgent group exchanges of armed force is controversial. See I.D. de Lupis, *The Law of War* (Cambridge: Cambridge University Press, 1987), pp. 35–8.

In contrast, certain governments seem far less constrained, as they tend more to adapt domestic 'peacetime' laws, e.g., when faced with violent social protest or behaviour they prefer to regard more commonly as 'criminal' or 'terrorist' and there are few if any international mechanisms to force a threatened state to apply laws of armed conflict domestically in relation to 'insurgents'. The surrounding doctrinal environment may prefer the view that laws of armed conflict are mere theory in situations of domestic unrest and, instead, support the right of states to exceed 'lawful' limits to restore good order. Even so, laws of armed conflict have been agreed by states at the international level and are thus a matter of inter-state customary law and/or treaty obligation. Moreover, as members of the official armed forces may themselves share close ties of kinship with dissident elements, the utilisation of force against those elements mandates the very highest levels of military order and loyalty to the government, which military attributes can be lost if laws of armed conflict are permitted to provide little of practical utility, as is now discussed.

## Times of war – a preliminary outline

The use of force within societies extends to violent revolution and certainly pre-dates modern laws of armed conflict. These laws have been developed largely from the mid-19th century to institutionalise predictable controls over the use of new technological developments and weaponry. As these laws evolved, a clear distinction between times of war and times of peace could develop, such that once a war began, the general law of peace was largely suspended and superseded by the more specialised laws of war and state neutrality.[3] The post-1945 political settlement attempted to alter this traditional practice by prohibiting inter-state aggression, which should have lessened the importance of the war–neutrality distinction. Even so, resorts to armed force by states have not slowed significantly. The difference today is that those resorts to use force are taken either in relation to a subject population or against persons deemed to be international criminals, such as 'terrorists'.

The rules regulating the lawful parameters of force thus remain relevant. Laws of armed conflict simply constitute another subset of public rules for human behaviour, albeit for use during exceptional events, i.e., those in which governmental coercion is a matter of life or death. The operation of 'laws' of armed conflict is also little different from that found in any other area of law. There is, however, one particularly useful feature of these laws: international humanitarian law, as this body of laws is denominated

---

3  See, e.g., E. Chadwick, *Traditional Neutrality Revisited: Law, Theory and Case Studies* (The Hague: Kluwer Law International, 2002).

today, binds not only states, but individuals as well. Individual criminal responsibility attaches to anyone found to have breached the relevant rules. Accordingly, their application as a behavioural parameter when curtailing or regulating violent events in human existence, e.g., revolution, can be particularly useful for the rule of law in general.

Contrariwise, the hierarchical nature of the international system mandates that only states have equal status, *inter se*. This status distinction then helps to explain why civil wars in particular tend to have a more indeterminate quality when the time arrives to apply law to them.[4] In other words, two separate situations are distinct: either there is an international armed conflict between states, in which the full scope of international laws of armed conflict is automatically applicable, or there is a non-international, domestic armed conflict, in which the scope and intensity of the force utilised should determine the source and scope of the law to be applied. This means that the precise scope of applicability of humanitarian laws can be somewhat complicated, while the implementation of laws of armed conflict in a violent struggle for self-determination can be even more complex, as well as controversial.

This indeterminacy of domestic armed force means that certain situations in which international standards should, in fact, apply to govern uses of military force might only be recognised as warranting the application of mere police or paramilitary force, within 'peacetime' criminal law frameworks.[5] The minimising effects of state powers to interpret their own local situations for purposes of legal enforcement powers can then create a more explosive situation, particularly in view of the twin exhortations on states found in the UN Charter, first in Article 2(4), to preserve each other's territorial integrity and political independence and, second, in Charter Article 2(7), not to interfere in the domestic affairs of each other. For example, and as summarised perceptively by Kiras:

> American President Franklin Roosevelt and British Prime Minister Winston Churchill could not possibly have known how truly strong and problematic the future whirlwind would be when they issued the Atlantic Charter in August 1941. Although most of its points appeared innocuous, the third point – the right of all peoples to self-determination – would cause the greatest difficulties. In particular, the leaders of socialist or nationalist movements . . . interpreted the

---

4 For example, as long ago as the American Civil War (1861–5), the alternative phrases 'War Between the States' and 'the Recent Unpleasantness' were used by the rebelling Southern Confederacy.

5 A third and more controversial possibility in the post-9/11 era is state self-defence against grave and repeated attack by terrorist forces. See 'The Chatham House Principles of International Law on the Use of Force in Self-Defence' [2006] 55 *I.C.L.Q.* 963.

Atlantic Charter as the basis for declarations of independence once the war was over.[6]

As with the operation of many areas of legal regulation, the laws of armed conflict are only as good as the extent to which they are respected, their rationale is comprehended, and their implementation in law restrains practical battlefield conditions. For this reason the primary concern in laws of armed conflict has generally not been the underlying cause of war, but, instead, the types and degrees of the force chosen to fight war. Accordingly, those liberation groups that do not receive international recognition or assistance for their 'rightful' cause are required first to earn a degree of international personality and recognition on (and off) the battlefield; they do this by demonstrating internal organisation, responsible leadership, control over territory, a commitment and ability to abide by humanitarian restraints and so on.[7] Once this occurs, the practicalities of battlefield reciprocity should ensure a measure of mutual self-discipline between the adversaries such that each instructs its own ranks to respect and abide by the relevant rules.[8]

Originally, the laws of armed conflict were developed in two main treaty formats: 'Hague' instruments impose obligations on governments to control and regulate the holders of command responsibility[9] and 'Geneva' instruments place obligations on governments to extend humanitarian protections to many – if not all – victims of armed conflict. There is thus an inbuilt status distinction between lawful combatants and non-combatants, e.g., civilians or soldiers who are *hors de combat*.[10] While the scope of this distinction has over time been reduced,[11] states continue to retain high levels of flexibility in the applicable law. For example, states often depend on reservations and declarations, that are appended to their treaty ratification, to make

---

6  J.D. Kiras, 'Irregular Warfare: Post-colonial Wars and the "Golden Age of Counterinsurgency"', in D. Jordan, J.D. Kiras, D.J. Lonsdale, I. Speller, C. Tuck and C.D. Walton (eds), *Understanding Modern Warfare* (Cambridge: Cambridge University Press, 2008), pp. 224, 257.

7  E.g., as required by Article 1(1) of additional Protocol 2 of 1977 to the four Geneva Conventions of 1949 and Relating to the Protection of Victims of Non-International Armed Conflicts.

8  The participation or *si omnes* clause was modernised in 1949 to make humanitarianism more universal. Common Article 2(3) to the four Geneva Conventions of 1949. See also Article 96(2) of additional Protocol 1 and Article 1(1) of additional Protocol 2 of 1977.

9  E.g., the International Military Tribunal (Nuremberg) ruled that, by 1939, the rules in Hague Convention IV of 1907 'were regarded as being declaratory of the laws and customs of war'. 'IMT (Nuremberg), Judgement and Sentences, 1 October 1946', reprinted in [1947] 41 *A.J.I.L.* 172, 248–9.

10  See the 1949 Geneva Conventions III and IV.

11  Cf. the 1899 and 1907 Hague Conventions Concerning the Laws and Usages of War, the four 1949 Geneva Conventions on the amelioration of the condition of victims of war, and the additional Protocols 1 and 2 of 1977 to the 1949 Geneva Conventions.

specific their future intentions or present interpretations of their international legal obligations. Variations in approach can then cause difficulties, while rules of customary international law on armed force are much less contestable.[12] Even so, obtaining redress for the breach of certain provisions requires a case to be made out in terms of state responsibility and/or individual criminal responsibility.

Inasmuch as states prior to 1945 were *bound* to comply with laws of war only if each and every hostile party to a conflict was party to the relevant instrument,[13] civil wars could be *treated* as full-scale belligerencies once their outbreak interrupted wider international and trade relations.[14] Any subsequent diplomatic recognition of the victorious party might then depend on evidence of wartime compliance with the relevant customary rules. In contrast, express reciprocity is no longer required in post-1945 'civil war' struggles, e.g., for self-determination, which have but rarely evinced mutual compliance with customary rules. 'Humanity in all circumstances' may be required today,[15] but in practical terms, there is far less scope available than in former times to assimilate civil wars into the obligations of international law (once a certain scale and intensity of force are reached), due in part to the strong international prohibition against the use of armed force – even though no 'law' is in fact capable of actually preventing armed hostilities should one party desire enough to use force against another.

Most fundamentally, it is the applicability of 'law' at all during 'war' which today is problematic.[16] The re-characterisation made in 1945, from 'war' to 'armed conflict' and/or a 'breach of international peace and security', reduces the chances that laws of armed conflict will be applied. The last two terms naturally sound better and a wider peace between states does indeed appear to have been largely maintained during the post-1945 era. The outbreak of armed hostilities has also caused less chance of complete rupture between states in diplomatic terms, as the prohibition of inter-state armed conflicts, per se, found in UN Charter Article 2(4), and the prohibition against interference found in Article 2(7), encourage the use

---

12 See J.-M. Henckaerts and L. Doswald-Beck (eds), *Customary International Humanitarian Law* (Cambridge: Cambridge University Press, 2005).

13 For example, defence council at Nuremberg argued that the 1907 Hague Convention IV was not formally applicable during the Second World War, due to the non-ratification of the Convention by several belligerents.

14 Cf. international attitudes to the Balkan wars (1912–13), as opposed to the Spanish Civil War (1936–9). E. Chadwick, 'Back to the Future: Three Civil Wars and the Law of Neutrality', in E. Chadwick, supra note 3, at p. 177.

15 For the ICRC interpretation of the words 'in all circumstances', see Y. Sandoz, C. Swinarski and B. Zimmerman (eds), *Commentary on the Additional Protocols of 8 June 1977* (Geneva: Martinus Nijhoff, 1987), pp. 37–8. Compare Article 96(2) of additional Protocol 1 of 1977.

16 See, generally, J.-J. Fresard, *The Roots of Behaviour in War: A Survey of the Literature* (Geneva: ICRC Publications, 2004).

of euphemism other than 'war'. Moreover, more or less subtle displays of force or other coercion remain available to further government policy,[17] including wide sovereign flexibilities the use of which can be characterised as states wish, initially at least.

Accordingly, governments today employ a wealth of alternative verbal strategies to assist them when formulating their future defence plans, which helps to reserve maximum flexibility for strategic choices in their use of the military instrument. If an armed conflict erupts, a panoply of euphemistic justification is then available. Inasmuch as states may be able to shift their burdens and responsibilities elsewhere, the requirements of public transparency can be much reduced. The outsourcing of military functions to specialist sectors of private industry extenuates the traditional links between governments, their military forces and the population at large, so the state ability to downplay the true nature of events represents a worrying development. The private sector might make available a greater range of choice to governments, e.g., by helping the latter to formulate and ensure an efficient private–public securitisation in military capacity, but public law frameworks of government responsibility can simultaneously be subverted, such that a total or partial immunity from prosecution for war crimes, grave breaches or other criminal law offences can be inbuilt in confidential commercial arrangements.[18]

This situation then makes it possible to argue that the heightened importance and emphasis placed on the maintenance of international peace and security in the post-1945 era and a strengthened, collective approach to ensuring existing state territorial boundaries and political independence, permit the contemporary assertion of extremely strong sovereign rights by individual states. Public–private arrangements hold the key for far less transparency in the official use of force itself, in terms of democratic mandate.[19] It should thus come as little surprise that a localised breach of the peace, e.g., in a struggle for equal rights and self-determination of 'peoples' (not 'states'), causes little concern to or distraction for the international community at large. A 'hands-off' attitude to domestic state affairs generally is equally apparent in the context of international terrorism, in view of localising laws to identify and prosecute 'terrorists'.[20]

---

17  Cf. the view of von Clausewitz's regarding war, as 'a mere continuation of (peace-time) policy by other means'. C.M. von Clausewitz, *On War*, A. Rapoport (ed.) (Harmondsworth: Penguin, 1968, first published 1832), Book 1, Ch. 1, Paragraph 24, p. 119.

18  See, e.g., C.J. Tams, 'The Use of Force against Terrorists' [2009] 20 *E.J.I.L.* 359; E. Chadwick, 'The 2005 Terrorism Convention: A Flexible Step Too Far?' [2007] 16(2) *Nottm.L.J.* 29; C. Walker and D. Whyte, 'Contracting Out War?: Private Military Companies, Law and Regulation in the United Kingdom' [2005] 54 *I.C.L.Q.* 651.

19  See, e.g., S. Shane, M. Mazzetti and R.F. Worth, 'Secret Assault on Terrorism Widens on Two Continents', *New York Times*, 14 August 2010 (US outsources its most important missions to an unaccountable, privately contracted army), nytimes.com.

20  See, e.g., N. Wong-Anan, 'Thai Court Orders Former Prime Minister Thaksin Arrested on Terrorism Charges', Reuters, 25 May 2010, www.uk.news.yahoo.com.

Moreover, certain territorial borders have in fact been reconfigured through the use of armed hostilities, such as the dissolution of the former territory of Yugoslavia, but the doctrinal environment adopted since 9/11 exhibits a much more marked willingness to emphasise the use of official force alone. Excessive force employed against 'terrorists' provides an apposite case. Little concern may be displayed either for the theory or practicality of individual rights of any description for 'terror' suspects. This raises a main concern that there has never before existed such a capacity in all states to deploy new, vertical controls over their subject populations, e.g., through increasingly sophisticated security technologies,[21] strict visa arrangements,[22] financial regulations[23] and so on, on the basis of international obligations. The steady erosion in the ability of individuals and groups to resist coercive state control thus risks the wider destruction of an important 1945 development: that of individual and people's rights.

Therefore, the greater evident fluidity and the flexibility and centrality reserved for official uses of force in the post-9/11 decade make it increasingly difficult to discern much of an underlying distinction between 'licit' and 'illicit' government acts.[24] Once private military or security firms are delegated to shoulder official functions, what restraints remain are locatable only through the traceability of official authorisation. The obligations required by the express ratification of humanitarian instruments can become quite lost in a public–private, moral–political 'anti-terrorist' hazard zone, as new theories of 'necessity', 'national survival', and/or 'security' serve only to cloud what may or may not remain of a shared international concept of forceful restraint and rights entitlements alike. In short, governments that overstep their mandates to govern undermine the very foundations of humanitarianism, military discipline and loyalty, as is now discussed.

## Laws of armed conflict

In terms of military strategy and tactics, an appropriate point of departure is the St Petersburg Declaration of 1868.[25] The International Military Commission convened at the St Petersburg Conference was composed of representatives of western European states, Russia, Turkey, Brazil and Persia.

---

21 Including the proliferation of 'no-fly' lists. See M. McIntire, 'Ensnared by Error on US Watch List', *New York Times*, 6 April 2010 (private security contractors choose from among 10,000 additional names in daily intelligence reports), nytimes.com.

22 Cf. Report, Kaczmarczyk and Okólski, 'International Migration in Central and Eastern Europe – Current and Future Trends', UN Expert Group Meeting on International Migration and Development, Population Division, Department of Economic and Social Affairs, UN Secretariat, New York, 6–8 July 2005, UN/POP/MIG/2005/12 (5 July 2005).

23 E.g., by means of the 1999 UN Convention on the Financing of Terrorism. See Chapter 5.

24 See, e.g., Comments, Byers, 'Terrorism, the Use of Force and International Law After 11 September' [2002] 51 *I.C.L.Q.* 401.

25 Text reprinted at [Suppl. 1907] 1 *A.J.I.L.* 16.

Discussion was centred on the prohibition or regulation of certain forms of new industrialised weaponry and, as none of the states objected generally to explosives in shells, the resulting Declaration specifically renounced the use against troops of exploding projectiles under 400 grammes in weight. These bullets, which had been developed initially to explode ammunition wagons, were subsequently modified to shatter on any impact such that they were likely to cause unnecessary suffering and inevitable death.[26] Crucially, however, the heads of state agreed to include in the Declaration's preamble a number of statements of principle, the most noteworthy of which is as follows:

> [The] Commission, having by common agreement fixed the technical limits at which the necessities of war ought to yield to the requirements of humanity . . . [is] authorised . . . to declare as follows:
>
> [. . .] That the only legitimate object which states should endeavour to accomplish during war is to weaken the military forces of the enemy;
>
> That for this purpose it is sufficient to disable the greatest possible number of men;
>
> That this object would be exceeded by the employment of arms which uselessly aggravate the sufferings of disabled men, or render their death inevitable.

The St Petersburg Declaration, as was usual at the time, was premised on an express reciprocity binding *all* the parties to a war. The applicability of rules of armed conflict in the contemporary era has also been modernised and supplemented far beyond this early and strictly reciprocal framework and humanitarianism is today a universal obligation. Even so, the relevant rules continue to be made dependent on whether an 'armed conflict' is recognised as such. Failing such recognition, the mantra of 'humanity in all circumstances' should, of course, still provide some protection, but for any situation requiring the use of official force, the relevant rules and their appropriate scope of applicability must first be determined on the basis of an international or non-international armed conflict or whether that conflict is of a lesser 'armed' variety such that domestic state criminal law frameworks may instead be deemed more appropriate.

Attention should be drawn to the concrete evidence of a state's willingness both to internalise and to reinforce humanitarian limits, as without 'law', military force merely provides a tool of coercion to governments. For example, at the most basic level, an international armed conflict is

---

26 A. Roberts and R. Guelff, *Documents on the Laws of War* (Oxford: Oxford University Press, 3rd edn, 2000), p. 53.

identified once two or more states exchange armed force. Whether or not that force attracts much international attention, the general treaty system in place requires an immediate cessation to the use of force and state compliance with fundamental UN requirements and obligations such as to settle the matter peacefully. Compliance then requires rapid remedial action to correct the cause of the hostilities, and/or to submit the matter to peaceful arbitration. This straightforward approach is in contrast to the more localised parameters for dealing with a non-international armed conflict, in that third states have no automatic right to interfere.[27] A non-international conflict is one that occurs within single state boundaries[28] and, typically, is less disruptive to international peace.

In the main, the vast majority of armed conflicts since 1945 have, in fact, been non-international, many waged by 'peoples' to achieve greater rights of self-determination. Examples range from the small scale, through to more consistent and/or intense exchanges of armed force between government forces and a non-state group or between such groups.[29] A 'just cause' however does not release the parties from humanitarian constraints, particularly as non-international conflicts are more easily euphemised as mere domestic disturbances that require only additional 'peacetime' emergency powers. Instead, all non-international armed conflicts should be guided from the very start at or above the minimal level provided by Common Article 3 to the four Geneva Conventions of 1949. Sidestepping political judgement for present purposes, as to the rights or wrongs of specific non-state groups resorting to armed force to attain rights entitlements, the minimal requirements of Common Article 3 are mandatory as they are considered to constitute customary international law.[30]

Nevertheless, the International Committee of the Red Cross has readily acknowledged during the post-1945 era that 'international customary law is applicable to all *states*'.[31] The ICRC also promotes the view that laws of war apply 'between states parties . . . *and states and other belligerent parties* accepting that treaty and applying its provisions', 'from the first acts

---

27 See, e.g., I.D. de Lupis, supra note 2, pp. 66–84.
28 Contrast UN Charter Articles 2(4) and 2(7). See also UN Charter Chapter VII, for Security Council powers in such an event.
29 Cf. the recent civil violence in Thailand. See, e.g., ILA Use of Force Committee, 'Final Report (Draft) on the Meaning of Armed Conflict in International Law', submitted at the ILA Annual Conference, The Hague, 15–20 August 2010, pp. 27–8, www.ila-hq.org.; B. Doherty, 'Bloodshed in Bangkok', *The Saturday Guardian*, 15 May 2010, p. 30.
30 *Military and Paramilitary Activities in and against Nicaragua (Nicaragua v. U.S.), Merits* [1986] ICJ Rep. p. 14 para. 218 (the 'elementary' rules of Common Article 3 are applicable in all circumstances, including in international armed conflicts). See also R. Abi-Saab, 'The "General Principles" of Humanitarian Law according to the International Court of Justice' [July–Aug. 1987] 259 *I.R.R.C.* 367.
31 Emphasis added. F. de Mulinen, *Handbook on the Law of War for Armed Forces* (Geneva: ICRC, 1987), p. 6.

of hostilities or unresisted occupation'.[32] Therefore, compliance with any Geneva instrument can be viewed through the modernised requirements of additional Protocol 1,[33] in Article 96(2):

> When one of the Parties to the conflict is not bound by this Protocol, the Parties to the Protocol shall remain bound by it in their mutual relations. They shall furthermore be bound by this Protocol in relation to each of the parties which are not bound by it, if the latter accepts and applies the provisions thereof.

However, while the ICRC promotes respect for humanitarian limits whether or not there is effective reciprocity in treatment, e.g., between liberation groups and those governments that refuse to recognise the scope of their mutual armed struggle, such an expectation may be misplaced. Doubt remains for many reasons as to whether sub-state groups are in fact even bound by the provisions of Common Article 3, for example. Struggling groups of any description have not generally been permitted to participate in the inter-state negotiations at which rules have been devised for use by states during non-international armed conflicts.[34] Their consent to those rules is thus not required. They may understand the purpose behind the relevant provisions, but might feel that compliance will not assist their cause positively, particularly as evidence is lacking of state reinforcement for doing so. This in turn affects the willingness of all parties to respect the relevant rules.[35]

The behavioural restraints contained in Common Article 3 to the four Geneva Conventions of 1949 constitute a bare minimum and in pertinent part provide as follows:

> *Article 3*: In the case of armed conflict not of an international character occurring in the territory of one of the High Contracting Parties, each Party to the conflict shall be bound to apply, as a minimum, the following provisions:

32  Emphasis added. *Ibid.*, pp. 6 and 7. See, e.g., Article 96(3) of additional Protocol 1 of 1977.
33  1125 UNTS 3 (1979); UKTS 29 (1999). See, e.g., M. Bothe, 'Commentary: 1977 Geneva Protocol 1', in N. Ronzitti (ed.), *The Law of Naval Warfare: A Collection of Agreements and Documents with Commentaries* (London: Martinus Nijhoff, 1988), p. 760.
34  Cf. the action of the Swiss Federal Council, which left it up to individual states parties to decide whether to accept the request by the Palestinian Liberation Organisation, made in a letter of 21 June 1989 addressed to the Swiss Federal Department of Foreign Affairs, to adhere to the four 1949 Geneva Conventions and two additional Protocols of 1977, www.icrc.org/ihl.nsf/Pays?ReadForm&c=PS.
35  Compare E. Chadwick, 'It's War Jim, But Not as We Know It: A "Reality-check" for International Laws of War?' [2003] 39(3) *Crime, Law and Social Change* 233.

(1) Persons taking no active part in the hostilities, including members of armed forces who have laid down their arms and those placed *hors de combat* by sickness, wounds, detention, or any other cause, shall in all circumstances be treated humanely, without any adverse distinction founded on race, colour, religion or faith, sex, birth or wealth, or any other similar criteria. To this end, the following acts are and shall remain prohibited at any time and in any place whatsoever with respect to the above-mentioned persons:

    (a) violence to life and person, in particular murder of all kinds, mutilation, cruel treatment and torture;

    (b) taking of hostages;

    (c) outrages upon personal dignity, in particular, humiliating and degrading treatment;

    (d) the passing of sentences and the carrying out of executions without previous judgement pronounced by a regularly constituted court affording all the judicial guarantees which are recognised as indispensable by civilised peoples.

(2) The wounded and sick shall be collected and cared for.

    [. . .]

The application of the preceding provisions shall not affect the legal status of the Parties to the conflict.

As can be seen, governments fighting in the vast majority of post-1945 armed conflicts have been legally obligated to implement only the most basic humanitarian protections; even then, protection is owed strictly only to those persons taking no part in the hostilities.[36] There are many controversial aspects of attempting through international law to restrain conduct during a non-international armed conflict and the application of Common Article 3 alters no pre-existing legal status held by either party to the conflict:[37] the state remains the only administrative unit lawfully entitled automatically to use armed force, while the mere resort to force of arms by an insurgent group certainly attracts nothing similar. Even so, broader Geneva concerns are still reflected generally, despite this fundamental distinction (i.e., between lawful combatants and non-combatants),[38] in terms of proportionality in attack, the prohibition of reprisals and so on.

---

36 *Nicaragua v. U.S.*, supra note 30, at para. 218.

37 But see UNGA Resolution 3103 (XXVIII), 12 December 1973, on basic principles of the legal status of the combatants struggling against colonial and alien domination and racist regimes.

38 Another distinction is made between soldiers and spies. See S. Shane, M. Mazzetti and R.F. Worth, 'Secret Assault on Terrorism Widens on Two Continents', *New York Times*, 14 August 2010 (troops put at risk of denial of Geneva protections), nytimes.com.

Many humanitarian anomalies were, in turn, produced during the many Cold War non-international armed conflicts by this quite minimal approach. States have often felt able – if not entitled – to exceed these Geneva parameters when acting domestically. A Diplomatic Conference was finally convened by the ICRC in Geneva in 1974 to supplement and expand the outdated approach. Lasting from 1974–7, the Conference produced two new Geneva Protocols, which supplemented and improved on the previous coverage of Articles 2 and 3 common to the four Geneva Conventions of 1949. Additional Protocol 1 of 1977, relating to the protection of victims of international armed conflicts,[39] extends combatant eligibility to many more violent actors, in practical recognition of new forms and types of warfare, even as those actors are still required to be organised under responsible command, and to attempt to comply with international rules for armed conflict.

Crucially, Protocol 1 Article 1(4) extends the application of Geneva provisions in full to:

> *[I]nclude* armed conflicts in which peoples are fighting against colonial domination and alien occupation and against racist regimes in the exercise of their right of self-determination, as enshrined in the Charter of the United Nations and the Declaration on Principles of International Law concerning Friendly Relations and Co-operation among states in accordance with the Charter of the United Nations.[40]

The decision to extend the scope of application of Article 1(4) provides the ultimate proof, if any were needed, that a 'people's' struggle for self-determination is not a mere domestic issue. This express inclusion of certain liberationist armed conflicts within the obligatory frameworks of international humanitarian law came at a cost, however, as it naturally caused consternation in some states not least because it seemed to recognise an entitlement to use 'terrorist', anti-government armed force on the basis of a 'cause'.[41] However, express ICRC sponsorship of Article 1(4) helped to ensure the entry into force of Protocol 1,[42] which gave the international community more oversight of the conduct of armed hostilities. The ICRC also made clear that a central safeguard remains: a liberation group needs at a minimum to have attracted some provisional level of international personality before its use of force can be viewed as legitimate. For this

---

39  Supra note 33.
40  Emphasis added. See UNGA Resolution 2625 (XXV) of 24 October 1970 (adopted by consensus). UNGA Resolution 3103, para. 3, supra note 37, contains the same conclusion.
41  See, e.g., J. Gardam, 'Protocol 1 to the Geneva Conventions: A Victim of Short-Sighted Political Considerations?' [1989] 17 *Mel.U.L.R.* 107; G. Best, *Humanity in Warfare: Modern History of the International Law of Armed Conflicts* (Littlehampton: Littlehampton Book Services Ltd, 1980), p. 321.
42  On 7 December 1978.

reason, the ICRC has stated that 'the mere existence of a government or resistance movement is not sufficient evidence of the international character of the conflict, nor does it establish that character'.[43]

Article 1(1) of Protocol 2, by way of contrast, makes the application of the two Protocols mutually exclusive. Protocol 2 also requires improved state self-regulation in non-international armed conflicts, but this is to be accomplished at a price – that of a tightly restricted scope of application. Protocol 2 applies only to armed conflicts:

> [W]hich take place in the territory of a High Contracting Party between its armed forces and dissident armed forces or other organised armed groups which, under responsible command, exercise such control over a part of its territory as to enable them to carry out sustained and concerted military operations and to implement this Protocol.[44]

In other words, to claim any entitlement to greater protections than those found in Common Article 3, the non-international conflict must be waged between a state and non-state group(s) within state territorial boundaries *and* the non-state group(s) must control a part of that territory *and* implement the Protocol. Article 1(1) clearly highlights the essential fact that international legal responsibility is entailed *only* within defined state territorial borders,[45] which reflects an exceedingly conservative approach in which the Protocol is made a practicable nonsense. Moreover, while Protocol 2 and Common Article 3 are similar in not defining the term 'armed conflict',[46] upper and lower thresholds for applicability are specified in Article 1(2) of Protocol 2. Protocol 2 does not apply to exchanges of armed force exceeding the upper limits of Article 1(2), at which point international Geneva provisions become available or if the use of force consists only of 'situations of internal disturbances and tensions, such as riots, isolated and sporadic acts of violence and other acts of a similar nature, as not being armed conflicts',[47] to which Common Article 3 may or may not apply.[48]

---

43 *The ICRC Commentary*, supra note 15, p. 508 (citation omitted). E.g., the ICRC viewed the Kosovo Liberation Army in the mid-1990s as a domestic group fighting only against Serbian 'police forces'. Cf. ILA Use of Force Committee, 'Final Report (Draft)', supra note 29, at pp. 19–21. See S. Boelaert-Suominen, 'The ICTY and the Kosovo Conflict' [2000] 837 *I.R.R.C.* 217.

44 Additional Protocol 2 Article 1(1).

45 See also additional Protocol 1 Article 3(b). Cf. M. Duffield, supra note 1, who discusses 'global' civil war.

46 Regarding contemporary difficulties in establishing the relevant thresholds, see ILA Use of Force Committee, 'Final Report (Draft)', supra note 29. See also M.E. O'Connell, 'Defining Armed Conflict' [2008] 13 *J.Con.&Sec.L.* 393.

47 For a discussion of this additional test, see A. Cullen, 'The Definition of Non-International Armed Conflict in the Rome Statute: An Analysis of the Threshold of Application Contained in Article 8(2)(f)' [2007] 12 *J.Confl.&Sec.L.* 419.

48 For a discussion of this point, see the ILA Use of Force Committee, 'Final Report (Draft)', supra note 29, at pp. 19–22.

Unfortunately, the ICRC explanation as to this new and express upper and lower limit of force is not entirely clear: if in regard to open struggle, the Protocol might (or might not) apply. As for acts of violence, which range from 'the spontaneous generation of acts of revolt, to the struggle between more or less organised groups and the authorities in power',[49] recourse to the police or similar forces to restore order may be all that is required. As examples of mere 'internal tension', the Commentary lists large-scale arrests and large numbers of political prisoners, regarding which latter:

> It should be noted that there is no legal definition of so-called 'political' prisoners. They may be referred to in very different ways depending on national legislation, for example, 'persons detained for security reasons', 'persons detained by order of the executive', etc.[50]

National legislation is, of course, the principle obstacle to rights of self-determination, even as an element of co-operation between a government and the governed could in contrast make violent struggles for self-determination a thing of the past. In turn, state ratification of additional Protocols 1 and 2 has been more leisurely,[51] which makes certain provisions uncertain as to the extent to which they are today entrenched in customary international law.[52] Even so, Common Article 3 of 1949 forms part of customary international law and remains theoretically available for situations in which the elusiveness of lawful limits on uses of state force within state territorial borders is in evidence.

As might therefore be expected, the many layered filters of individual state decision making and discretion generally enable states themselves to determine what and whether particular rules bind them in certain circumstances, and the atrocities of 9/11 are but a reminder of the primitive role still played by force in the world today. Unless there is an authoritative declaration, such as from the ICJ[53] or the UN Security Council

---

49 *The Commentary*, supra note 15, p. 1355, quoting the ICRC submission to the Conference of Government Experts in 1971 (citation omitted).
50 *Ibid.*, p. 1355 n. 29.
51 But is steadily increasing. See, e.g., UNGA Resolution 63/125 of 15 January 2009 on the 'Status of the 1977 Geneva Protocols', UN Doc. A/RES/63/125, 63rd session, Agenda item 76.
52 But see, e.g., J.-M. Henckaerts and L. Doswald-Beck (eds), supra note 12. Cf. C. Greenwood, 'Customary International Law and the First Geneva Protocol in the Gulf Conflict', in P. Rowe (ed.), *The Gulf War 1990–1991 in International and English Law* (New York: Routledge, Sweet & Maxwell, 1993), p. 63.
53 See, e.g., *Legal Consequences for States of the Continued Presence of South Africa in Namibia (South West Africa) Notwithstanding SC Resolution 276 (1970) (Advisory Opinion)* [1971] ICJ Rep. 16, at 31 (principle of self-determination applicable for all the UN, and specifically to peoples and territories which 'have not yet attained independence'). See also UNGA Resolution 63/3 of 8 October 2008.

acting under UN Charter Chapter VII,[54] it remains largely for states alone to manage their own compliance with international law and rules of armed conflict. Accordingly, the enduring rarity of recognition that Common Article 3 applies or is enforced in certain less sophisticated or less popular non-international armed conflicts remains of concern. Non-enforcement, etc., may be explained by a widespread lack of education, infrastructure, and/or judicial capacity. Conversely, non-enforcement may be attributable to a disregard of humanitarianism itself, in relation to particular enemies, as is now discussed.

## Prevention of breaches of laws of armed conflict

### In general

The fundamental problem with governmental non-recognition of domestic 'armed conflicts', as such, is as follows. State duties to fulfil the obligations imposed by even minimal levels of humanitarian law often fall foul of broader government strategic considerations. On the one hand, many rules of armed conflict must of necessity depend on realistic, sliding scales of military flexibility under battlefield conditions. Once humanitarian rules are implemented, no derogation beyond *military* necessity and proportionality is available in general.[55] In other words, field commanders may only conduct their operations within more specialised frameworks of necessity and proportionality. This inability to derogate from humanitarian prohibitions militates not only against government instincts in their shorter term strategies to react immediately and excessively to shows of insurgent force; the legal parameters for action when *military* necessity and proportionality are concerned require far higher standards of care than might otherwise be thought.[56]

As civilians are able only to seek protection from somewhat indeterminate human rights norms if an 'emergency situation' is recognised, rather than an 'armed conflict',[57] the spirit of the 1868 St Petersburg Declaration is hardly satisfied, as that instrument makes quite clear that the means or methods of armed force adopted should not 'uselessly aggravate the sufferings of disabled men, or render their death inevitable'. On the other hand,

---

54 See, e.g., the jurisprudence on the issue by the International Criminal Courts for the former Territory of Yugoslavia and Rwanda, established pursuant to UNSC Resolutions 827 of 25 May 1993 and 955 of 8 November 1994, respectively.

55 See, e.g., Preamble to Protocol 2: 'international instruments relating to human rights offer a basic protection to the human person'.

56 See, e.g., Article 15(1) of the 1950 ECHR. See W. Abresch, 'A Human Rights Law of Internal Armed Conflict: The ECtHR in Chechnya' [2005] 16 *E.J.I.L.* 741.

57 See, e.g., C. Warbrick, 'The Principles of the ECHR and the Response of States to Terrorism' [2002] 3 *E.H.R.L.R.* 287.

even as many more specific humanitarian rules have been agreed since 1868, the widespread *non*-recognition of humanitarian law applicability certainly affords governments more malleable standards with which to gauge their available choices of action, particularly in situations that move in and out of different stages and intensities of violence or conflict.[58] It can equally be posited that the retention of both strategic and terminological flexibilities in respect of non-international armed conflicts can, in fact, be used to mollify humanitarian sentiments: the use of counter-force does after all both weaken and disable an opponent.

The 1949 Geneva Conventions and additional Protocol 1 of 1977 have long provided for the prosecution of perpetrators of grave breaches and war crimes in international armed conflicts,[59] but states hesitate or refuse to do so largely for political reasons and subsequent international inaction too often rewards a recalcitrant state. Little recourse is made to UN Charter arrangements, which, in any event, afford little concrete solution, particularly as UN Security Council powers for maintaining international peace and security pursuant to Charter Chapter VII tend to operate well only where there is sufficient political will.[60] The UN General Assembly is constrained from making binding recommendations and should not make any recommendation at all once it has been notified that the Security Council is dealing with a matter.[61] A highly conservative ICJ proceeds with extreme caution when asked to adjudicate either a contentious dispute or to deliver an advisory opinion, which concerns armed hostilities.[62] Lastly, creative euphemism is always available to downplay the nature of various situations occurring within state territorial boundaries.

## The adjudication of atrocity

Obviously, the Charter arrangements of 1945 reflect the political relations of their time, yet a major concern since has been to create an international *legal* order – one that is capable of 'rising above' mere diplomacy or other political arrangement. As post-Cold War era non-international armed conflicts increased in number and ferocity, this concern surrounding an international legal order appears to have imbued certain states with a renewed

---

58 See, e.g., Current Development, Okowa, 'Case Concerning Armed Activities on the Territory of the Congo (*Democratic Republic of the Congo v. Uganda*)' [2006] 55 I.C.L.Q. 742.
59 1949 Geneva Convention I Article 49, Convention II Article 50, Convention III Article 129, Convention IV Article 146, and 1977 additional Protocol 1 Article 85.
60 UN Charter Article 27(3).
61 UN Charter Articles 10–12 and 14.
62 See, e.g., Speech by H.E. Judge Rosalyn Higgins, (former) President of the ICJ, to the 61st Session of the UNGA, 26 October 2006, reprinted by Oxford University Press, ukcatalogue. oup.com/product/9780198262350.do.

sense of urgency to deter the incidence of extreme and systematic acts of violence, and it can be stated with much more certainty today that atrocity is no longer so well tolerated. New judicial capacity has been made available, such as the ad hoc tribunals created by UN Security Council action to prosecute war criminals, perpetrators of crimes against humanity and/or genocide in the former territory of Yugoslavia and in Rwanda[63] or the more localised mixed law tribunals, e.g., in Lebanon and Cambodia.[64] Many dilemmas of 'international justice' have also today secured a partial solution with the ratification and entry into force of the 1998 Rome Statute for an International Criminal Court,[65] created outside UN arrangements to exercise jurisdiction over 'the most serious crimes of concern to the international community as a whole'.[66]

It has been recognised since the International Military War Crimes Tribunals held in Nuremberg and Tokyo after the Second World War that individuals can be subjected to prosecution under humanitarian law irrespective of personal status and can be held individually criminally responsible.[67] There is now an even broader impetus behind the harmonisation of domestic laws with international standards prohibiting crimes of war, humanity and genocide, and the basis of jurisdiction in the multilateral Rome Statute of 1998 is on 'complementarity'. This means that national criminal jurisdictions in states that are willing and able to prosecute violent actors may do so.[68] The very formation of the ICC was thus intended to be only an additional means with which to end impunity[69] and one that can potentially sidestep the political deadlocks that occur so frequently in UN Security Council political decision making under Charter Chapter VII.[70] What is also new is the uncoupling of acts of genocide and

63 UNSC Resolutions 827 of 25 May 1993, and 955 of 8 November 1994, supra note 54.
64 Special Tribunal for Lebanon, established pursuant to UNSC Resolution 1757 of 30 May 2007; Extraordinary Chambers in the Courts of Cambodia for the prosecution of persons belonging to the Khmer Rouge, approved in UNGA Resolution 57/228 B of 13 May 2003 and established pursuant to Agreement between the UN and the Royal Government of Cambodia signed in Phnom Penh on 6 June 2003.
65 Opened for signature 17 July 1998; entered into force 1 July 2002; text reprinted in [1998] 37 I.L.M. 1002.
66 Rome Statute Articles 1 and 2.
67 'IMT (Nuremberg), Judgement and Sentences', supra note 9. See also Rome Statute Articles 1, 25 and 27.
68 Rome Statute Article 17.
69 Consider J.P. Cerone, 'Dynamic Equilibrium: the Evolution of US Attitudes Toward International Criminal Courts and Tribunals' [2007] 18 *E.J.I.L.* 277; J. Kyriakakis, 'Corporations and the ICC: The Complementarity Objection Stripped Bare' [2008] 19(1) *Crim.L.F.* 115.
70 E.g., the decision to withdraw the United Nations Observer Mission established in 1993 for Georgia (UNOMIG), following disagreement in the Security Council regarding further support. UNSecGen'l, UN Doc. SG/SM/12342, Press Release of 30 June 2009.

crimes against humanity from situations of armed conflict for purposes of jurisdiction, which allows alleged perpetrators to be tried for crimes committed at any time.[71]

Rome Statute Article 5 lists the following heads of jurisdiction: crimes of genocide, against humanity, of war and of aggression. The most contentious is the crime of aggression. The crimes in issue were in large part established or given substance immediately after the Second World War, but the use and application of the phrase 'crimes against the peace' or 'aggression' at Nuremberg is still deemed today to be insufficiently precise. The ICC thus requires both a new definition and the formulation of precise jurisdictional preconditions, in accordance with Rome Statute Articles 121 and 123. When the Rome Statute entered into force in 2002, a Special Working Group on the Crime of Aggression was appointed by the ICC's Preparatory Commission to work on these tasks, and after meeting formally on a twice-yearly basis, it did, in fact, arrive at a draft 'definition' tentatively based on UNGA Resolution 3314 (XXIX) of 14 December 1974.[72] This definition was approved by the Revision Conference held in Uganda from 31 May–11 June 2010,[73] but, as various 'triggers and filters for referrals' remain contentious, the 'crime' is yet to be made operative.[74]

Thus, since the end of the Cold War, the legal environment has certainly evolved to discourage the breach of well-known international standards of wartime behaviour. In terms of individual criminal liability, the post-1945 principle of non-interference in domestic state affairs has, to a certain extent, been shrunk.[75] Traditional approaches to sovereign powers of domestic control are increasingly coded by new and concrete international moves to punish those aiding, facilitating, etc., specific large-scale wartime atrocities regardless of their underlying 'cause'. The recent impetus by states to

---

71  See P. Akhavan, 'Reconciling Crimes against Humanity with the Laws of War' [2008] 6 *J.I.Cr.J.* 21.
72  See Report of the Special Working Group on the Crime of Aggression, 9–13 February 2009, ICC-ASP/7/20/Annex II and Addendum 1 (Appendix 1).
73  Resolution RC/Res. 6, 'The Crime of Aggression', Annex 1: 'Amendments to the Rome Statute' Articles 15bis and 15ter (adopted 11 June 2010 by consensus), www.icc-cpi.int/iccdocs/asp_docs/Resolutions/. Contrast Note, Boeving, 'Aggression, International Law, and the ICC: An Argument for the Withdrawal of Aggression from the Rome Statute' [2005] 43 *Colum.J.Transnat'l.L.* 557.
74  See Resolution RC/Res. 6, 'The Crime of Aggression', Annex 1, supra note 73. See, e.g., C.L. Sriram, 'State Aggression is Finally a Crime . . . But How is it Punished?', *The Guardian*, 14 June 2010, guardian.co.uk.
75  Consider J.P. Cerone, supra note 69; B. Tuzmukhamedov, 'Symposium: ICC and Non-Party States. The ICC and Russian Constitutional Problems' [2005] 3 *J.Int'l.Cr.J.* 621; L. Jianping, and W. Zhixiang, 'Symposium: ICC and Non-Party States: China's Attitude Towards the ICC' [2005] 3 *J.Int'l.Cr.J.* 608. Cf. the provision made in Rome Statute Article 98 for so-called 'immunity' or 'impunity', agreements and utilised heavily by the USA. D. Scheffer, 'Article 98(2) of the Rome Statute: America's Original Intent' [2005] 3 *J.Int'l.Cr.J.* 333.

ratify and implement the Rome Statute finally makes express the most fundamental, longstanding state obligations, the breach of which will no longer be tolerated.[76] The ICC has shortcomings, but the attempt to prevent and alleviate the suffering inflicted by extreme forms of violence – a goal long sought in humanitarian and human rights instruments – is certainly better than nothing and better late than never. Most crucially, it is only by making any perpetrator and/or instigator, of whatever rank, fully accountable for such actions that high-level impunity may cease.

### *'Borderline' situations*

Even in states that have ratified and implemented the Rome Statute, contentious issues remain, e.g., the potentially exculpatory aspects of amnesties and truth commissions.[77] In contrast, domestic trial under post-9/11 'new' domestic criminal laws contemplates the prosecution of increasing numbers of actors for 'new' types of prohibited violence, as has become particularly apparent in the international action adopted to deter the new conflicts arising ostensibly in connection with the Al Qaeda phenomenon. The ICC regime unfortunately reinforces this distinct framework by helping to perpetuate the international–domestic distribution of legal power. For example, after the US Congress rapidly approved the use of military force against Afghanistan in the wake of the 9/11 terrorist attacks, the US also overturned its 1976 ban on political assassination[78] and began to search for those persons it considers to be militant enemies. According to one recent report in the mainstream US press:

> At least by American government calculations, the killing of an Al Qaeda member is an act of war, not assassination. The ban on assassination, in effect since President Gerald Ford's executive order of 1976, would apply only to 'politically inspired killings of people who are not combatants'. To be a lawful target, a terrorist must be 'engaged in armed combat with the United States'.[79]

This US attitude that Al Qaeda members are 'unlawful combatants', to be hunted down and murdered, raises a central problem for international

---

76 See, e.g., E. Chadwick, 'A Tale of Two Courts: The "Creation" of a Jurisdiction?' [2004] 9 *J.Confl.&Sec.L.* 71.

77 See, e.g., D. Roche, 'Truth Commission Amnesties and the International Criminal Court' [2005] 45 *Br.J.Crim.* 565.

78 See, e.g., S. Shane, 'U.S. Approves Targeted Killing of American Cleric', *New York Times*, 6 April 2010, nytimes.com; N. Melzer, *Targeted Killing in International Law* (Oxford: Oxford University Press, 2008).

79 S. Shane, 'Government Hit Squads, Minus the Hits', *New York Times*, 18 July 2009, nytimes.com.

justice: an 'act of war', so-called, should, of course, always be accomplished in accordance with international law,[80] while the identification, proscription and prosecution of 'terrorists' are regulated by domestic state criminal laws. This legal distinction forms the subject of succeeding chapters, but, for present purposes, it is sufficient to note that the assassination policy indicated here is pursued within an overarching US reluctance to view 'terrorists' and their acts as ever coming within the framework of laws of armed conflict.[81] In this, there is certainly no hint of the humanitarian spirit promoted by the 1868 St Petersburg Declaration, but is, instead, rather more akin to the treatment meted out for 'war treason' in occupied territory, before 1949.[82] It must thus be kept uppermost in mind that many of those involved in ongoing armed conflicts of whatever ilk have never encountered, not to mention internalised, any higher 'law' than their own side's military might.[83]

Irregular fighters of any description are often unable or unwilling to comply with humanitarian or human rights norms and/or are simply unaware of certain prohibitions.[84] Overstepping the limits of law is easily done even when those limits are well known.[85] 'Unprivileged' combatants and unrecognised armed conflicts thus continue to raise old questions about new uses of force, despite the attempt at St Petersburg to 'fix [. . .] the technical limits at which the necessities of war ought to yield to the requirements of

---

80   In relation to 'terrorist' means and methods of warfare, see Article 33 of Geneva Convention IV, Articles 43, 44 and 51 of Protocol 1 and Articles 4 and 13 of Protocol 2. See also ILA Use of Force Committee, 'Final Report (Draft)', supra note 29, p. 25.

81   See S. Schmemann, 'The World; Prisoners, Surely. But POWs?', *New York Times*, 27 January 2002, nytimes.com; F. Johns, 'Guantanamo Bay and the Annihilation of the Exception' [2005] 16 *E.J.I.L.* 613.

82   Which offence traditionally extended to treacherous acts by private individuals or soldiers in disguise. J.E. Edwards and L. Oppenheim, *Land Warfare: An Exposition of the Laws and Usages of War on Land, for the Guidance of Officers of His Majesty's Army* (London: His Majesty's Stationery Office, 1912), para. 167.

83   Cf. Article 47 of Geneva Convention 1, Article 48 of Convention II, Article 127 of Convention III and Article 144 of Convention IV of 1949. See also Article 83(1) of additional Protocol 1 of 1977.

84   But see Article 3 of the 1907 Hague Convention IV Respecting the Laws and Customs of War on Land. Contrast Rome Statute Article 25(4): 'No provision in this Statute relating to international criminal responsibility shall affect the responsibility of states under international law'. See also Rome Statute Article 33.

85   See J. Rikhof, 'Fewer Places to Hide? The Impact of Domestic War Crimes Prosecutions on International Impunity' [2009] 20 *Crim.L.For.* 1. Contrast Case Comment, Rasiah, 'The Court-martial of Corporal Payne and Others and the Future Landscape of International Criminal Justice' [2009] 7(1) *J.Int'l.Crim.J.* 177; T.W. Pittman and M. Heaphy, 'Does the US Really Prosecute Its Service Members for War Crimes? Implications for Complementarity before the ICC' [2008] *Leid.J.I.L.* 165; P. Rowe, 'Military Misconduct during International Armed Operations: "Bad Apples" or Systemic Failure?' [2008] 13 *J.Confl.&Sec.L.* 165; A.P.V. Rogers, 'War Crimes Trials under the Royal Warrant: British Practice 1945–1949' [1990] 39 *I.C.L.Q.* 780.

humanity'.[86] In 1868 this exhortation was not considered applicable to fighting 'savage tribes',[87] whereas for purposes of ICC prosecutorial neutrality, 'humanity in all circumstances' is required. Even so, the ICC must first look to the elements of crimes within differing violent contexts (whether international, non-international, mere civil disturbance, etc.), rather than to official characterisations of that violence by one or other state.

Persistent status gaps remain in legal coverage nonetheless.[88] Status distinctions arise from within the constitutional or commercial arrangements put in place by individual states to accommodate their own government powers and the use of force. Should these distinctions prove abusive, legal blurring is produced, in that like cases are not treated as like. Even as decolonisation started the process of transforming peoples into nation-states, the development of friendly relations between states themselves was 'based on principles of equal rights and self-determination', yet bi- and multilateral defensive arrangements have not been made redundant. Existing territorial boundaries and political independence are not secure. The intervening decades have only led states to deepen and extend their own mechanisms to contain, repress and control captive populations. The virtual ban in place today on free and spontaneous migration effectively traps those who inhabit territories split on ideological, nationalist, and/or religious lines, or in danger of being 'ethnically cleansed'.

Accordingly, the rhetoric of self-determination is likely to continue fuelling armed conflict no matter what the characterisation attributed to that conflict may be, as is now discussed.

## Problems in identifying an 'armed conflict'

It was noted at the start of this chapter that individual states tend to view the domestic applicability of even minimal laws of armed conflict within their own territorial boundaries more as theory than as an obligation. In any event, a link to an armed conflict is no longer required today to prosecute genocide and crimes against humanity. However, a refusal to countenance the existence of a domestic armed conflict does nothing to promote the rule of law – one in which ascertainable legal limits to official uses of force exist – which also can undermine the content of human rights law. Of course, official rights to kill without warning or to detain without trial may appear at first sight to be far more limited in peacetime, but as UN Charter Article 2(7) permits, the greater malleability of domestic peace-time rules leads many governments to indulge in overly broad approaches

---

86 Albeit found in the Declaration's Preamble.
87 E. Colby, 'How to Fight Savage Tribes' [1927] 21 *A.J.I.L.* 279, at 287.
88 See, e.g., L. Moreno-Ocampo, 'Now End this Darfur Denial', *The Guardian*, 15 July 2010 (ICC issues three charges of genocide against Sudan President Omar Al-Bashir), guardian.co.uk.

when seeking to control their own 'emergency situations' and 'terrorists' through official force.

For this reason alone, the term 'armed conflict' has long needed an ascertainable definition, i.e., one in which certain express elements can be specified for neutral and transparent application, regardless of a conflict's political context. The use of military force and rhetoric in recent years in more unusual international situations, such as the post 9/11 'war on terror', as well as of the means and methods utilised to pursue violent formats of force adopted for it,[89] led the Executive Committee of the International Law Association in May 2005 to create a new committee to study the meaning of the term 'armed conflict' in international law.[90] The remit for this purpose of the ILA's new Use of Force Committee was quite narrow and did not include wider issues such as entitlements to self-determination or the application of international humanitarian law. The Use of Force Committee pursued the narrow question of 'the meaning of the term "armed conflict" in international law' by examining and evaluating, *inter alia*, the present status of general principles of international law, international custom, treaties, judicial decisions and the commentary of publicists.

By August 2008 the Committee's preliminary findings could be presented.[91] As might be expected, the Committee concluded that, as a minimum, an armed conflict exists for purposes of international law when evidence of the following two criteria is present:

- the existence of organised armed groups
- fighting of some intensity.

These basic criteria are refreshingly essentialist, in that they indicate only a situation of fact. While it can be argued that mere facts provide insufficient information, the very simplicity of facts permits neutral transparency, regardless of political context. For example, it is normally a matter for states to decide whether domestic state criminal laws should attach to a 'situation of internal disturbances and tensions'[92] or whether laws of armed conflict should apply instead. As recognised in pertinent part on the Committee's webpage:[93]

> Of course there is no immutable, scientifically-definable line between these socially-constructed concepts [war and peace], and, therefore,

---

89 E.g., it was quickly argued that 'the events of 11 September have set in motion a significant loosening of the legal constraints on the use of force'. Comment, Byers, supra note 24, p. 414.
90 See M.E. O'Connell, supra note 46.
91 ILA Committee on the Use of Force, 'Initial Report on the Meaning of Armed Conflict in International Law', 2008, www.ila-hq.org/en/committees/index.cfm/cid/1022.
92 Article 1(2) of additional Protocol 2.
93 Accessed 18 July 2010.

a perennial challenge for international law has been understanding what armed conflict is and determining when the rules relevant to armed conflict apply.

The Committee submitted its final report to the ILA Annual Conference, held from 15–20 August 2010 in The Hague,[94] for purposes of which it had conducted extensive research in order to identify significant state practice and *opinio juris*. Due to the narrowness of the underlying task, the final report distinguishes between different types of armed conflict for purposes only to analyse the definition of 'armed conflict' itself. The final report does not deviate from the original two characteristics highlighted earlier, but after having adopted a highly rigorous approach literally to hundreds of post-1945 violent situations, the Committee noted the many legal consequences of an armed conflict in general, as follows:

> In addition [to laws of armed conflict], states that provide asylum to persons fleeing the violence of armed conflict will have the duty to do so; treaty obligations may be implicated; the law of neutrality may be triggered; arms control agreements are affected, and UN forces engaged in armed conflict will have rights and duties not applicable in operations outside of armed conflict. These are just some of the areas of international law that are affected by the outbreak of armed conflict. Plainly, the existence of armed conflict is a significant fact in the international legal system, and, yet, the Committee found no widely accepted definition of armed conflict in any treaty. It did, however, discover significant evidence in the sources of international law that the international community embraces a common understanding of armed conflict.[95]

In finding that '[a]ll armed conflict has certain minimal, defining characteristics that distinguish it from situations of non-armed conflict or peace', the Committee made clear that, in the absence of all of these characteristics, 'states may not, consistently with international law, simply declare that a situation is or is not armed conflict based on policy preferences'.[96] The tendency by states to use the political labelling process, in order to disregard their more inconvenient legal obligations, is thus expressly acknowledged.

For purposes of the 'war on terror', the final report notes that 'it cannot be assumed – as in the past – that a state engaged in armed conflict is free to attack its adversary anywhere in the area of war'.[97] The report concludes:

---

94 ILA Use of Force Committee, 'Final Report (Draft)', supra note 29.
95 *Ibid.*, p. 1.
96 *Ibid.*, pp. 1–2.
97 *Ibid.*, p. 32.

Perhaps most importantly states may only claim belligerent rights *during* an armed conflict. To claim such rights *outside* of an armed conflict risks violating fundamental human rights that prevail in non-armed conflict.[98]

These conclusions have serious implications for the overall distribution of power in the UN era. While, on the one hand, states place themselves under international obligations to act lawfully, it is imperative to the good working of the UN system, on the other, that states retain their social and political powers to maintain order domestically. Until the publication of the ILA Report, it had generally been thought that this latter consideration includes the power to construct local meanings to distinguish 'emergency situations' from 'armed conflict', in order to react appropriately in each case. Not only is this sovereign power entrenched in individual state constitutional arrangements that are vital to attributing differential rights and privileges to individuals, but further, sovereign powers of social construction have heretofore also allowed states to set – and exceed – their own limits on the use of force, particularly in domestic contexts.

Accordingly, a longstanding sovereign state power to create and/or maintain gaps in perception between the fact of hostilities (ICRC approach) and the reason for or rationale behind those hostilities (the US view over the past decade, for example), illustrates the crucial importance to governments of retaining control of their own official labelling processes when the time arrives to promote their preferred frameworks of analysis in terms of legal consequences at the international level. It is thus of huge potential import that the final conclusions of the ILA's Use of Force Committee point essentially to the same criteria as those utilised in the ICRC's humanitarian-but-pragmatic approach to armed violence and, more recently, in the prosecutorial regime of the ICC's Rome Statute of 1998. Accordingly, to paraphrase Professor Brownlie, when international principles are at issue, UN organs should keep uppermost in mind the reasons for their discretion, and disregard a strict approach to UN Charter Article 2(7).[99]

Therefore, although it may seem odd today that the characterisation of so recurring a human event as 'war' should still cause uncertainty in government, military and legal circles, it is also relatively easy to understand why this is so. International society is not ready, perhaps, for more centralised control over individual states and certain domestic situations

---

98  *Ibid.*, p. 33.
99  E.A. Laing, 'The Norm of Self-Determination, 1941–1991' [1993] 22 *Int.Rel.* 209, at 222, quoting Brownlie in 1973 (citation omitted). See also M.N. Shaw, *International Law* (Cambridge: Cambridge University Press, 6th edn, 2008), p. 1148: 'international law treats civil wars as purely internal matters, with the possible exception of self-determination conflicts'.

may, in fact, require forceful 'cooling down' by government force. However, it is equally important to recall that 'human' and 'humane' limits exist. In other words, once government reaction becomes the problem rather than the solution, any further breakdown in lawful government limits developed since 1945 in terms of *military* 'necessity' and 'proportionality' can endanger *all* governments, particularly when considering the growth in support for theories of 'corrective' or 'remedial' self-determination.

## Conclusion

State disagreement, or incoherence, regarding 'self-determination' points at many levels to the contradictions perennially in play between hierarchically organised, 'equal' sovereign states. While it may be true that many struggles for self-determination have been defeated by overwhelming government force, the social, political and/or economic phenomenon of self-determination is being continuously reinvented. The social, and political, constructions cast over war, as highlighted earlier, further illustrate how one non-state entity may be viewed as heroic to some when struggling to attain greater rights entitlements, while another may not. In turn, not only do many post-Cold War anti-terror laws effectively neutralise certain liberationist causes, but further, they blur the peace–war distinction that is so crucial to prevent self-interested governments from coining legally meaningless terms such as 'unlawful combatant' or 'terrorist' and the institution of excessive policies, e.g., shoot to kill, which are unlawful under both human rights laws and laws of armed conflict.

In turn, the condemnation by states of 'unauthorised' violence, while turning a non-interfering, blind eye to 'authorised' violence within states, encourages impunity as regards the lawful limits of popularly mandated government action. For so long as the characterisation of force remains within the sole remit of a UN Organisation, organised itself to permit social deviation between states, the new ICC must remain controversial for its alternative authorisation to interfere in state domestic affairs, even as it attempts to seek justice and redress for the victims of atrocity, by whomever caused. The Great Powers long ago declared that the means employed to weaken the enemy during war must not be used simply to make death inevitable, neither should means be employed that needlessly prolong suffering. Whether or not those limits on force are respected in fact, or are truly effective during war, it is difficult to think that those same rules have no role to play whatsoever in peacetime. However, if the latter is indeed the case, the meaning of the rule of law in general is more likely to need constant re-evaluation, such that the war–peace distinction can be further minimised to become a simple matter of interpretation, as is now discussed.

# 4 'Peace' is 'war'

## Introduction

The issue explored in this chapter is the interrelationship during 'peace-time', so-called, of law, force and violent struggle once the politics of self-determination are involved. The qualifier 'so-called' is utilised to convey more a sense that identifying a 'war' can actually be highly problematic in practice, as discussed in Chapter 3.[1] In turn, to begin with a clear distinction made between a situation of 'war' or 'peace' is a logical first step, as either entails its own set of lawful rights and duties, inasmuch as the latter flow from a UN Charter that expressly prohibits inter-state uses of force directly as a matter of treaty obligation, while it leaves the operation of human rights and self-determination to individual state control. However, even though state control over domestic implementation preserves an invaluable sovereign right, one main drawback is that it also affords an opportunity for states to manipulate certain social constructions surrounding terms such as 'peace', equality and rights.[2]

A good example of terminological imprecision is in regard to the ongoing inter-ethnic strife between Uzbeks and Kyrgys, in the southwest corner of the former Socialist Republic of Kyrgyzstan. Recent unrest there has been alternatively described as 'ferocious ethnic conflict', 'rioting' and an 'internal (armed) conflict',[3] as the ethnic Uzbek minority, along with many

---

1 See, e.g., the ILA Use of Force Committee, 'Final Report (Draft) on the Meaning of Armed Conflict in International Law', submitted at the ILA Annual Conference, The Hague, 15–20 August 2010, p. 16, www.ila-hq.org.

2 Contrast *ibid.*, pp. 1–2 ('states may not, consistently with international law, simply declare that a situation is or is not armed conflict based on policy preferences'), www.ila-hq.org. See also the ILA Committee on the Use of Force, 'Initial Report on the Meaning of Armed Conflict in International Law', 2008, p. 2, www.ila-hq.org/en/committees/index.cfm/cid/1022; 'The Chatham House Principles of International Law on the Use of Force in Self-Defence' [2006] 55 *I.C.L.Q.* 963, pp. 963–4.

3 L. Harding, 'Kyrgyzstan Begs Russia to Send in Troops', *The Observer*, 13 June 2010, p. 11 (Russia willing to act only in conjunction with the UN). Contrast the exclusion of 'riots' from the coverage of Article 1(2) of additional Protocol 2 of 1977.

other peoples in the former Soviet Union, have tried (and so far failed) since the 1990s to gain territorial autonomy. Many other such situations have been described inaccurately over recent decades,[4] as it is commonplace for a wide variety of social grievance, ranging far beyond colonialism, to be at the heart of a longstanding struggle for self-determination. Nonetheless, it is somewhat unusual for complete territorial secession to be the original motivation of many liberation groups;[5] the likely prospect of social upheaval and the difficulties of attracting subsequent recognition would daunt most peoples.

Instead, the goal that is more likely to be sought involves an idea of *moral victory within* an existing state, such as to improve the conditions of daily life, effect societal change and/or achieve a sense of justice. In response, the post-9/11 era has witnessed instead numerous examples of the use of government force against social protest of many types, curtailments of individual rights of association and expression and the stripping-out of due process rights and rights of defence from 'terrorist' suspects. The resulting lack of clarity regarding the outer limits of permissible forceful action by states can then make it hardly appropriate to use the term 'peace'. More-over, the terms 'peace' and 'war' have not often been self-explanatory at all since 1945: the expansionist has seen little but constant war;[6] the reductionist, 'peace' as simply the absence of 'war'.

Accordingly, after a brief account of the manipulation of terms such as 'war' and 'peace', specific issues such as the purpose of official force, the role of commercial arrangements when utilising that force and the creation of 'suspect communities within' are developed in the sections that follow.

## 'Peace' as the absence of 'war'?

Assuming for purposes of argument that law 'is not a natural fact but a characterisation we give to an agglomeration of complex facts and cir-cumstances',[7] it is obvious that a 'peaceful' world order might depend on strong and stable inter-state relations, as is promoted in the UN Charter and premised on equal sovereign rights. In turn, strong sovereign rights make it a matter of self-interest to co-operate on a trans-boundary basis

---

4 H. McDonald, 'Seven Days: Dismissed as Yobs, these Rioters could be Terrorism's Next Generation', *The Observer*, 18 July 2010, p. 32.

5 Consider, e.g., M. Weller, *Escaping the Self-Determination Trap* (Leiden: Martinus Nijhoff Publishers, 2008); L. Brilmayer, 'Secession and Self-Determination: A Territorial Inter-pretation' [1991] 16 *Yale J.Int.L.* 177. Cf. A. Kolers, *Land, Conflict, and Justice: A Political Theory of Territory* (Cambridge: Cambridge University Press, 2009).

6 'War in the Gulf', *Greenpeace Campaign Report* (London: Greenpeace, February 1991).

7 M. Krygier, 'The Fall of European Communism: 20 Years After' [2009] 1 *H.J.R.L.* 195, p. 203. See also G. Skapska, 'The Rule of Law, Economic Transformation and Corruption After the Fall of the Berlin Wall' [2009] 1 *H.J.R.L.* 284.

via multilateral or regional instruments, as trans-boundary instruments allow states to retain more individual control over the implementation, interpretation and enforcement of substantive provisions[8] than do universal obligations. Accordingly, the post 9/11 'war on terror' has proven to be exceedingly useful to states, as the vast majority of international anti-terror codifications rest on trans-boundary arrangements, e.g., for extradition and judicial co-operation.

A state acquires formal treaty obligations in relation to other state parties once that state gives its consent to be bound. Where necessary, the bound state must then ensure that a treaty's substantive provisions have local effect, but the constitutional provisions of certain states first require enabling legislation to incorporate those provisions internally. Moreover, inasmuch as domestic laws take effect by means of the mechanisms and procedures provided in individual state constitutional arrangements, there will be variation between states as to the scope, substance and effect of law. Variation is useful, as it can make the law more receptive to local conditions and cultural standards, even as greater malleability can also be injected into what otherwise would be externally imposed obligations, as is now outlined.

## Domestic implementation

The main advantage offered by humanitarian laws during a non-international armed conflict, as discussed in Chapter 3, is that they should apply as a matter of universal treaty obligation in relation to a situation of fact, i.e., once exchanges of armed force display organisation and intensity, at which point the effect of the underlying customary international law provides inter-state standards and makes the prohibitive core of war law non-derogable. International human rights laws, by way of contrast, tend somewhat to operate as if they had been agreed on a trans-boundary basis, in that their enforcement is more likely to accord with local values.[9] Human rights obligations should also contain a core of non-derogable rights, such as rights to life and against torture or slavery, but as the substance of those rights is instead more amenable to subjective interpretation, their enforcement engages less external scrutiny.[10]

---

8  See, e.g., N. Boister, 'Transnational Criminal Law?' [2003] 14 *E.J.I.L.* 953.

9  This is a general proposition and it is not intended to disregard the role of regional human rights courts such as the ECtHR. However, the UN Human Rights Committee, established under Part IV of the ICCPR of 1966, has no powers to make binding decisions on the merits of rights cases. See M.N. Shaw, *International Law* (Cambridge: Cambridge University Press, 6th edn, 2008), pp. 314–22.

10  For expansion of this point, see C. Antonopoulos, 'The Relationship Between International Humanitarian Law and Human Rights' [2010] 63(2) *R.Hell.deDr.I.* (2010) [forthcoming].

Domestic standards for implementing trans-boundary obligations thus afford more flexibility to states. This means that it can be quite complex to describe a hostile domestic situation, which moves factually between the characteristics of 'war' and 'peace' over a period of time, both politically (for external consumption) and in formal legal terms (for internal purposes), which explains why the issue of international rules for civil wars in Common Article 3 to the four Geneva Conventions of 1949 remains controversial.[11] Accordingly, the internationally obligatory nature of Common Article 3 has had a perverse effect: states rely instead on the principle of non-interference in their domestic affairs, the modern version of which is found in UN Charter Article 2(7). In other words, it can be anticipated that a threatened state will certainly prefer not to recognise the applicability of even minimal international standards for civil war, inasmuch as the latter require restraint when using official force to restore domestic order and no more so than during a self-determination 'revolution'.

Even though it might appear today that the logic of revolution no longer has any role to play in a post-Cold War era 'against terror',[12] influential support for self-determination has been expressed since quite early in the UN era, along the lines that the international principle of self-determination sits higher in the legal hierarchy than the principle of non-interference.[13] Assuming this to be accurate, it would then appear that the conduct of a modern non-international armed conflict for self-determination should not be the responsibility of single-state judgement alone, particularly in view of the ruthless, widespread, and protracted nature of such conflicts.[14] Be that as it may, the competing strength of the non-interference principle helps to illuminate the reason why the realities underpinning the use of terms such as 'peace' and 'war' can become practically indistinguishable once related international laws are implemented domestically.

In short, Common Article 3 has the potential to embarrass states. High-intensity and organised exchanges of official and insurgent armed force are utilised, but laws of armed conflict are not respected or applied as no 'war' is recognised; 'peace' is hardly an appropriate characterisation either, once

---

11 See, e.g., Armed Activities on the Territory of the Congo (*Democratic Republic of the Congo v. Uganda*) [2005] *ICJ Rep.* 168.

12 See, e.g., *Peacekeeping Operations: Principles and Guidelines* (UN, 2008), p. 13 (UNSC peacekeeping authorisations as 'statements of firm political resolve'). Cf. *UN Peacekeeping 2009: Overview*, para. 57 (lack of Security Council consensus terminates UN mission in Georgia in June 2009).

13 E.A. Laing, 'The Norm of Self-Determination, 1941–1991' [1993] 22 *Int.Rel.* 209, at p. 222, quoting Brownlie in 1973 (citation omitted). See also UNGA Resolution 3103 (XXVIII), of 12 December 1973, on the international status of combatants struggling against colonial and alien domination and racist regimes.

14 See, e.g., ICRC Report, 'Protection of the civilian population in periods of armed conflict', 26th International Conference of the Red Cross and Red Crescent (Geneva: ICRC, 15 September 1995) (civilian suffering increases as civil conflicts become more complex).

domestic 'emergency powers' have been activated. The term 'aggression' has no relevance on associated rights and duties, as that term of art generally applies only to acts perpetrated by states against other states, even as state practice broadens self-defence for use against 'terrorists'. In any event, a state-focused right of self-defence sits uncomfortably alongside the extension in Geneva Protocol 1 of 1977 to 'some' liberationist struggles, as it is particularly contentious to argue that laws of armed conflict could extend analogous rights of self-defence to mere peoples;[15] to do so would practically ensure the non-applicability in such struggles of rules for international armed conflict.

Accordingly, the legal variations between states represent the purpose of state boundaries. Variation in the field of 'peacetime' criminal laws is particularly useful,[16] e.g., when authorising the use of domestic force to re-establish order and/or to re-impose local notions of social discipline. For example, state flexibility in anti-terrorist legal frameworks is sourced in domestic criminal laws. Requiring more from a threatened government could otherwise pose too great a risk of moral equivalence between a government and its non-state adversary. Moreover, even though governments may be criticised by other states for the breach of general customary international law duties in respect of the most basic levels of individual human rights entitlements (which include notional limits on state uses of armed force), 'margins of appreciation' remain available for government discretion in specific circumstances.

The upshot is that ensuring 'humanitarian treatment in all circumstances' is easier said than done. If a margin of appreciation is utilised during 'peace', a hard core of non-derogable rights *might* hold firm, but most rights can be eroded or eliminated as 'emergency powers' take effect. If the margin is utilised during 'war', minimal protections may be fixed in law, but the most the latter can promise is that a civilian population will not be attacked as an express military objective.[17] In turn, the most dangerous development under modern conditions is that governments rely increasingly on euphemism to misapprehend the true nature of armed force. International rules of war are diluted by 'war on terror' rhetoric and human rights are deemed less important than national security. Official authorisation to perpetrate acts in 'peacetime' that are only permitted during armed conflict thus facilitates the integration of struggles for self-determination into the anti-terror agenda, as is now discussed.

---

15 See, e.g., Editorial, 'Interpretive Guidance on the Notion of Direct Participation in Hostilities under International Humanitarian Law' [June 2009] 872 *I.R.R.C.* 819.

16 In that different systems of political control create crimes peculiar to each. H. Kelsen, *The Communist Theory of Law* (New York: Frederick A. Praeger, Inc., 1955), p. 102.

17 See Ipsos Report, 'ICRC Survey: Our World. Views from the Field' [2010], www.icrc.org/web/eng/research-report-240609.

## Euphemistic transition

As every wordsmith knows, a more sophisticated means of communication can be built with euphemism. In terms of international conventional law, treaty provisions will contain either peremptory ('shall') or permissive ('may') provisions, as there will often be a strong political rationale for utilising such terms to remove or inject clarity or discretion. Similarly, inasmuch as domestic legislation determines the domestic enforceability of local law, more precise wording may or may not be utilised, depending on the basis for operation of the underlying legal system. In turn, certain legal obstacles, such as prohibitions against killing, can normally be waived when official powers are utilised in special cases, e.g., for purposes of war or to restore domestic order through force. At that point, general government powers to interpret the appropriate source of law to be applied will require political choices as to the appropriate criteria for 'necessity', as discussed in Chapter 3. Accordingly, whenever a government must resort to euphemism to describe a situation of domestic unrest, the equal application of law is at its weakest.

Law, of course, is a superior tool for winning a 'conflict' and victorious governments mould the law. States that utilise force purportedly in lawful self-defence against non-state actors thus immediately possess superiority in terms of law,[18] as legal doctrine usually accepts the use of official armed force against 'terrorists', however the latter may be identified.[19] Moreover, in that the UN Charter is essentially concerned with restraining, if not preventing, the use of aggressive armed force between sovereign states,[20] states continue to retain customary rights of 'necessity of self-defence', pursuant to UN Charter Article 51, particularly as the terminology employed in Article 51 is not expressly confined to state action. State rights of self-defence which are wider than international duties not to perpetrate aggression do little to lessen the use of armed force in the contemporary 'war on terror' era.

The practicalities of adopting force in state self-defence make it all too easy for states then to re-designate autonomously the lawful parameters for their subsequent action. In other words, if a state strategically can orient its use of official force against terrorists towards 'winning' quickly and still characterise that forceful action as 'self-defence', it has a better

---

18 See 'Chatham House Principles', supra note 2, Principle F, at pp. 969–71; C. Antonopoulos, supra note 10, (Israeli intifada, and Operation 'Cast Lead'); M. Bothe, 'Terrorism and the Legality of Pre-Emptive Force' [2003] 14 *E.J.I.L.* 227, pp. 229–33.
19 'Chatham House Principles', supra note 2, pp. 969–71.
20 UNGA Resolution 3314 (XXIX) of 14 December 1974 Article 1. See also Resolution RC/Res. 6, 'The Crime of Aggression', Annex 1: 'Amendments to the Rome Statute' Articles 15bis and 15ter (adopted 11 June 2010 by consensus), www.icc-cpi.int/iccdocs/asp_docs/Resolutions/.

chance to assert that it is 'a matter that is conclusively and exclusively determined by the state concerned'.[21] At this point, it becomes all too easy to see how the recent integration of self-determination struggles into criminal anti-terrorist arrangements represents a breathtaking liberty taken with euphemism, as it replaces international opinion and regulation with autonomous state policy. Accordingly, the logic of rapid victory mandates a degree of terminological blurring in order to characterise any force utilised under frameworks of 'peace' and to reduce international scrutiny.

Once official force is aimed against liberation fighters deemed domestically to be 'criminals' (and/or 'terrorists'), any subsequent prosecution will be conducted under domestic criminal laws, rather than via the more rigorous procedures of a court martial or other military tribunal.[22] This practice also explains the recent penchant of certain states for adopting extremely broad, anti-terrorist criminal laws, as those laws can transform the true nature and extent of force authorised. While this trend in legislation reflects core sovereign powers to deal with what may, in fact, be only a temporary situation, they arise fundamentally from the central function assigned to state governments in the UN Charter: that of maintaining domestic order, one way or another. There is thus evident a new, independent, autonomous sovereign right to shape and give substance to the requisite self-authorisations for forceful action in the domestic sphere.

Self-authorisation is, of course, attributable organically to the essence of man-enforced laws, both in terms of procedural and substantive legal variation. State autonomies make more understandable the ongoing inability of states collectively to define and criminalise terrorism at the international level, as the scope of terms such as 'state terror', 'liberation war' and 'armed conflict' remains highly contentious.[23] Legal flexibility also plays a central role in the domestic implementation of certain specific, and sensitive, issues in individual human rights, including those of self-determination, inasmuch as these rights should condition the use of centralised government powers over the modalities of individual life. Accordingly, while the *principles* of equal rights and self-determination permit states to agree mutually that 'all

---

21  C. Antonopoulos, supra note 10, at p. 2.
22  For example, only the USA has attempted to institute military commissions for 'terrorists' held at Guantanamo Bay, Cuba. See, e.g., F. Johns, 'Guantanamo Bay and the Annihilation of the Exception' [2005] 16 *E.J.I.L.* 613. Cf. C. Aradau and R. Van Munster, 'Exceptionalism and the "War on Terror": Criminology meets International Relations' [2009] 49(5) *Brit.J.Crim.* 686.
23  See, e.g., E. Wong, 'Chinese Separatists Tied to Norway Bomb Plot', *New York Times*, 9 July 2010 (Uighur 'Al Qaeda' separatists), nytimes.com; H. Sherwood, 'Netanyahu Accuses Turkey of Ignoring Gaza Flotilla Warnings', *The Guardian*, 9 August 2010 (Israeli Raid in Self-defence against Terrorists, Israeli Prime Minister Tells Inquiry), guardian.co.uk; D. Gritten, 'Dubai Killing Shines Unwelcome Light on Mossad', 26 February 2010 (assassination of Hamas leader), news.bbc.co.uk.

peoples' are so entitled,[24] the disunity displayed by states in relation to details in effect entrenches sovereign powers, such that the concrete application of rights principles can be left to domestic arrangements and, of course, 'events'.[25]

The 'war on terror' is thus made in structural terms for extension to and inclusion of the many struggles by peoples for their rights of self-determination, particularly as the political intertwining of 'terrorist' acts and self-determination tactics is longstanding in certain official circles. One need only recall the controversy surrounding the extension of international laws of armed conflict to include those peoples fighting for their self-determination in accordance with the UN Charter, as found in Article 1(4) of additional Protocol 1 of 1977 to the four Geneva Conventions of 1949. The absence in international law of a comprehensive definition for either the terrorist or self-determination phenomenon thus exposes a fundamental sovereign power to preserve a strong domain within which to employ force without external interference, which implies that the main advantage to states of re-categorising liberation fighters as criminal 'terrorists' is once again that of flexibility.

Indeed, a High-Level Panel at the UN, tasked by the UN's Secretary General to assess existing restraints over state uses of military force, reported in 2004 that 'we believe that the Charter of the United Nations, properly understood and applied, is equal to the task'.[26] The latter phrase – 'properly understood and applied' – reveals the gap left for state choice, within which euphemism plays its part. Further, the principle of non-interference fits comfortably within such space in view of the inter-state friction surrounding many contemporary details of the international order.[27] The retention by each state of sovereign powers to act internationally against groups and individuals in line with its own law-and-order approach thus reinforces the rationale for state territorial borders in the first place: the governed can

---

24  UNGA Resolution 2625 (XXV) of 14 October 1970. See also *Legal Consequences for States of the Continued Presence of South Africa in Namibia (South West Africa) Notwithstanding SC Resolution 276 [1970] (Advisory Opinion)* [1971] ICJ Rep. 16, at pp. 31–3.

25  See, e.g., *Accordance with International Law of the Unilateral Declaration of Independence in Respect of Kosovo (Advisory Opinion)* [22 July 2010] ICJ, General List No. 141. Cf. D. Kumbaro, 'Final Report. The Kosovo Crisis in an International Law Perspective: Self-Determination, Territorial Integrity, and the NATO Intervention' (Brussels: NATO Office of Information and Press, 16 June 2001), p. 39 (reference to self-determination made continuously by Kosovo since 1990).

26  Report, Secretary General's High-Level Panel on Threats, Challenges and Change, 'A More Secure World: Our Shared Responsibility', UN Doc. A/59/565 (2004), at p. 13.

27  E.g., the UNSC draft resolution on unrest in Burma, UN Doc. S/2007/14, UN Doc. S/PV.5619, 12 January 2007, vetoed by China, Russia and South Africa for concerning a domestic question posing no threat to regional peace and security. See C. Focarelli, 'The Responsibility to Protect Doctrine and Humanitarian Intervention: Too Many Ambiguities for a Working Doctrine' [2008] 13 *J.Con.&Sec.L.* 191, at pp. 208–9.

be controlled by local enforcement capabilities,[28] while 'enemies' found outside can be dealt with summarily as 'international terrorists' who possess few, if any, 'rights'. Accordingly, the state solidarity demonstrated immediately after 9/11 against international terrorism can easily coexist with inter-state disunity regarding the identification of specific terrorists, which latter may include groups struggling for self-determination.

## The limits of state violence and force

In the past, Lauterpacht defined 'security' in defensive terms, as 'a system of obligations to enforce by common international action the existing limitations upon the right to go to war'.[29] In contrast, states individually have long been in charge of their own domestic security arrangements and maintain domestic order largely by unilateral action. Much has changed, however, since 1989, when certain of the former Communist states began to demonstrate a degree of enthusiasm for liberal democracy and the market economy, and many wanted inclusion in that club alongside the West by the mid-1990s. Unfortunately, the west responded by attempting – at least initially – to impose certain preconditions aimed rather more at 'constituting a specific limitation of post-Communist political power'[30] than at helping to entrench substantive parameters of justice.[31]

Many liberationist and terrorist causes alike were thus forced to become more flexible[32] and certain ones negotiated political accommodations with their governments. By way of contrast, it was perhaps to be expected that the new insecurities in power politics facilitated the rise of less predictable potential adversaries, which also meant that further attempts to refine the 'right' of self-determination within colonial contexts were fatally damaged. Even so, the asymmetry which has been evident ever since, whether in 'rights' to use armed force or in merely the 'power' to do so, has, in turn, had a real impact on those who struggle for self-determination, as is now discussed.

### *Privatised coercion*

The greater the scope for government flexibility when consolidating and utilising military capabilities, the less likely it is they will be inclined to

---

28  See, e.g., I. Detter De Lupis, *The Law of War* (Cambridge: Cambridge University Press, 1987), pp. 67–71.

29  H. Lauterpacht (ed.), *Oppenheim's International Law, Vol. II* (London: Longmans, 7th edn, 1952), p. 93 n. 1.

30  Krygier, supra note 7, p. 211 (citing Priban).

31  Contrast R.A. Miller, 'Self-Determination in International Law and the Demise of Democracy?' [2002–2003] 41 *Colum.J.Transnat'l.L.* 601, who argues that the emergence of new states in the immediate post-Cold War era by no means represented a democratic revolution.

32  See, e.g., S. Tisdall, 'Rogue States and Terrorist Threats Identified in Attempt to Boost Spending', *The Saturday Guardian*, 13 January 2001, p. 3.

agree or to legislate for fixed parameters of self-restraint. Accordingly, the use of official force is authorised by the legislative and/or executive branches of states, sanctioned by the judiciary and made effective in military and police powers.[33] Force is used to bolster government power and to prevent a slippage from power, as can be seen in the ongoing military presence of Russian forces in the Caucasus,[34] the military repression in Burma and, more recently, the extraordinary police powers adopted for post-election violence in Iran. Force is used by newly restored governments, as in Iraq, or Afghanistan.[35] It is used by well-established states to end cross-border insurgencies,[36] as in Israel, which has for decades controlled occupied Palestinian areas and 'terrorists' by means of superior force.[37]

Therefore, and assuming for purposes of argument that governments everywhere utilise forceful means of some description at one time or another, it may be thought that the domestic use of official force is generally acceptable. The prevention of disruption, e.g., by 'criminals' and 'terrorists', is what government is for, after all, and the maintenance of order helps to strengthen societal trust and economic stability. However, even as the post-1945 era dawned, the numbers of non-state violent actors proliferated, which prompted many governments to study, develop and adopt counter-insurgent strategies and security mechanisms; not to do so would only have encouraged the continuing emergence of such violent actors.

Devlin references labour relations as the 'litmus test' of state violence.[38] Similar to the way in which the military instils discipline in soldiers, individuals in civil society are also subjected to forms of societal discipline. Institutionalising disciplined industrial relations prompts speculation as to further efficiencies to be gained from 'litmus tests', which may incorporate *pre-emptive* and *anticipatory* forms of government or private control over individuals. Giddens, for example, notes that 'there are close substantive connections between the surveillance operations of nation-states and the

---

33  See R.F. Devlin, 'Law's Centaurs: An Inquiry into the Nature and Relations of Law, State and Violence' [1989] 27 *O.HallL.J.* 219.

34  Cf. E. Stepanova, 'Islamist Terrorism in the Caucasus and Central Asia', in A.P. Schmid and G.F. Hindle (eds), *After the War on Terror: Regional and Multilateral Perspectives on Counter-Terrorism Strategy* (London: RUSI Books, 2009), p. 104.

35  See, e.g., R. Barrett, 'Legitimacy, Credibility and Relevance: The Tools of Terrorists and "Counter-Terrorists"', in *After the War on Terror*, supra note 34, pp. 8, 24 (Taliban also exploit local desire for peace and security based on an effective and fair justice system).

36  See, e.g., F. Bhutto, 'Eyewitness 2009: Pakistan Signs a Deal with Militants, 13 April', *The Observer Magazine*, 27 December 2009, p. 26 (deal struck with Islamic militants in the Swat valley).

37  See, e.g., J. Ging, 'Eyewitness 2009: Israelis Shell a UN Compound in Gaza', *The Observer Magazine*, 27 December 2009, p. 31.

38  R.F. Devlin, supra note 33. See, e.g., Reuters, Moody and Clarke, 'Police Clash with Workers in First Unrest at World Cup', 14 June 2010, news.yahoo.com (riot police use tear gas and rubber bullets against security stewards protesting about pay).

altered nature of military power in the modern period',[39] pre-eminent among which is surveillance. In turn, financial markets gladly fund government security arrangements and surplus or used capacity generates additional sources of profit.

The many uses of government surveillance capabilities then make it easier to understand why and how the military–industrial complex has transmogrified into a security–industrial one. The markets for technological weaponry and security alike are huge and lucrative, as illustrated over many years in the proliferation of corporate weapons fairs, exhibitions, dealers, suppliers, developers, etc. As increasingly sophisticated technologies are made available to governments and commerce alike, their use is made operational in any civil arena in which groups and individuals, and information about them, connect. This not only allows governments as well as private concerns to monitor the daily lives of certain individuals more closely but, further, to do so with coercive means that are not overtly forceful. Once a subject population becomes inured to frequent identity checks, the retention of greater amounts of personal information and tighter restrictions on movement, the sheer ubiquity of government and workplace monitoring can make it seem that surveillance generally is acceptable, both politically and/or morally, as a social choice.

Nonetheless, this growth in government-sanctioned surveillance capability carries heightened risks for certain groups and individuals. The contracting-out to private concerns of many official functions includes government functions that carry powers to utilise armed force.[40] Contracting-out involves processes in which a multitude of banking and other financial interests are prominent, but which only rarely make provision for wider public scrutiny. The commercial confidentiality inherent to contracting-out thus helps to inject into the exercise of official force a more polymorphic character as public accountability is subsumed. By way of illustration, Hughes notes that:

> In January 2003 investors were invited to give their cash to men who promised they could make big profits from the aftermath of the terrorist attacks of 11 September 2001. Potential shareholders were told that the war on terror 'offer[s] substantial promise for homeland security investment'. . . . Uniquely, this new application of force depended heavily on private companies: from the wars in the Middle East to the

---

39 A. Giddens, *The Consequences of Modernity* (Cambridge: Polity Press, 1990), p. 60.
40 See generally S. Hughes, *War on Terror, Inc.: Corporate Profiteering from the Politics of Fear* (London: Verso, 2007), for examples of the transfer to corporations of former government activities, including the running of prisons, immigration controls, and so on. See also C. Walker and D. Whyte, 'Contracting Out War? Private Military Companies, Law and Regulation in the U.K.' [2005] 54 *I.C.L.Q.* 651.

databases and systems of detention at home, the new weapons in the 'war on terror' were both supplied and operated by corporations.[41]

Obviously, in this (somewhat euphemistic) conjoining of high-end politics, the military, and private profit, is open to abuse, particularly as 'everything depends on the hearts of men' who provide and use technological, forceful means.[42] However, once individual 'consent' tacitly accepts the adoption and use of overly intrusive, public and private domestic 'security' controls, competing rights and associated freedoms are reduced. The reduction of individual rights then has broad implications, producing a far more dangerous proposition: commonly held social values are not the central concern of state security. It is, in fact, the case that reduced rights entitlements release certain putative limits on official uses of force.[43] Accordingly, it can certainly be argued in the post-9/11 era that a broad approach to public coercion reflects a readiness by governments to substitute their publicly accountable responsibilities with commercial self-interest.

## Self-determination

Law in general is shown to be subordinate to state power when it is confirmed only through the 'characterisation [a government chooses] to give to an agglomeration of complex facts and circumstances'.[44] Therefore, while the act of ratifying an international or regional human rights treaty, for example, makes compliance with that treaty a matter of inter-state obligation,[45] the actual enforcement of the rights provided forms but an additional tool of individual state regulation, particularly as criticism by states of each other on this basis is relatively rare. In the context of the 'war on terror', individual rights entitlements are even more disposable once political opponents are branded and characterised as 'terrorists' by similarly minded states, which makes it even less likely that individuals or groups will find protective content in rights and moves entitlements to the centre ground of social conflict.

As noted earlier, the retention by governments of strong sovereign flexibilities when using force domestically is not conducive to state self-restraint. It is for this reason that the importance to civil society of neutral

---

41 S. Hughes, supra note 40, pp. 1 and 5.
42 J.L. Kunz, 'The Chaotic Status of the Laws of War' [1951] 45 A.J.I.L. 37, at p. 41.
43 See, e.g., L.K. Donohue, *The Cost of Counterterrorism: Power, Politics, and Liberty* (Cambridge: Cambridge University Press, 2008).
44 M. Krygier, supra note 7, p. 203.
45 See, e.g., *Certain Criminal Proceedings in France (Republic of the Congo v. France) (Provisional Measure Order of 17 June 2003)* [2003] *ICJ Rep.* 102 (interim measures requested by the Congo rejected in legal proceedings filed by French human rights organisations concerning Congolese crimes against humanity and torture).

and non-discriminatory treatment is likely to remain at the core of struggles for self-determination. Official force used under 'peacetime' conditions thus demonstrates both the asymmetries of social hierarchy and the effects of those asymmetries on evaluations of government risk. For example, even after the Cold War ended and certain states decommissioned their competition to sponsor struggles for self-determination, the task in government circles of containing liberationist group sentiment endured. The difference today is that the task of containment enjoys broad 'anti-terrorist' frameworks regarding new types of 'stateless' terrorist group, e.g., those seeking and securing support instead by means of shared religious or ideological affiliations and/or a sense of common grievance.[46]

In turn, certain struggling groups have been more susceptible to the propaganda of global jihad than others, as well as to the additional funding that membership attracts. For example, and as noted by Stepanova, in the context of the ongoing Chechen conflict:

> The rise of Islamist extremism was in some ways counterproductive for the separatist insurgency. Radical Islam did not gain a popular mass following in Chechnya: in fact, it might have even reduced the appeal of the separatist cause among Chechens dismayed by attempts to impose Sharia law. . . . Politically, nothing facilitated the Kremlin's efforts to integrate the war in Chechnya into the global war on terrorism more than the Islamisation of the radical separatists. The Islamisation of the insurgency led to . . . blurring their political goals. In contrast to the mid-1990s, the stated political demands of the terrorists (the release of militants and the withdrawal of Federal troops from Chechnya) no longer appeared to reflect some of their broader, underlying goals such as the . . . undermining of the credibility of the Federal government and its fragile system.[47]

Inasmuch as some separatist groups have made overtures to wealthier patrons in order to secure additional resources, despite the destabilising, ideological visions of those patrons, the growth in influence of corporate ideology in government security arrangements also imbalances essential social aims and objectives. As First World governments in the 1990s renewed their interest in preventing international crime generally, the adoption of wide anti-terror laws simply effected a 'collapse [of] the political into the criminal'.[48] In turn, the nationalist, and/or anti-western bias adopted in response in

---

46  France was reportedly the first state to detect this radical change in the nature of terrorism. B. MacIntyre, 'Anti-terror War Stepped up Despite Sanctions Split', *The Times*, 31 July 1996, p. 10.

47  E. Stepanova, supra note 34, p. 107.

48  Book Reviews, Sedley, 'Enemies of All Mankind', *L.R.B.*, 24 June 2010, p. 33.

much of the Third World produced practitioners of new forms of terrorist violence, which in turn increased personal risk all over again. Inasmuch as the *rule* of law is rather more important than its mere existence, it is of particular concern that a heightening of personal risk by anti-terror legislation reduces the often subtle distinction between procedural neutrality on the one hand, and substantive justice on the other.[49]

The blanket condemnation of all 'unauthorised' non-state violence and the blind eye turned to 'authorised' violence, also assume the acceptability of new forms of state security for use in a less well-anchored post-Cold War environment no longer so conditioned by the basic individual need to protect oneself and others.[50] The succeeding waves of anti-terror agendas during the post-Cold War era generally thus pose deep challenges to human rights and rights of self-determination, including the human right to resist repression. Accordingly, if in fact 'national' security is the value pursued by policies of national security, it is on the generation of 'new enemies within'[51] and 'suspect communities'[52] that the security 'industry' will concentrate, as is now discussed.

## Creation of 'suspect communities'

As noted earlier, the post-9/11 'war on terror' has rejuvenated 'the very old trend of states resorting to the notion of "terrorism" to stigmatise political, ethnic, regional or other movements they simply do not like'.[53] This stigmatisation process is made effective in broader police powers,[54] tightened immigration controls,[55] official compromise on the prohibition of torture[56] and so on. The close attention paid by states to prevent acts of terrorism

---

49 For a brief discussion on this point, see M. Krygier, supra note 7, at pp. 199–201 (viewpoint of L. Balcerowicz).

50 See, e.g., Y. Shany, 'Symposium: Self-Defence: Looking at International Law through the Prism of Domestic Criminal Law. The Analogy's Limit: Defending the Rights of Peoples' [2009] 7 *J.Int'l.Crim.J.* 541.

51 Cf. a brief discussion of useful 'triggers' in determining terrorist conduct, in Report of the Special Rapporteur, 'Promotion and Protection of Human Rights', Commission on Human Rights, 62nd session, agenda item 17, UN Doc. E/CN.4/2006/98, paras 32–42. See also UNSC Resolution 1566 (2004).

52 C. Pantazis and S. Pemberton, 'From the "Old" to the "New" Suspect Community: Examining the Impacts of Recent UK Counter-Terrorist Legislation' [2009] 49 *Br.J.Crim.* 646.

53 Report of the Special Rapporteur, supra note 53, para. 56(a).

54 For a discussion of the U.K.'s 'Operation Kratos' for post-2002 operational police strategies, including a specialist arms unit and 'shoot to kill' strategy, see D. Kostakopoulou, 'How To Do Things With Security Post 9/11' [2008] 28 *Oxf.J.L.Stud.* 317, at 336.

55 See, e.g., M. Duffield, 'Global Civil War: the Non-Insured, International Containment and Post-Interventionary Society' [2008] 21 *J.Ref.St.* 145.

56 E.g., P. Walker, 'Shot Guinea Ruler', *The Guardian*, 5 December 2009, p. 24 (UN investigates pro-democracy massacre); Reuters, Maltezou and Melander, 'Greek riots anniversary', 6 December 2009, news.yahoo.com.

then produces a double-edged sword: international obligations to co-operate provide but one rationale for tighter regulation,[57] while variations in approach by different states provide the seeds for future friction.[58] The utilisation of state security mechanisms to protect the state as a whole also produces conflicts of interest with individual human rights guarantees, in that national security normally pre-empts individual rights.[59] As a result, a government that is intent on entrenching state powers, e.g., by extending official control over many of the social aspects of individual daily life, can easily do so.

The case of the UK is apposite. The UK plays host to a multitude of ethnicities, among which Muslim communities are prominent. The UK has a highly developed approach to civil liberties and human rights; its sophisticated judicial system, well-disciplined military apparatus and parliamentary system of governance all help to ensure that it remains possible for counter-terrorism measures to be produced legitimately in the UK; first, in terms of procedure and, second, in terms of substantive credibility and with clear relevance to actual – as opposed to mere potential – threats.[60] Nonetheless, the content and impact of certain anti-terrorist measures on specific groups and individuals require closer inspection.

International obligations exist today that require the outright prohibition of certain terrorist groups as 'criminal', per se.[61] Such proscription presumes that a group's organisational aims as well as its acts constitute an automatic danger, even though there should, at a minimum, be some evidence that an individual is, in fact, sympathetic to and/or involved with a proscribed group. Moreover, forming groups goes to the very essence of what it means to be human. Groups are based on a plethora of connecting ties or linkages such as family, ethnicity, religion, community, profession, political view, hobby or otherwise, and surveillance operations also target social 'buffer zones', e.g., 'those individuals who act as protectors, advisers and promoters in the police force, the legal system or in the political and economic world'.[62] Globalised communications networks further ensure that

---

57  See, e.g., C. Harding, 'The Offence of Belonging: Capturing Participation in Organised Crime' [2005] *Crim.L.R.* 690, at p. 697 (constant demand for new domestic legislation).
58  See, e.g., the EU Council Framework Decision of 13 June 2002 on the European Arrest Warrant and the Surrender Procedures Between Member States [2002] OJ L584/190, p. 1.
59  See, e.g., C. Warbrick, 'The Principles of the ECHR and the Response of States to Terrorism' [2002] 3 *E.H.R.L.R.* 287.
60  For expansion of this basic point, see R. Barrett, 'Legitimacy, Credibility and Relevance: The Tools of Terrorists and "Counter-Terrorists"', in *After the War on Terror*, supra note 34, p. 8.
61  National proscription has now been joined by UN sanctions regimes, including proscribed lists, e.g., in UNGA Resolution 60/288, UN Global Counter-Terrorism Strategy, 20 September 2006, U.N. Doc. A/RES/60/288. See also Chapter 6.
62  C. Harding, supra note 57, p. 692, citing the European Council's Joint Action, adopted 21 December 1998, [1998] OJ L351/1, p. 12.

human linkages multiply rapidly, producing theories such as the so-called 'six degrees of separation'.

Official profiling strategies for gauging behavioural patterns also cause concern[63] and a government that wishes to do so may cast the net of 'social dangerousness' very widely indeed.[64] However, once captured, prosecution by the state for suspected membership in a proscribed group entails trial as an individual, at which point the benefits of group membership are lost.[65] Even the voicing of social issues depends on social organisation and personal inclination, the prerequisites for which are language, communication, education, culture, etc., and yet the UK has been criticised for certain anti-terrorist surveillance operations, in that they 'chill' group activities and social participation. As noted by McCulloch and Pickering, the key weapon of civil society against its government is public censure (broadly construed), but censure is difficult to formulate or express when individuals are deterred from associating together and their social networks are disrupted.[66]

At the extreme, official authority to suppress dissent can create the requisite legal environment to sustain excessive personal intrusion and, indeed, methods of state terror.[67] As criminal suspicion is cast by legislation over wider groups or activities, the political isolation of 'suspect communities' that results can then transform a social issue into an additional security concern.[68] Self-determination, as the principle pertains to groups struggling for stronger rights or greater autonomy, is clearly implicated in this 'chilling' process. Accordingly, differentiations between individuals and the groups to which they belong that are incorporated in legislation reflect the ability of governments to protect certain persons to the detriment of other persons. For example, Articles 5–7 and 9 of the Council of Europe's 2005 Terrorism Convention exempt 'lawful' government action, however

---

63 See, e.g., R. Youngs, 'Germany: Shooting Down Aircraft and Analyzing Computer Data' [2008] 6 *Int.J.Const.L.* 331; C.J.M. Safferling, 'The Response to Terrorism in Some Western Countries: Terror and Law' [2006] 4 *J.Int.Crim.J.* 1152.
64 C. Harding, supra note 57, p. 692. See also J. Wadsley, 'Painful Perceptions and Fundamental Rights – Anti-Money Laundering Regulation and Lawyers' [2008] 29(3) *Comp.Law.* 65; T. Thompson, 'Software that Can Predict Violent Crime to Help Police', *The Observer*, 25 July 2010, p. 10.
65 R.F. Devlin, supra note 33.
66 J. McCulloch and S. Pickering, 'Suppressing the Financing of Terrorism' [2005] 45 *Br.J.Crim.* 470, at p. 472.
67 See, e.g., E. Barry, 'Draft Law Revives Practice of Soviets', nytimes.com, 16 July 2010 (draft law revives Soviet KGB practices used against dissidents).
68 See Press Release, UN Dept. of Public Information, 'Sixth Committee is Told Aim Is "Not to Attack a People"', UN Doc. GA/L/3364 (9 October 2009). See also D. Bonner, 'Responding to Crisis: Legislating Against Terrorism' [2006] 122 *L.Q.R.* 602; P. Hillyard, *Suspect Community: People's Experiences of the Prevention of Terrorism Acts in Britain* (London: Pluto Press, 1993).

defined.[69] In other words, the official power to identify prohibited 'expressions of support for terrorist offences' permits the exemption from prosecution of those who wield that very power.[70]

Such auto-exemptions from the scope of certain laws by governments can cover both civil servants and private commercial concerns to which government responsibilities have been contracted-out, which process creates an inbuilt double standard finding legitimacy only in formal, procedural terms. The resulting potential for political bias and arbitrariness found in many areas of legal regulation, e.g., in social welfare provision, immigration, education and sport, to name but a few, then is seen to reinforce only a government's ability to protect itself against its political opponents, rather than protect the governed against violence or other damage. The ability to censure government publicly is thus crucial to resolving many grievances of many liberation groups that are usually premised on local factors, even when based purportedly on a wider agenda.[71]

To continue with the example of the UK, the Irish Republicans in Northern Ireland are well known for campaigning violently for a united Ireland, yet it can easily be argued that this goal arose from a deep apprehension and experience of ethnic discrimination by the Protestant majority in the province over their minority Catholic neighbours. Modern British anti-terrorist legislation was designed originally to deal with this localised violence, and date from the Prevention of Violence Act (Temporary Provisions) 1939, on which the Prevention of Terrorism (Temporary Provisions) Act 1974 was based in part.[72] Nonetheless, these early laws were ultimately 'predicated on the British state's historical construction of the Irish as dangerous following colonisation'.[73] In other words, the Catholic population in Northern Ireland has been subjected to differential treatment in English legislation in relation to the rest of the UK for many years.

Even as British 'anti-terrorist' legislation continued largely on this temporary basis, the legislation was expanded and made permanent in 2000 in a Prevention of Terrorism Act intended more broadly to deter terrorism in general. Developments in British provisions since 9/11 have been

---

69  Explanatory Report to the 2005 Terrorism Convention, para. 83, accessed at conventions. coe.int/Treaty/EN/Report/Html/196htm. Cf. the delay to discussion in the UN Sixth Committee on the criminal accountability of UN officials and experts while on mission (documents A/64/183 and A/64/183.Add.1). Press Release, UN Dept. of Public Information, supra note 68.

70  E. Chadwick, 'The 2005 Terrorism Convention: A Flexible Step Too Far?' [2007] 16(2) *Nottm.L.J.* 29, at p. 31.

71  See, e.g., M. Sterio, 'On the Right to External Self-Determination: "Selfistans", Secession, and the Great Powers' Rule' [2010] 19 *Minn.J.I.L.* 137.

72  See D. Bonner, supra note 68.

73  C. Pantazis and S. Pemberton, supra note 52, at p. 647.

accomplished at breakneck speed,[74] and Pantazis and Pemberton assert that Britain in recent years has substituted its Irish 'suspect community' with a Muslim one. They identify a 'suspect community' generically as follows:[75]

> [A] sub-group of the population [. . .] is singled out for state attention as being 'problematic'. Specifically in terms of policing, individuals may be targeted, not necessarily as a result of suspected wrong-doing, but simply because of their presumed membership to that sub-group. Race, ethnicity, religion, class, gender, language, accent, dress, political ideology or any combination of these factors may serve to delineate the sub-group.[76]

Differentiating, official action is typical of the treatment received by many groups who struggle for rights of self-determination. As for government containments of 'problematic' communities, Pantazis and Pemberton cite several criminological studies that criticise the use of public resources by government to manipulate official discourse analysis and to collect excessive amounts of personal information in order to construct and profile difference.[77] Moreover, as judicial deference can be further entrenched by legislation that requires the judicial system to treat foreign nationals differently,[78] the scene is set for a political construction of offender and victim communities alike.

Other states have adopted a similar approach to Britain's, as indicated in a report to parliament by Lord Carlile in 2007 which examined the issue of definition.[79] Certain states, such as Turkey for example, have experienced 'terrorist' struggles for self-determination for many years. Similar to the UK and Northern Ireland, Turkey has long dealt with separatist forces, mainly in its Kurdish regions, as well as with other movements agitating for constitutional change and has adopted a broad legislative approach to terrorism and the maintenance of public order, in general. However, and somewhat in contrast to Britain,[80] Turkish legislation has focused on the direct curtailment of certain rights, such as the freedom of expression, regarding which it has lost several cases before the European Court of Human

---

74 At least 11 acts or orders have come into force in whole or in part since 2000.
75 C. Pantazis and S. Pemberton, supra note 52.
76 *Ibid.*, p. 649.
77 See also J. Wadsley, 'Painful Perceptions and Fundamental Rights – Anti-Money Laundering Regulation and Lawyers' [2008] 29(3) *Comp.Law.* 65 (more onerous UN rules for information gathering than is required by EC Directives).
78 See, e.g., A. Kavanagh, 'Judging the Judges Under the Human Rights Act: Deference, Disillusionment and the "War on Terror"' [2009] *P.L.* 287.
79 Lord Carlile of Berriew, QC (Independent Reviewer of Terrorism Legislation), 'The Definition of Terrorism', Cm. 7052 (London: Her Majesty's Stationery Office, 15 March 2007).
80 Specifically, the Terrorism Act 2000, as amended by the Anti-Terrorism, Crime and Security Act 2001.

Rights. Russia, too, has an ever-broadening definition of terrorism and has similarly found itself on the losing side before the Court, e.g., for Russia's failure to take advantage of the derogation regime provided in Article 15 of the European Convention on Human Rights when conducting armed hostilities in the North Caucasus.[81]

Such cases can be contrasted with the example of Germany and the strong role played by its Federal Constitutional Court in guaranteeing rights. Although several perpetrators or supporters of the attacks on 9/11 had lived in Germany, there has not been much of a domestic terrorist problem there since the 1970s, other than sporadic attack by the remnants of the Rote Armee Fraktion (RAF), or against non-German targets, e.g., the Israeli Olympic team in Munich in 1972, and the 'La Belle' night club in Berlin in 1986.[82] However, the German Parliament did pass a number of statutes in the aftermath of 9/11 to enhance surveillance and information gathering, to increase police powers, to shoot down passenger airplanes suspected of being used as weapons and so on. Nonetheless, although the overall effect of German legislation makes its domestic law coverage similar to that in the UK, Germany has no specific definition of terrorism. Instead, an essential criterion for prosecution concerns whether the suspect group aims to destroy the basic values of the democratic state or the peaceful coexistence of peoples, which is an extremely sophisticated safeguard for individual human rights.

Safferling points to ways in which German legislation allows the term 'terrorist' to range broadly to include organisations that aim to kill, kidnap or sabotage both foreign and national targets, although the Criminal Code distinguishes between EU and non-EU organisations. Review by the German Federal Constitutional Court also remains possible, such as the successful challenge brought against the Air Security Act of 11 January 2005, which purported to give the Federal Government lawful authority to shoot down hijacked planes.[83] In that case, the Court held the relevant provision to violate the right to life under Article 2(1) of the Basic Law. Similarly, the Constitutional Court held that orders to collect and compare personal computerised data were unlawful, unless they were designed to protect a high-ranking interest against a concrete danger, as they violated both

---

81 See W. Abresch, 'A Human Rights Law of Internal Armed Conflict: the ECHR in Chechnya' [2005] 16 *E.J.I.L.* 741; R. Draper, 'Human Rights and the Law of War' [1972] 12 *Vir.J.I.L.* 326.

82 Safferling notes that the main substantive concerns between 1980 and 2000 were political crimes in the former GDR, war crimes during the Yugoslav dissolution wars and organised economic crimes. However, the German Criminal Procedural Code was still heavily modified in order to take account of new technical means of surveillance. C.J.M. Safferling, 'Terror and Law: German Responses to 9/11' [2006] 4 *J.Int'l.Crim.J.* 1152.

83 Judgement of 15 January 2006, www.bverfg.de/entscheidungen/rs2006215.1bvr035705.html (in German).

Article 2(2) of the Basic Law (protection of the free development of the personality)[84] and the right of privacy under Article 8 of the ECHR.

What is thus remarkable about the operation and interpretation of German law, in contrast to that in the UK, is that German constitutional rules provide expressly for the judicial override of discretionary governmental powers. Thus, by locating and enforcing a clear line between liberty and security, political discretion is narrowed when assessing 'lawful' proportionality and made subject to rights limitations. Of course, more remote German history is replete with political abuses of law, and national sensitivities on this point in the post-1945 era have mandated that all persons and communities within the state retain their rights not only under the Basic Law, but also are able to work within society to alter those rights lawfully, if so desired. In turn, this helps to create what Youngs terms a:

> [M]ilitant or fortified democracy in the sense that . . . [the constitutional order] contains elements that are intended to act as a defence against forces that would destroy it.[85]

Most importantly, perhaps, such cases illustrate that in the UK, as in many other states, any comparable demonstration of the strength of law over politics would be institutionally impossible due to the deliberate omission of sufficiently enabling mechanisms in the relevant constitutional and/or statutory order.

## Conclusion

Demands for self-determining autonomy are raised by people 'who[m] history has assaulted'.[86] However, complete territorial secession is rarely the original motivation of many such peoples. Moreover, in that the international community leaves the concrete application of rights principles to domestic arrangements, secessionist demands are more often made once discrete communities are forced to endure high levels of discrimination or other state-organised oppression over a long period of time.[87] This is why ongoing attempts to confine the entitlement to rights to self-determination to former colonial or analogous non-self-governing lands are a nonsense: to do so effectively treats such groups as objects and not *subjects* of international law. Accordingly, the list of peoples around the world who

---

84 Judgement of 4 April 2006, brought on complaint of a Moroccan Muslim student at the University of Duisburg and discussed by R. Youngs, 'Germany: Shooting Down Aircraft and Analysing Computer Data' [2008] 6 *Int.J.Const.L.* 331, pp. 338–48.

85 R. Youngs, supra note 84, p. 347.

86 S. Barry, 'Upfront', *The Observer Magazine*, 4 October 2009, p. 10.

87 As in the case of Kosovo. See *Kosovo Advisory Opinion* [22 July 2010] ICJ, General List No. 141, supra note 25.

at present are struggling for greater rights entitlements is long and growing.[88] The recent 'Troubles' in Northern Ireland illustrate well the dynamics involved, as does the ongoing conflict in Chechnya.

The customary rights of state self-defence against each other are confined to a necessity that is 'instant, overwhelming, leaving no choice of means, and no moment for deliberation',[89] while 'lawful' action to deprive an individual in 'peacetime' of his or her right to life is similarly premised on 'absolute necessity'. Just as there is no more right to eliminate a people than there is a right to oppress or to discriminate against them, such parameters for 'necessity' do not include standing state policies to assassinate political opponents or 'shoot to kill' in either context. Nonetheless, state sovereign powers to act unilaterally in pursuit of their own versions of 'peacetime' law and order illustrate the principal rationale for state territorial borders. Governments (and their commercial associates) can monitor the daily life of those within and a subject population is conditioned over time to the sheer ubiquity of official forms of coercion. Commonly held social values can be subtly 'chilled' by state security mechanisms, and public censure of government behaviour is silenced when met by state violence.

As the UN's Sixth Committee debated measures against terrorism in October 2009, it was reminded by the Sudanese representative that the objective in fighting terrorist actions is 'not to attack a people'.[90] Perhaps not, but several state representatives on the Sixth Committee were equally adamant that the global fight against terrorist actions must be clearly differentiated from legitimate struggles by peoples for their rights of self-determination. This has yet to occur. The heavy international rights obligations placed on each state when fighting terrorism are more easily accomplished by developed states than by developing ones, the international principle of non-intervention allows *all* governments to control their own domestic spheres, and different state governments generate different means

---

88 Of many noted in by the press in 2009 alone, see, e.g., D. Walsh, 'Strategic Balochistan Becomes a Target in Taliban War', *The Guardian*, 22 December 2009, p. 17 (autonomy and rights to control gasfield revenues demanded since 1948); J.M. Paoletti, 'Post-Colonial Self-Determination: Basques and Catalans in Contemporary Spain' [2009] 15 *Buff.H.R.L.R.* 159; L. Harding, 'Rebellion in the Caucasus', *The Observer*, 29 November 2009 (violent independence struggles); Reuters, Gergely, 'Northern Irish Dissidents Forming "New IRA"', 14 December 2009, uk.news.yahoo.com; Reuters, Chandran, 'Violent Protests Shut Down Hyderabad', 9 December 2009, uk.news.yahoo.com (demands for separate state); S. Dagher, 'Kurds Defy Baghdad', *New York Times*, 10 July 2009, nytimes.com (new Kurdish constitution); B. Serrano, 'Tribal Gunmen Abduct Dozens', 10 December 2009, uk.news. yahoo.com (pro-independence Islamist, Muslim and Communist militant insurgencies); S. Carrell, 'Salmond under Attack', *The Guardian*, 1 December 2009, p. 17 (Scottish independence referendum scheduled). See also P. Epstein, ' "Autonomous Colonisation" – the Case for Western Sahara' [2009] 15 *Ann.Surv.Int'l.&Comp.L.* 107.
89 The Caroline Case [1837] 29 *B.F.S.P.* 1137–8.
90 Press Release, UN Dept. of Public Information, supra note 68.

with which to contain those categories of citizens and groups they do not like on grounds of 'security'.[91] As highlighted earlier, the word 'peace' hardly seems appropriate.

Meanwhile, as identified by Stepanova earlier in this chapter, the willingness of many liberation groups to accept aid and assistance from Al Qaeda affiliates, or similar, leads not only to a loss of clarity in liberation agenda but further endangers what international goodwill there might otherwise have been to support a people's resistance against injustice and oppression, as is now illustrated by a comparison of the content of contemporary anti-terrorist instruments.

---

91 See, e.g., N. Watt and H. Sherwood, 'David Cameron: Israeli blockade has Turned Gaza Strip into a "Prison Camp"', *The Guardian*, 27 July 2010, guardian.co.uk.

# Part 3

It is our domestic legislation, and not an international act. Each country has the right to perfect its own legislation, including that which affects special services. And we will do this.

(Dmitri A. Medvedev)

## 5  The growth in linkage between self-determination and terrorism: international and regional instruments

### Introduction

The bipolar east and west tended to opt for an informal, arm's-length 'partnership' during much of the post-1945 era, and the two main blocs generally managed to avoid open interference or confrontation in one another's spheres of influence. However, once the Soviets had pulled out of Afghanistan in the late 1980s, and the Cold War ended, a new international environment of territorial and/or political insecurity began to unfold. Islamist extremists in Afghanistan were already noticeable for their use of intimidation and terror to subdue their followers. Even as the more traditional types of self-determination struggle, as in Northern Ireland, were dissipating, new violent actors began to appear within many more multi-ethnic states and, with the spread of their influence, the characteristics formerly attributed to 'terrorists' slowly began to alter.

As the Cold War thawed, many states and organisations seemed more willing than previously to intervene in regional trouble spots, particularly when no one party to a conflict could reduce trans-boundary violence and/or contain radical extremism. The new spirit of deferral to international 'good offices' necessitated greater involvement by the UN, and Security Council authorisations for 'peacekeeping', 'peacemaking', 'peace enforcement', and 'peace-building' exercises became commonplace.[1] In turn, the growing dangers of extremism and intolerance during the 1990s began to supplant self-determination in codifications at the international level. Expressions of support for peoples seeking rights of self-determination survived, if at all, only in regional instruments. In reality, however, not a great deal changed in terms of inter-state obligation,[2] as support for self-determination preserves

---

1 *Peacekeeping Operations: Principles and Guidelines* (UN, 2008), p. 17. See also Report of the UNSecGen'l, *UN Peacekeeping 2009: Overview*, UN Doc. A/6/41, Pt. 2, para. 47 (17 peacekeeping operations currently deployed across five continents), www.un.org/en/peacekeeping/documents/pko_2009.pdf.

2 E.g., as of 9/11, only Botswana, Sri Lanka, the UK and Uzbekistan had joined the International Convention for the Suppression of the Financing of Terrorism, New York, 9 December 1999, in force 10 April 2002.

a much-needed forum for inter-state dissent amid condemnations of indiscriminate violence.[3] It would take the shocking atrocity of 9/11 for *all* states to be required to carry the heavy burdens of a 'global' anti-terrorist agenda.

It is thus the purpose of this chapter to describe in brief the most notable international and regional anti-terrorist treaties, inasmuch as they may or may not make direct and/or indirect reference to rights of self-determination. This is done primarily to illuminate the evolving linkages made in official discourse to ethnicity, extremism and terrorism, which linkages ultimately help states to disparage the significance of a 'right' of self-determination, inasmuch as the latter is symptomatic of the relative inattention paid by states generally to inequality, discrimination, equal human rights and societal intolerance. Moreover, a brief review is also made of enduring state support for rights of self-determination, as is made clear in continuing negotiations at UN level to agree a comprehensive convention against international terrorism.[4]

## International instruments

To begin, one treaty from the League era has had an enduring influence over post-1945 anti-terrorism efforts: the Convention for the Prevention and Punishment of Terrorism of 1937.[5] Twinned with the first Convention for the Creation of an International Criminal Court,[6] the Terrorism Convention was an attempt to deter a spate of attacks against heads of state, diplomats and other public officials.[7] The Convention specifically defines the phenomenon of terrorism in the context of criminal acts of 'an international character' directed against a state. For this purpose, the Convention adopts first a generic definition in Article 1(2), which provides as follows:

> In the present Convention, the expression 'acts of terrorism' means criminal acts directed against a state and intended or calculated to create a state of terror in the minds of particular persons, or a group of persons or the general public.

---

3  See, e.g., UNGA Resolutions 49/60 of 9 December 1994, and 51/210 of 17 December 1996, on measures to eliminate international terrorism.
4  UNGA Doc. A/59/894 (59th session, agenda item 148 'Measures to eliminate international terrorism'), Appendix II, 'Draft comprehensive convention against international terrorism: Consolidated text prepared by the coordinator for discussion', www.ilsa.org/jessup/jessup08/basicmats/unterrorism.pdf.
5  7 Hudson, *International Legislation*, No. 499, at 862. Never entered into force.
6  7 Hudson, *International Legislation*, No. 500. Never entered into force.
7  Keesings Archives, p. 1394, notes that 'during the past 80 years more than 100 Monarchs, Presidents, and Heads of Government have been assassinated'.

Articles 2 and 3 then enumerate specific instances of international terrorism, such as causing death, harm, or loss of liberty to heads of state, the destruction of public property, conspiracy and assistance. The public at large is protected against 'wilful act[s] calculated to endanger' their lives,[8] but not 'grievous bodily harm or loss of liberty'.[9] What is of note today regarding this early effort in 1937 to define terrorism is the anticipation of more modern challenges, such as differential individual status, self-determination, freedom fighters, 'state terror' and acts of the armed forces. For example, the distinction made in protection between heads of state and the public at large somewhat parallels that differentiating soldiers and civilians, in that the former are more likely to be targeted due to their position, while the latter should never be.

Further, the Terrorism Convention was not intended to apply to acts of the armed forces, although this was not made express in the final draft, as it was thought originally that members of the armed forces could be subsumed within the protections afforded to persons charged with official functions. However, Saul notes, in the context of civil war specifically that it was also felt strongly at the time that members of the armed forces should be excluded from the 1937 Terrorism Convention 'because the Committee . . . believed that "the question of civil war . . . is clearly outside the scope of the Convention"'.[10] This belief in turn merely reflects the more long-standing framework for regulating 'war' pursuant to international laws, while acts of terrorism are prosecuted under domestic criminal law – a division that is still utilised today to distinguish between (lawful) belligerent and (unlawful) insurgent status.

Nonetheless, inasmuch as indiscriminate tactics were developed for use by the conventional armed forces during the major wars of the 20th century, certain prohibitions in laws of armed conflict have broken down, such that insurgent/terrorist acts have also broadened in terms of their indiscriminate effects. As noted by Walzer:

> The increasing use of terror by far left and ultranationalist movements represents the breakdown of a political code first worked out in the second half of the nineteenth century and roughly analogous to the laws of war worked out at the same time. Adherence to this code did not prevent revolutionary militants from being called terrorists, but in fact the violence they committed bore little resemblance to contemporary

---

8  Article 3(3), Terrorism Convention.
9  Article 2(1), Terrorism Convention.
10  B. Saul, 'The Legal Response of the League of Nations to Terrorism' [2006] 4 *J.Int'l.Crim.J.* 78, at p. 94, citing L.o.N. (C.I.R.T.), Report adopted by the Committee on 26 April 1937 (Geneva), Third Session, L.o.N. Doc. V. Legal 1937.V.1, at 2. See also E. Chadwick, 'A Tale of Two Courts: the "Creation" of a Jurisdiction?' [2004] 9(1) *J.Confl.&Sec.L.* 71.

terrorism. It was not random murder but assassination,[11] and it involved the drawing of a line that we will have little difficulty recognising as the political parallel of the line that marks off combatants from non-combatants.[12]

The 20th century witnessed many episodes in which an element of 'total war' was unleashed by states on each other as well as on civilians and there has been a general sense of loss in constraint regarding the use of official force generally. As previously discussed in Chapter 3, laws of war arose to ensure that belligerent rights could only be claimed by state forces or by a non-state group whose use of force displayed a certain scope and intensity, in order, subsequently, to attribute international responsibility for breach of the relevant rules. Even though, prior to 1949, humanitarian restraint was generally a matter of strict reciprocity, the rules tended to be followed for the most part during the First World War, even as the means and methods for 'total warfare', such as mustard gas, were utilised. During the Second World War, inasmuch as the main war aims were driven more by political than by military guidelines, relatively inexpensive terrorising war tactics both at home and abroad were widely employed. Kamikaze pilots, Nazi genocide and Allied carpet bombing spring to mind as examples of the means utilised to commit mass murder.

The bipolar nature of much of the UN era facilitated the spread of 'totality' in terms of the means and methods of armed force, even as a new era had dawned in which individuals and peoples had greater rights expectations. Moreover, states have never been expressly prohibited from utilising force against their own populations,[13] but as certain states began to utilise terror, excessive internal state force or forms of state-sponsored violence, it was soon clear to the UN community at large that peoples would struggle for their self-determination in ways that were at once understandable and deplorable.[14] Certainly, it is not difficult to find constant reminders to states that they should not utilise or sponsor terrorist acts, but a broad exposure to the terrorist imagination had been assured by the return home of demobbed soldiers after the Second World War, who could then pass the efficacies of utilising terror techniques to post-Second World War revolutionaries,[15] as is now highlighted.

---

11 E.g., the SR Combat Organization, the PPS Combat Organization and Bolshevik combat groups carried out numerous assassinations, targeting civil servants and police between the years 1904–7.
12 M. Walzer, *Just and Unjust Wars: A Moral Argument* (New York: Basic Books, 1977, 2d edn), p. 198. See also M. Howard, *'Temperamenta Belli:* Can War Be Controlled?', in J.B. Elshtain (ed.), *Just War Theory* (Oxford: Blackwell, 1992), at pp. 23, 30–3.
13 See generally A. George (ed.), *Western State Terrorism* (Cambridge: Polity Press, 1991).
14 See, e.g., Q. Wright, 'Subversive Intervention' [1960] 54 *A.J.I.L.* 521; A. Fraleigh, 'The Algerian Revolution as a Case Study in International Law', in R.A. Falk (ed.), *The International Law of Civil War* (London: Johns Hopkins Press, 1971), at p. 179.
15 M. Walzer, supra note 12, p. 198.

*Pre-1980 instruments*

General Assembly resolutions throughout the 1960s and 1970s slowly gained in momentum, to support first the right of self-determination,[16] then, a right by peoples to use all available means to achieve it[17] and, ultimately, an entitlement of 'all peoples' to their self-determination.[18] In turn, the many known contradictions between human rights entitlements and state non-interference simply created more space in which 'peoples' living far beyond those under so-called 'salt-water' imperialism could seek redress, if not yet all subjects of historic conquest or other perceived injustice. Ultimate proof was provided, if any were needed, that a 'peoples' struggle for self-determination should no longer be considered a mere domestic issue once international humanitarian laws of armed conflict were adapted in full in 1977 to apply expressly to a 'new' yet 'classic' trilogy of liberation struggles – colonialism, foreign occupation and/or racist regimes.[19]

Nonetheless, a core difficulty remained: many non-international armed conflicts were not recognised as 'war', so threatened governments could refuse even to consider the minimal application of humanitarian constraints. At their most basic level, the extension of laws of armed conflict to non-international armed conflicts was met in many government quarters with a strong counter-argument that the extension was equivalent to affording undeserved recognition to 'rebels' and 'terrorists',[20] despite the Geneva initiatives having constituted only a practical recognition of the scale and intensity of liberationist armed struggles, and the consequential dangers to innocent civilians. Nonetheless, by affording such recognition to 'terrorists', there was a risk that affording preferential treatment would have knock-on effects on more controversial issues found in abstract theory, ideology, practicality and power politics, which, in turn, were likely to make self-determination far less safe for governments. Accordingly, the attempt to extend laws of armed conflict to struggles for self-determination led many states to stonewall even longer, making liberationist struggles somewhat more certain to occur.

Broader international concern about the sheer scale of liberationist force did, in fact, help to shift inter-state consensus away from the mere condemnatory in order to 'manage' the new generation of liberation causes, e.g., post- or non-colonial 'peoples', who equally felt empowered by human rights entitlements to seek greater political accommodations and/or to

---

16  See, e.g., UNGA Resolutions 2588 B (XXIV) Article 1 of 15 December 1969, 2787 (XXVI) Article 1 of 6 December 1971 and 2955 (XXVII) Article 1 of 12 December 1972.

17  See, e.g., UNGA Resolutions 3070 (XXVIII) Article 2 of 30 November 1973 and 3246 (XXIX) Article 3 of 29 November 1974.

18  UNGA Resolution 2625 of 1970 (the 'Friendly Relations' resolution).

19  Article 1(4) of the 1977 Protocol 1 additional to the four Geneva Conventions of 1949.

20  See, e.g., H.-P. Gasser, '*Agora*: the US Decision Not to Ratify Protocol 1' [1987] 81 *A.J.I.L.* 912; J. Gardam, 'Protocol 1 to the Geneva Conventions: A Victim of Short-Sighted Political Considerations?' [1989] 17 *Mel.U.L.R.* 107.

achieve system change, whether or not by force, while other politically transformative, violent groups by way of contrast may merit rather more a blanket public condemnation of unlawful violence, such as the Baader Meinhof gang in Germany or the Red Brigade in Italy. Nonetheless, there would be little distinction made in the sectoral instruments of the 1960s and 1970s between 'terrorist' group acts and those perpetrated by peoples in struggles for self-determination. These early instruments seek instead to prohibit specific crimes on a universal basis, as now outlined.

### Convention on Offences and Certain Other Acts Committed on Board Aircraft (Tokyo 14 September 1963)

The 1963 Convention refers expressly to neither 'terrorism' nor 'self-determination'. Its purpose was to encourage states to ensure that criminal jurisdiction would be applied on board flag-flying aircraft. In particular, the aircraft commander was to be afforded express rights to restrain any person who endangered or was about to endanger flight safety.

Liberation or civil wars fought at the time were in Portuguese Guinea, North Yemen and Sudan.

### Convention for the Suppression of Unlawful Seizure of Aircraft (The Hague 16 December 1970)

The 1970 Convention refers expressly to neither 'terrorism' nor 'self-determination'. Due to a recent spate of aircraft hijackings, its purpose was to define 'hijacking', to criminalise it, and to impose an 'extradite or prosecute' obligation on states.

The contemporaneous terrorist environment for aircraft at the time included an Israeli attack on Beirut airport on 28 December 1968, in which 13 Middle East Airlines planes were destroyed. This was purportedly in retaliation for recent separatist Palestinian (PFLP) attacks on El Al flights. Hijackings recorded during 1969 included a plane owned by El Al (Zurich, 2 February) and Trans-World Airlines (Damascus, 29 August). Otherwise, separatist Irish (IRA) terrorism was ongoing, while in London, the department store Marks & Spencer was bombed. By way of contrast, the first three Baader Meinhof bombs were detonated in Berlin in late 1969.

### Convention for the Suppression of Unlawful Acts Against the Safety of Civil Aviation (Montreal 23 September 1971)

The 1971 Convention refers expressly to neither 'terrorism' nor 'self-determination' and was intended to criminalise the placing of an explosive device on an aircraft.

This initiative was adopted in reaction to alleged PFLP liberationist sabotage the previous February in Switzerland and Germany; the PFLP also hijacked three planes subsequently in September. Otherwise, the Bangladesh Liberation War was unfolding, in which former East Pakistan and India were allied against West Pakistan, and resulting in the secession of East Pakistan as Bangladesh. Idi Amin seized power in Uganda and forcibly expelled the Indian minority of some 35,000 people.[21] Sri Lanka (named Ceylon at the time) put down an insurgency.

*Convention on the Prevention and Punishment of Crimes Against Internationally Protected Persons, Including Diplomatic Agents (New York 14 December 1973)*

The 1973 Convention refers expressly to neither 'terrorism' nor 'self-determination'. It was formulated in the interests of reinforcing inter-state co-operation and friendly relations by seeking to criminalise the murder or kidnap of certain public officials and attacks on them or their premises or means of transport, in addition to prohibiting threats and participation in respect of the relevant crimes.

Otherwise, the Turkish consul general and the consul had been murdered earlier in January, while in April bombs exploded in Paris outside the Turkish consulate and Turkish Airlines offices. In December the Spanish prime minister was killed by a Basque separatist (ETA) car bomb and Carlos, a notorious terrorist–outlaw who often aided the Palestinian cause, attempted to assassinate the chairman of Marks & Spencer. The fourth Arab–Israeli ('Yom Kippur') war took place in the most recent phase of the Middle East dispute, which had been ongoing since 1948, and the 'dirty war' was continuing in Chile and Argentina.

*International Convention Against the Taking of Hostages (New York 17 December 1979)*

For the first time, the principle of equal rights and self-determination of peoples *is* expressly reaffirmed in the Preamble to the Hostages Convention and there is no express labelling of hostage taking as 'terrorism'. The Convention characterises the offence by means of the classic triangular structure of terrorist tactics (i.e., politically inspired, etc., attack on A, to make B change its position regarding C). Article 1(1) phrases this structure as 'to compel a third party . . . to do or abstain from doing any act as an explicit or implicit condition for the release of the hostage'.

In 1975 the more infamous hostage-taking incidents included the seizure of the Indonesian consulate, and a train in Amsterdam by the Moluccans, a separatist group from the South Moluccas islands in the Banda Sea. A Palestinian group led by Carlos seized the OPEC headquarters in Vienna.

21 P. Keatley, 'Obituary: Idi Amin', *The Guardian*, 18 August 2003, guardian.co.uk.

In June 1976 the Israelis carried out a raid on Entebbe, Uganda, to rescue passengers held hostage on board an Air France jet hijacked by Palestinians and, in 1977, the Moluccans seized a Dutch school and another train. Ongoing liberation or civil wars at the time included those in Angola, Cyprus, Ethiopia, Indonesia, Iraq and the Lebanon. The Philippines and Turkey experienced insurrections. The Cambodian genocide occurred in 1975.

### 1980s' instruments

As can be seen, the causes behind 'terrorist' acts were ignored for the most part, as was the issue of self-determination. Instead, this early pattern in anti-terrorist codifications sought to develop a global net over certain acts by encouraging all states to harmonise specific criminal definitions and co-operative arrangements in domestic law. Using this globalising technique, the 'extradite or prosecute' formula gained in favour, at the expense of the political offence exemption to extradition. However, ongoing political and ideological divisions between states meant that the number of ratifying states required for these early anti-terrorist instruments to enter into binding force remained relatively low. Accordingly, coverage was by no means comprehensive for many years, particularly as certain groups who perpetrated these acts were not always considered at the diplomatic level to be 'terrorists' at all, but instead, 'freedom fighters'.

The maintenance of inter-state comity and friendly relations also meant that it was fairly easy for states to sidestep the 'extradite or prosecute' obligation. For example, should a state be sympathetic to the cause pursued by an alleged offender in its custody yet receive a request for his extradition to stand prosecution, the requested state might prefer not to extradite him or her to the requesting state, but instead, itself comply with the fundamental legal obligation to prosecute, at which point an indulgent, 'light-touch' investigation is likely to lead nowhere but to acquittal. The principle conventional instruments of the 1980s would subsequently follow this initial framework and aim at deterring specific, internationally harmful acts, as outlined in the following.

### Convention on the Physical Protection of Nuclear Material (adopted in Vienna 3 March 1980; opened for signature in Vienna and New York 3 March 1980)

The 1980 Nuclear Convention refers expressly to neither 'terrorism' nor 'self-determination' and criminalises the possession, use, transfer theft, etc., of nuclear material. The preamble expressly recognises the importance of physically protecting nuclear material intended for military purposes. Article 2 states the convention applies to 'nuclear material used for peaceful purposes while in international nuclear transport' and, subject to certain exceptions, 'while in domestic use, storage and transport'. Proof of a triangular terrorist motive is not required but constitutes one alternative in Article 7, and there is an 'extradite or prosecute' provision in Articles 8 and 9. Annex I categorises nuclear materials in accordance with their requisite physical protection during international transportation. Subsequent amendments placed obligations on states parties to co-operate when locating and recovering stolen material and when working to mitigate the consequences of accident or sabotage.

*Protocol for the Suppression of Unlawful Acts of Violence at Airports Serving International Civil Aviation, supplementary to the Convention for the Suppression of Unlawful Acts Against the Safety of Civil Aviation (Montreal 2 February 1988)*

The Montreal Air Protocol does not refer expressly to 'terrorism' or to 'self-determination'. Its purpose was to extend the provisions of the 1971 Montreal Convention on the Safety of Civil Aviation to terrorist acts at airports serving international civil aviation.

Relevant terrorist acts involving aviation at the time included the planting by Sikh insurgents of suitcase bombs on separate Air India and Air Canada (ultimately intended for Air India) flights out of Toronto in June 1985; one suitcase bomb exploded over the Irish Sea, killing over 300 people; the second exploded on the ground in Tokyo, killing two. Later that year, in December, the Abu Nidal gang attacked El Al airline counters in Rome and Vienna airports. In April 1986, El Al security personnel discovered a smuggled bomb in carry-on luggage. On 21 December 1988, Pan Am flight 103 was blown up over Scotland, killing nearly 300 people. A Libyan agent was subsequently convicted of planting the bomb in a suitcase and imprisoned in Scotland, but he was returned to Libya on compassionate grounds in 2009. Ongoing insurrections or civil wars were in Peru (Communist Shining Path), Syria (Muslim Brotherhood), Sri Lanka (Tamils), Sudan, South Yemen, Somalia and Burundi.

*Convention for the Suppression of Unlawful Acts Against the Safety of Maritime Navigation (Rome 10 March 1988)*

The Maritime Navigation Convention is one of the few international instruments at the time to refer both to terrorism and self-determination; the bipolar rivalry between the superpowers mandated the inclusion of neither or both, as the US generally condemned liberation wars as terrorism and the Soviets did not. The convention was intended to establish a legal regime for international maritime navigation similar to that applicable in international aviation. The preamble refers to acts of terrorism several times, and in terms that are specific to UNGA Resolution 40/61 of

9 December 1985, which authorised the International Maritime Organisation to 'study the problem of terrorism aboard or against ships with a view to making recommendations on appropriate measures'.

The convention preamble recalls that this General Assembly resolution 'unequivocally condemns, as criminal, all acts, methods and practices of terrorism wherever and by whomever committed' and that the resolution refers only indirectly to self-determination, in that the UN is urged 'to pay special attention to all situations, including colonialism, racism and all situations involving flagrant violations of human rights and fundamental freedoms and those involving alien occupation which may give rise to international terrorism'. Proof of a triangular terrorist motive is not required, but instead constitutes one alternative. The 'extradite or prosecute' obligation is found in Article 10.

Notable maritime acts of terrorism at the time included the seizure in October 1985 of the Italian cruise liner *Achille Lauro* by members of Al-Fatah and the interception by the French navy in late October 1987 of the *Eksund*, which was transporting Libyan weapons to the IRA.

*Protocol for the Suppression of Unlawful Acts Against*
*the Safety of Fixed Platforms Located on the Continental Shelf*
*(Rome 10 March 1988)*

The 1988 Protocol refers expressly neither to 'terrorism' nor to 'self-determination'. Its purpose, as noted in its preamble, is to extend the 1988 Maritime Navigation Convention in relation to fixed platforms on the continental shelf.

*Post-Cold War instruments*

Despite frequent condemnation throughout the Cold War, many non-international armed conflicts were effectively enabled by third state sponsorship or other outside assistance. The superpowers may have avoided direct attack on each other, but each was fundamental in provoking or facilitating the destabilisation of international relations elsewhere in proxy wars, as in Vietnam, Angola and Afghanistan. With the collapse of the bipolar world order, a renewed interest in peace could grow such that states were pressured increasingly not to sponsor insurgent force and, by this point, the threat of terrorist activity had certainly altered in focus, even as neither terrorism nor self-determination could be comprehensively defined at the international level, as it was naturally too useful to states to conflate the two.

Further complicating the scene are the seeds of Islamic jihad, inasmuch as they carried a different strain of resistance theory entirely on becoming more visible in the late 1970s. For example, Benda, writing in the early 1970s, describes a generational shift in many colonial, post-colonial, and non-colonial lands, between a younger generation increasingly exposed through education to Western influences and their more traditional elders. In so doing, Benda discerns among this younger, newly educated class both an envy of and resentment against the west, which is illustrated by the following characteristics:

> [N]on-western intelligentsias, insofar as they are politically active . . . tend to be social revolutionaries whose ideological aims as often as not militate against the *status quo*. Since, by definition, most of these aims are western-derived and transplanted to a social environment inherently still far more conservative than is true of the more advanced industrial societies of the west, the task of social engineering becomes far more radical. . . .
>
> Thus, 'feudalism' as well as colonialism – rule by entrenched native classes or rule by foreigners – can be blamed on the political, military and economic preponderance of the western world.[22]

Jason Burke, a reporter for *The Observer*, seemingly agrees with Benda, as noted in his post-9/11 book on Al Qaeda:

> Thirty years ago a new Islamic political ideology began to resonate amongst millions of young men and women across the Muslim world. This ideology was a sophisticated and genuine intellectual effort to find an Islamic answer to the challenges posed by the West's cultural, economic and political superiority. Over the decades that ideology has changed and mutated into something different. Once, Islamic activists thought primarily in terms of achieving power or reforming their own nation. There was room in their programme for gradualism and compromise.[23]

Even so, notable examples of extremist Islamic violence provoked wider attention when they were perpetrated during the 1980s, such as the hijackings by Islamic jihad gunmen of a Kuwaiti jet to Tehran in December 1984 and of a Trans-World Airlines jet out of Athens in June 1985. Burke adds that:

> The word or phrase 'al-Qaeda'[24] was certainly in use by the mid 1980s among the Islamic radicals drawn from all over the Muslim

---

22 H.J. Benda, 'Elites', in F. Tachau (ed.), *The Developing Nations: What Path to Modernization?* (Chicago: Harper & Row, 1972), pp. 105, 107–9.

23 J. Burke, *Al-Qaeda: Casting a Shadow of Terror* (London: I.B. Taurus & Co. Ltd., 2003), p. 5.

24 The phrase is Arabic in origin and means 'a base, as in a camp or a home, or a foundation, such as what is under a house. It can mean a pedestal that supports a column. It can also mean a precept, rule, principle, maxim, formula, method, model or pattern'. *Ibid.*, p. 7.

world to fight the Soviets in Afghanistan alongside the local resistance groups. . . .

However, the word 'al-Qaeda' was also used by the most extreme elements among the radicals fighting in Afghanistan, particularly those who decided that their struggle did not end with the withdrawal of the Soviets from the country in 1989.[25]

Meanwhile, many anti-terrorist General Assembly resolutions, such as Resolution 46/51 of 9 December 1991, continued to repeat formulaically the Assembly's continued support for self-determination, in terms of 'the inalienable right to self-determination and independence of all peoples under colonial and racist regimes and other forms of alien domination and foreign occupation, and upholding the legitimacy of their struggle, in particular the struggle of national liberation movements', even as the UN Official Documents System contains documentary evidence of the veritable explosion in General Assembly and Security Council Resolutions throughout the 1990s, which also condemn the growing number of acts of indiscriminate violence that still were often perpetrated in support of separatist causes. As the new form of Islamic extremism unfolded and tasked itself with ridding Western interests and influence from Muslim or other lands,[26] the 1990s – a decade of revolutions, both peaceful and violent – erupted in a struggle for political supremacy consequent on the disbanding Soviet Union; the Middle East remained turbulent, Irish republicans continued to bomb the British mainland, as Basque separatists did Spain, political assassinations occurred in many parts of Asia and Africa and political strife spread in Latin America.[27]

However, of crucial importance to more modern times is the tendency observed by Stepanova,[28] and highlighted in Chapter 4, for certain groups that happen to be predominately Muslim, such as the Chechens, effectively to sabotage their own chances of achieving their self-determination by sacrificing their worldwide goodwill when accessing, co-operating and colluding with local extremist Islamic networks in order to obtain additional publicity, support and finance. Therefore, as stronger linkages were made in official circles between 'terrorism' and other forms of group criminality such as money laundering and people trafficking, an anti-Western bias displayed in certain terrorist acts did little to increase their communication

25  *Ibid.*, pp. 7–8.
26  Such as the simultaneous bombings of two American embassies in Africa on August 7, 1998 attributed to Al Qaeda, which killed over 200 people and wounded thousands.
27  See, e.g., the case studies in D.J. Whitaker, *The Terrorism Reader* (London: Routledge, 2001).
28  E. Stepanova, 'Islamist Terrorism in the Caucasus and Central Asia', in A.P. Schmid and G.F. Hindle (eds), *After the War on Terror: Regional and Multilateral Perspectives on Counter-Terrorism Strategy* (London: RUSI Books, 2009), p. 104.

value, but instead, helped to shift the international focus onto their preferred modalities, technologies and communications systems, such as the internet, which opened the door to states for the next stage of co-ordinated action: the automatic equating of terrorism and *unauthorised* violence of any kind, which naturally includes prohibited acts by peoples struggling to achieve self-determination.

After the 9/11 atrocities, the opportunity has not been missed to bolster anti-money laundering efforts by linking them to terrorist funding, even though money may be laundered by 'white-collar' professionals and the source of terrorist funding may be entirely 'clean'.[29] The Security Council was quick to pass onto states blanket international *legal* obligations to ratify the relevant treaties,[30] to take certain additional precautions and even to upgrade their deterrence capabilities against the financing of terrorism prior to joining the relevant international instruments. While the older instruments have an intrinsic value in terms of formulating and influencing the trends yet to come, in terms of a new, post-9/11 conventional approach to take account of these changed circumstances at the international level, existing codifications would be adapted, as with the 2005 Protocol to the 1988 Convention for the Suppression of Unlawful Acts against the Safety of Maritime Navigation,[31] and the 2005 Protocol to the 1988 Protocol for the Suppression of Unlawful Acts Against the Safety of Fixed Platforms Located on the Continental Shelf.[32] In turn, new instruments would be drafted for purposes of providing an even greater breadth of coverage, a brief review of which now follows in chronological order.

### 1991 Convention on the Marking of Plastic Explosives for the Purpose of Detection

The Plastics Explosives Convention was negotiated in the aftermath of the 1988 bombing of Pan Am flight 103 over Lockerbie, Scotland, by use of a Semtex radio cassette bomb contained in a loaded suitcase.[33] The sources of the Pan Am bomb's components were ultimately traced and blame was attributed to Libyan agents. Terrorism is naturally referred to at many points in the 1991 instrument, but by this time, rights of self-determination are certainly not. Instead, the convention was intended to obligate states to

---

29 See, e.g., O. Elagab, 'Control of Terrorist Funds and the Banking System' [2006] 21(1) *J.Int'l.Banking.L.&Reg.* 38. Contrast M.M. Gallant, 'Tax and Terrorism: A New Partnership?' [2007] 14(4) *J.Fin.Cr.* 453.
30 E.g., UNSC Resolution 1373 (28 September 2001), UN Doc. S/RES/1373 (2001).
31 To criminalise the use of a ship as a device to perpetrate an act of terrorism or to transport dangerous materials for such purposes.
32 To adapt the 2005 Maritime Navigation Protocol for the Fixed Platforms Convention.
33 See, e.g., A. Cramb, 'Lockerbie Bombing: The Evidence', *The Daily Telegraph*, 13 August 2009, Telegraph.co.uk.

control and limit the use of unmarked and undetectable plastic explosives, to prohibit and prevent their manufacture and territorial movement, to destroy, consume, mark, or render permanently ineffective within three years all stocks of unmarked explosives not held by the military or police and to do the same with those held by the military or police within 15 years.

## 1997 International Convention for the Suppression of Terrorist Bombings

The preamble to the Bombing Convention mentions 'terrorism' at many points and refers to the Declaration on Measures to Eliminate International Terrorism, annexed to UNGA Resolution 49/60 of 9 December 1994/17 February 1995, which unequivocally condemns all acts of terrorism driven by intolerance and extremism as criminal and unjustifiable. Resolution 49/60 targets states as well as individuals and groups for such acts of terrorism, but self-determination, per se, is ignored, and the activities of the armed forces are expressly excluded from the coverage of the convention. The Bombing Convention was intended expressly to extend universal jurisdiction to the unauthorised use of bombs and explosives in public places – a practice that was increasingly widespread.[34] Proof of a triangular terrorist motive is not required but constitutes one alternative. By this point, the 'extradite or prosecute' formula is standard.

## 1999 International Convention for the Suppression of the Financing of Terrorism

Rather predictably, the 1999 Financing Convention refers only to terrorism and not to self-determination. Standard clauses are repeated, but as the central concern is to tighten existing prohibitions against money laundering generally, banking confidentiality and many practices used in globalised finance are severely curtailed.[35] The convention obliges ratifying states to take steps in particular to identify, freeze and seize terrorists' funds.[36]

---

34 Of note, the first non-Islamic suicide bomber is reputed to have been Syrian in March 1985, as was the first female suicide bomber, in April 1985.
35 See, e.g., R. Bosworth-Davies, 'The Influence of Christian Model Ideology in the Development of Anti-Money Laundering Compliance in the West and Its Impact, Post 9-11, Upon the South Asian Market: An Independent Evaluation of a Modern Phenomenon' [2008] 11(2) *J.MoneyLaund.Contr.* 179; J. Rehman, 'Islamic State Practice, International Law and the Threat from Terrorism – A Critique of the "Clash of Civilizations" in the World Order' [2007] 18(2) *Crim.L.F.* 253.
36 Megret notes that these provisions also require the West to 'turn [anti-terror] weapons against itself, its fiscal paradises ... and its many pockets of hypocrisy'. F. Megret, '"War"? Legal Semantics and the Move to Violence' [2002] 13 *E.J.I.L.* 361, at p. 385. Cf. A.V. Orlova, 'Russia's Anti-Money Laundering Regime: Law Enforcement Tool or Instrument of Domestic Control' [2008] *J.MoneyLaund.Contr.* 210.

Over time, the operation of this convention has been particularly controversial, particularly as compliance with most of its obligations was made mandatory pursuant to Charter Chapter VII in UNSC Resolution 1373 on 28 September 2001. The measures indicated in Resolution 1373 are supplemented by the FATF[37] and the United Nations Counter-Terrorism Implementation Task Force. Of primary concern for present purposes is the impact of these new rules on local banking practices and traditions, as well as their effects on the economic survival of many peoples who depend on alternative financial arrangements such as *hawala* rather than on Western-style banking practices.[38]

### 2005 International Convention for the Suppression of Acts of Nuclear Terrorism

The end of the Cold War created a new black market in dangerous materials and the post-9/11 anthrax attacks in the US fuelled wider fears regarding weapons of mass destruction. The possibility of terrorist access to so-called 'dirty' bomb-making materials and equipment has become a particular concern. Therefore, while the 1980 Nuclear Material Convention obligated states to secure the physical protection of military use nuclear material, the coverage of the 2005 Nuclear Convention is aimed at preventing terrorist access to civil nuclear power plants and nuclear reactors. The preamble condemns terrorism unequivocally and the activities of the armed forces are expressly excluded from its coverage. Article 2 makes it an offence to possess and/or use nuclear material or a nuclear device unlawfully, but in the case of use, proof of a triangular terrorist motive constitutes one alternative form of evidence. Attempt, organisation and co-operation are similarly criminalised. Article 7(1)(a) obliges states parties to prevent and counter preparations to commit the Article 2 offences either within or outside their respective territories.

## Main regional instruments

The international instruments outlined in brief already have been formulated as penal measures and thus emphasise the criminality of certain activities which are only occasionally referred to as 'terrorism'. However, once the UN General Assembly had taken the opportunity in Resolution 40/61 of 9 December 1985 to 'unequivocally condemn [. . .], as criminal, all acts, methods and practices of terrorism wherever and by whomever committed',

---

37 The Financial Action Task Force on Money Laundering is an intergovernmental organisation close to the OECD and in 2004 produced Special Recommendations on Terrorist Financing.

38 See, e.g., T. Viles, 'Hawala, Hysteria and Hegemony' [2008] 11(1) *J.MoneyLaund.Contr.* 25.

the stage was set to play down the UN General Assembly support of the 1970s for liberation movements and associated uses of force to achieve self-determination,[39] even though Resolution 40/61 still urged states to seek redress for 'all situations, including colonialism, racism and all situations involving flagrant violations of human rights and fundamental freedoms and those involving alien occupation which may give rise to international terrorism'. It could thus be speculated that attitudes had changed once many former colonial and non-self-governing territories were admitted as full members to the UN – in that they had no wish to encourage their own home-grown separatists.

Somewhat in contrast, the regional anti-terrorism instruments are much more likely to emphasise rights of self-determination alongside support for UN anti-terrorism activity. Regions tend not to encourage their own struggles for self-determination but, instead, support those occurring elsewhere, due largely to geopolitical and cultural divisions, and accordingly, to occasional difficulty when separating the political from the violent.[40] The continued existence of parallel support also helps to reinforce the point that customary international law does not, and cannot, prohibit revolution. Inasmuch as any lingering desire to conflate prohibited revolutionary violence and belligerent rights can be cured in 'extradite or prosecute' obligations and defendant rights clauses, the inclusion of a so-called 'human rights' exception to extradition keeps a back door open for failures to prosecute. The main regional treaties listed, and translated, by UNODC are as follows.[41]

### Alphabetical listing of main regional instruments

#### Association of South East Asian Nations: ASEAN Convention on Counter Terrorism, 2007

ASEAN member states are Brunei, Cambodia, Indonesia, Laos, Malaysia, Myanmar, the Philippines, Singapore, Thailand and Vietnam. Self-determination is not mentioned in the preamble to the 2007 Convention, but in its condemnation of terrorism, it is reaffirmed 'that terrorism cannot and should not be associated with any religion, nationality, civilisation or ethnic group'. Terrorist offences are defined in Article 2 as those provided for in the international instruments outlined above. Rights of defence are provided in Article 8 in accordance with national law, and rehabilitation programmes are contemplated in Article 11 as follows:

---

39 See, e.g., UNGA Resolutions 3070 (XXVIII) Article 2 of 30 November 1973 and 3246 (XXIX) Article 3 of 29 November 1974.
40 See, e.g., *T v Secretary of State for the Home Department* [1996] AC 742 (UKHL) (acts of violence are not political crimes for purposes of political asylum, if intended to terrorise and injure persons having no connection to government).
41 United Nations Office on Drugs and Crime (UNODC), www.unodc.org.

The Parties shall endeavour to promote the sharing of best practices on rehabilitative programmes including, where appropriate, social reintegration of persons involved in the commission of any of the offences covered in Article II of this Convention with the objective of preventing the perpetration of terrorist acts.

The 'prosecute or extradite' clause in Article 13 is unconditional and Article 14 permits no political offence exception to extradition for the Article 2 offences.

### Commonwealth of Independent States: Treaty on Co-operation Among State Members of the CIS in Combating Terrorism, 1999

The CIS was created in December 1991 and its members at present are Armenia, Azerbaijan, Belarus, Georgia, Kazakhstan, Kyrgyzstan, Moldova, Russia, Tajikistan, Turkmenistan, Ukraine and Uzbekistan.[42] As might be anticipated, the CIS Convention does not refer to rights of self-determination, neither is there any mention of defence rights of an accused. Struggles for self-determination are essentially ignored as valid concerns, as all non-state group violence has been integrated with terrorism for purposes of the cumulative definition found in Article 1, as 'an illegal act punishable under criminal law committed for the purpose of undermining public safety, influencing decision-making by the authorities *or* terrorizing the population'. This definition is exemplified by a list of specific acts and 'other acts classified as terrorist under the *national legislation* of the parties *or* under universally recognised international legal instruments aimed at combating terrorism' (emphasis added).[43] Article 4(1) is peremptory and provides that 'the parties shall not regard the acts involved as other than criminal', and the tone adopted generally throughout the convention is peremptory ('shall'/'shall not').

### Co-operation Council for Arab States of the Gulf: Convention Against Terrorism, 2004

The Arab Co-operation Council consists of, Bahrain, Kuwait, Oman, Qatar, Saudi Arabia and the United Arab Emirates. The preamble to the

---

42  There is also an agreement to co-operate to combat terrorist crime, in particular its organised forms, in an Additional Protocol of 2004 to the Agreement among the Governments of participating states in the Organisation of the Black Sea Economic Co-operation. The BSEC was formed in June 1992; state members are Albania, Armenia, Azerbaijan, Bulgaria, Georgia, Greece, Moldova, Romania, Russia, Turkey and Ukraine.
43  'Technological terrorism' is also of concern and is defined as 'nuclear, radiological, chemical or bacteriological (biological)' means of attack to 'achieve political, mercenary or any other ends'. CIS Convention Article 1.

2004 Convention refers to the growing incidence of terrorism and that it 'cannot be justified under any circumstances, notwithstanding its motives or objectives'. Self-determination is 'the right of peoples to struggle by various means against foreign occupation and against aggression', which perhaps more reflects concern for such longstanding situations as are sustained by the Palestinian and Afghan peoples. Article 1 defines terrorist acts as any 'act of violence or threat thereof, notwithstanding its motives or intentions, perpetrated . . . with the aim of terrorizing or harming people or imperilling' their lives, freedom, security, environment, public or private facility or property or attacking a national resource. The international instruments are listed.

In line with the self-determination concerns contained in the preamble, Article 2(a) exempts from coverage by the convention '[s]truggle by various means, including armed struggle, against foreign occupation and aggression and aimed at liberation and self-determination in accordance with the principles of international law', unless directed 'against the territorial integrity of any Contracting State'. Chapter 3 is devoted to preventing the support and financing of terrorist activities. The political offence exception to extradition is not allowed and no rights of defence are indicated.

*Council of Europe: European Convention on the Suppression of Terrorism, 1977, and Protocol of 2003; Convention on the Prevention of Terrorism, 2005*

As can be seen from the dates, the Council of Europe, which at present has 47 members, has a long history of anti-terrorism activity, due to a number of separatist movements active over several decades. Self-determination is not mentioned in the 1977 convention. The 1977 instrument is intended more to specify extradition arrangements, as it attempts to exclude or minimise the importance of the political offence exception in relation to the codified international terrorist offences and those endangering internationally protected persons, kidnapping, hostage taking, explosives, firearms, attempt and conspiracy. Articles 5 and 8(2) contain a 'human rights' exception to obligations for extradition and mutual co-operation, if based on a requested state's suspicion that extradition is sought to prosecute or punish a person due to his race, religion, nationality or political opinion.[44] Article 7 contains the 'extradite or prosecute' obligation, but Article 13(1) permits states to reserve the right *not* to extradite in respect of any offence 'which it considers to be a political offence, an offence connected with a political offence or an offence inspired by political motives'. Denmark, Italy, Norway and Sweden expressly made such a reservation.

---

44 ECtHR case law related to terrorism is also provided on the UNODC website.

The 2003 Protocol updates the 1977 Convention by adding the new international anti-terrorist instruments to the original 1977 list and makes other amendments, as well as including torture and the death penalty in the 1977 Convention Article 5 human rights exceptions to extradition. Previous reservations made pursuant to Article 13, if renewed, can now be applied only on a case-by-case basis for three years and, even then, a non-extraditing state must still submit an accused for prosecution before its own courts.

The 2005 Convention, by way of contrast, extends the breadth of offences to include the full list of UN instruments and, by criminalising in Article 5 a new offence of 'public provocation to commit a terrorist offence'. Article 6 covers 'recruitment for terrorism', Article 7, 'training for terrorism' and Article 9, various ancillary offences. Article 8 does not require an offence actually to have occurred. Article 12 contains human rights safeguards and Article 13 provides for victim support and compensation.[45]

### European Union: various

The UNODC website provides extensive details of EU resources on deterring acts of terrorism, including various instruments and case law reports. The EU at present consists of 27 member states, which have pooled together their individual sovereign powers over many areas of competence. A number of regulations, directives and decisions have been handed down by EU institutions in relation to terrorism, such as Council Decision 2002/996 JHA,[46] of 28 November 2002 establishing a mechanism for evaluating the legal systems and their implementation at national level in the fight against terrorism, Council Regulation 881/2002 EC of 27 May 2002 imposing certain specific restrictive measures directed against certain persons and entities associated with bin Laden, the Al Qaeda network and the Taliban (subsequently amended), and Directive 2005/60 EC of the European Parliament and of the Council of 26 October 2005 on the prevention of the use of the financial system for the purpose of money laundering and terrorist financing (subsequently amended).

The EU's institutional policies include the Council Common Position 2001/931 CFSP,[47] of 27 December 2001 on the application of specific measures to combat terrorism, Council Decision 2007/124 EC of 12 February 2007 establishing for the period 2007–13 the Specific Programme 'Prevention, Preparedness and Consequence Management of Terrorism and other Security related risks' as part of the General 'Security and Safeguarding Liberties'

---

45 See, e.g., E. Chadwick, 'The 2005 Terrorism Convention: A Flexible Step Too Far?' [2007] 16(2) *Nottm.L.J.* 29.
46 Judicial and home affairs.
47 Common foreign and security policy.

Programme, and Council Decision 2008/633 JHA, of 23 June 2008 concerning access for consultation by designated authorities of member states and by Europol of the Visa Information System to prevent, detect and investigate terrorist offences and other serious criminal offences.

Judicial competence is shared selectively between the EU's member states and the central Court of Justice and the General Court (formerly the Court of First Instance), in that the Union courts deal solely with European areas of competence. This means that the implementation by member states of Union laws, regulations or decisions can normally be reviewed by the central courts, which helps to conform and stabilise relevant European interpretations for use in all member states. For example, in relation to EU legislation regarding terrorism, many recent cases brought before the Court of Justice have involved requests for annulment of financial freezing orders or orders pertaining to criminal association.[48]

*League of Arab States: Arab Convention on the Suppression of Terrorism, 1998*

The 1998 Arab Convention affirms in the preamble:

> [T]he right of peoples to combat foreign occupation and aggression by whatever means, including armed struggle, in order to liberate their territories and secure their right to self-determination, and independence and to do so in such a manner as to preserve the territorial integrity of each Arab country.

The Arab League expresses conditional commitment to human rights protections, 'based as they are on co-operation among peoples in the promotion of peace'. Article 1 defines terrorism as 'any act or threat of violence, whatever its motives or purposes, that occurs for the advancement of an individual or collective criminal agenda', which causes terror, fear or damage. Article 2(a) is the precursor of that in the 2004 Arab Co-operation Convention in excluding struggles for self-determination, and Article 3 refers to the offences contained in six international instruments (including the 1982 UN Law of the Sea Convention). Chapter 2 provides for extradition and does not require double criminality. Defence or other rights of an accused are not specified.

---

48 E.g., Case T-308/01, *Omar Mohammed Othman v Council of the European Union and Commission of the European Communities* (11 June 2009) (several EC Regulations annulled); Case C-355/04 P, *Segi and Others v Council of the European Union* (Grand Chamber, 27 February 2007) (no jurisdiction to entertain action for damages), eur-lex. europa.eu/LexUriServ/LexUriServ.do?uri=CELEX:62002B0338:EN:H.

*Organisation of African Unity: Convention on the Prevention and Combating of Terrorism 1999, and Protocol of 2004*

The AU has 53 member states.[49] The convention reaffirms both 'the legitimate right of peoples for self-determination and independence' and a 'rejection of all forms of terrorism irrespective of their motivations' in the preamble. 'Terrorist act' is defined in Article 1(3) and proof of the triangular terrorist motive is not required but constitutes one alternative. Self-determination is distinguished from terrorism in Article 3, as follows:

> Notwithstanding the provisions of Article 1, the struggle waged by peoples in accordance with the principles of international law for their liberation or self-determination, including armed struggle against colonialism, occupation, aggression and domination by foreign forces shall not be considered as terrorist acts.
>
> Political, philosophical, ideological, racial, ethnic, religious or other motives shall not be a justifiable defence against a terrorist act.

Article 7 provides for defence rights, to be 'exercised in conformity with the national law of the state in whose territory . . . the alleged offender is present' and Article 8 makes provision for states parties to refuse either to extradite or prosecute an alleged offender. The 2004 Protocol is intended to bolster an 'African Union Plan of Action on the Prevention and Combating of Terrorism in Africa', formulated in 2002. Its preamble expresses grave concern at the increase worldwide in terrorist acts and at 'the growing risks of linkages between terrorism and mercenarism, weapons of mass destruction, drug trafficking, corruption, transnational organized crimes, money laundering, and the illicit proliferation of small arms'.

*Organisation of American States: Convention to Prevent and Punish Acts of Terrorism taking the Form of Crimes Against Persons and Related Extortion that are of International Significance, 1971; Inter-American Convention Against Terrorism, 2002*

The 1971 OAS Convention is of interest due to its historic terms of reference, as the preamble refers to OAS Resolution 4 of 30 June 1970, which declared such 'serious common crimes' as extortion, murder and kidnapping to be 'strongly condemned acts of terrorism'. For this reason, it is largely an extradition, criminal enforcement and co-operation agreement.

---

49 There is also the Economic and Monetary Union of West Africa, formed in January 1994, for which UNODC holds three minor instruments, in French. For the Economic and Monetary Community of Central Africa, formed initially in June 1959, two minor instruments are listed, also in French.

As for the 2002 Inter-American Convention, the economic harm caused by terrorism is recognised in the preamble. Article 1 indicates the aim is to prevent, punish and eliminate terrorism, relevant offences being those indicated in the international instruments, as per Article 2. The financing of terrorism, the seizure and confiscation of terrorist funds, and money laundering are the subject of Articles 4–6. The political offence exception to extradition is made inapplicable in Article 11, but Article 14 provides a human rights exception, and defence rights are protected in Article 15.

### Shanghai Organisation Co-operation: Shanghai Convention on Combating Terrorism, Separatism and Extremism, 2001

China, Kazakhstan, Kyrgystan, the Russian Federation, Tajikistan and Uzbekistan are states parties to this convention, which is intended to deter 'terrorism, separatism and extremism'. It is largely defensive in tone, procedural, and provides for mutual co-operation measures. Article 1(1)(a) applies the international instruments and, interestingly, Article 1(1)(b) prohibits other acts, including those 'intended to cause death or serious bodily injury to a civilian, or any other person not taking an active part in the hostilities in a situation of armed conflict', 'when the purpose of such act . . . is to intimidate a population, violate public security or to compel public authorities or an international organization to do or to abstain from doing any act'. The definitions given for 'separatism' and 'extremism' go to the heart of struggles for self-determination: separatism 'means any act intended to violate state territorial integrity', while extremism includes acts 'aimed at seizing or keeping power through the use of violence or changing violently the constitutional regime of a state' and organising and participating in 'illegal armed formations'. No defence or other rights of the accused are mentioned, neither are human rights generally.

### South Asian Association for Regional Co-operation: Regional Convention on Suppression of Terrorism, 1987, and Additional Protocol of 2004

Bangladesh, Bhutan, India, Maldives, Nepal and Sri Lanka are signatories to this 1987 convention. The preamble condemns all acts of terrorism due to their impacts, including those on socioeconomic development and political stability. The condemnation of state-sponsored terrorism in UNGA Resolution 2625 (XXV) is explicitly recognised and the convention is largely an 'extradite or prosecute' arrangement.

The 2004 Protocol seeks to update the 1987 convention in conformity with the provisions of UNSC Resolution 1373 of 28 September 2001 and, in particular, those applicable to the financing of terrorism. Protocol Article 17 contains a human rights exception to extradition, but nothing further is expressed regarding human rights. Pakistan is added to the Protocol signatories.

## Other instruments

### *Organisation of Islamic Conference*

#### *Convention of the OIC on Combating International Terrorism, 1999*

As a final example, there is the convention of the Islamic Conference. The Islamic Conference is not geographically confined, but instead its member states and observers range geographically and institutionally, across the Middle East, Africa, Asia and Europe, as well as the participation of organisations such as the UN. The 1999 convention was intended as much to publicise the 'tenets of the tolerant Islamic Sharia' as to reject violence, terrorism and extremism.

The preamble of the 1999 Convention emphasises the 'protection of human rights' inasmuch as they parallel global co-operation and principles to maintain peace, 'unambiguously' condemns terrorism in all its forms and manifestations 'whatever its origin, causes or purposes, including direct or indirect actions of states', and confirms 'the legitimacy of the right of peoples to struggle against foreign occupation and colonialist and racist regimes by all means, including armed struggle to liberate their territories and attain their rights to self-determination and independence'.

Self-determination struggles are excluded from coverage in Article 2(a), examples of which are more extensive than in the preamble: 'Peoples' struggle includ[es] armed struggles against foreign occupation, aggression, colonialism and hegemony, aimed at liberation and self-determination in accordance with the principles of international law'. Extradition may be refused according to Article 6(1) 'if the crime . . . is deemed by the laws enforced in the requested Contracting State as one of a political nature', and Article 6(7) permits the non-extradition of pardoned offenders. Otherwise, the convention aims to support a broad area of Islamic co-operation, as in the 'education and information field' indicated at the fourth point in Article 4, which emphasises the need to 'promot[e] the true image of tolerance of Islam'. The convention also applies to the internationally prohibited offences and provides details for extradition procedures.

## Ongoing efforts

### *A UN instrument*

#### *UN Draft Comprehensive Convention on International Terrorism*

The task of maintaining international peace in the post-Cold War state-centric world altered in focus onto 'common enemies' such as terrorists, yet, as is clear from what is discussed above, there is as yet no comprehensive definition of terrorism. Starting with UNGA Resolution 40/60 on

9 December 1994, states were encouraged to develop a more comprehensive legal framework covering all aspects of terrorism, and they subsequently concluded the 1997 Bombing Convention, the 1999 Financing Convention, and the 2005 Nuclear Terrorism Convention.[50] The UN's Sixth (Legal) Committee and the Ad Hoc Committee established pursuant to UNGA Resolution 51/210 of 17 December 1996 were asked to work on negotiating a draft Comprehensive Convention on International Terrorism, which they have done since 1997, but the main difficulties remain the definition of terrorism and its relationship to liberation groups, state sponsorship of terrorism, and the activities of state armed forces.[51] At present, the Ad Hoc Committee pursuant to UNGA Resolution 64/118 of 16 December 2009 is continuing its work and discussing pursuant to UNGA Resolution 54/100 whether to convene a high-level conference under UN auspices.

The draft convention is intended mainly as a law enforcement instrument based on an 'extradite or prosecute' regime and to operate in parallel with the existing sectoral instruments by filling in any gaps in their coverage. Although the definition of terrorism remains under negotiation, the value of a comprehensive definition is deemed to reside in the linkage between the prohibited acts in draft Article 2 and the triangular terrorist motive. As noted by the General Assembly by the Ad Hoc Committee's Coordinator in 2010:

> The purpose of the conduct, by its nature or context, should be to intimidate a population, or to compel a government or an international organization to do or to abstain from doing any act.[52]

The act or offence of terrorism, currently in Article 2, is broadly drafted, in that the only essential characteristic is to cause harm. Terrorism is perpetrated by 'any person' unlawfully and intentionally:

> [C]ausing or threatening to cause violence by means of firearms, weapons, explosives, any lethal devices or dangerous substances, which results, or is likely to result, in death or serious bodily injury to a person, a group of persons or serious damage to property – whether for public use, a State or Government facility, a public transportation system or an infrastructure facility.[53]

---

50  See 'Background, etc., Draft Comprehensive Convention on International Terrorism', accessed at 'Inventory of International Nonproliferation Organizations and Regimes, Center for Nonproliferation Studies', (Last Updated: 5/27/2009), http://cns.miis.edu/inventory/pdfs/intlterr.pdf.

51  See, e.g., M. Hmoud, 'Negotiating the Draft Comprehensive Convention on International Terrorism: Major Bones of Contention' [2006] 4 *J.Int'l.Crim.J.* 1031.

52  UN Doc. A/65/37, Fourteenth Session, 14–16 April 2010, p. 14.

53  'Obligations', in 'Background, etc., Draft Comprehensive Convention', supra note 50.

Prohibited acts include attempt, participating, organising or contributing to an act of terrorism and the commission, etc., of any offence prohibited by the sectoral conventions. The draft convention obligates states not to sponsor acts of terrorism elsewhere and to exercise due diligence to prevent their territories from being used by terrorist groups. Ongoing disagreement continues to surround the scope of application of the convention, particularly with regard to draft Article 18. Article 18 excludes from coverage those activities of the armed forces that should be regulated by other rules of international law. There is uncertainty whether the convention should apply to situations of foreign occupation, and whether Article 18 is intended to cover all activities of the armed forces, including those in 'peacetime'. As official activity can be unlawful as easily as lawful, a further paragraph was added to draft Article 18 in 2007 to make clear that certain conduct could be considered unlawful under *any* legal regime. However, it is for the parties and their judicial authorities to make decisions in specific cases.

The main contention voiced about self-determination in the draft Comprehensive Convention is that the definition of terrorism should be kept distinct from legitimate struggles by peoples for their rights to self-determination and that, accordingly, the root causes of terrorism are important to address. In its 2010 report to the General Assembly,[54] the Ad Hoc Committee stressed that the draft convention 'should distinguish between acts of terrorism and the legitimate struggle of peoples in the exercise of their right to self-determination under foreign occupation and colonial or alien domination'.[55] As regards the root causes of terrorism, some delegations suggested also that the draft convention should include the notion of *state* terrorism, including acts committed against innocent civilians, but as the convention is intended to rely on the 'extradite or prosecute' regime, other delegations considered that the notion of state terrorism has to be avoided. Nonetheless, the General Assembly was warned in the report that certain states would predicate their approval of the draft on the inclusion of 'activities undertaken by national liberation movements'.[56]

## Conclusion

As can be seen from the brief summaries given in this chapter, the earlier anti-terrorist instruments were drafted during the anti-colonial heyday of the Cold War. For example, after 1946, the year in which eight UN member states (Australia, Belgium, Denmark, France, the Netherlands, New Zealand, the UK and the US) indicated the 72 non-self-governing

54 UN Doc. A/65/37, supra note 52.
55 *Ibid.*, pp. 6–7.
56 *Ibid.*, p. 7.

territories over which they had control, eight had gained their independence by 1959, while only 16 remained as of 2007.[57] From roughly the same point in time (the late 1940s), the 11 territories placed under the UN Charter Trusteeship System were able to exercise their self-determination, and completed the task by 1994, when Palau joined the UN as its 185th member state. Accordingly, at some point during the Cold War or soon after, most former colonies, non-self-governing territories and/or trust territories were, in fact, able to exercise their self-determination or begin preparations for doing so.[58]

The UN proclaimed an International Decade for the Eradication of Colonialism, to last from 1991–2000. Early in the following decade, the General Assembly declared the Second International Decade for the Eradication of Colonialism (2001–2010), and called on member states to redouble their efforts to achieve complete decolonisation.[59] However, while it might have originally been hoped that such progress could be achieved more or less smoothly and consensually, that was only rarely the case. Instead, the norm for colonial, as well as non-colonial, and post-colonial, contexts of self-determination has exhibited more often than not a necessity to use oppositional violence or armed force. Particularly once the Soviet Union began to collapse, many new actors emerged who sought effective territorial and political power or independence for their peoples, in circumstances far removed from those grudgingly assented to by prevailing international sentiment or legal theory as potentially 'legitimate' cases of self-determination.

Even with the rise of pan-Islamic extremism, which served only to muddy the self-determination waters, one underlying theme has become increasingly clear – that of a general breakdown in constraint in state uses of armed force, whether or not during a 'recognised' armed conflict, which breakdown has found its echo in a similar breakdown in constraint in terrorist tactics. Where once the military forces of a state fought wars conventionally, e.g., by targeting only enemy soldiers, early 'terrorist' groups assassinated and/or otherwise targeted only those persons who represented the state in some capacity. Today, both the armed forces and terrorists are much less discriminating in terms of their uses of force; remaining differences lie mainly in their respective access to military resources, but many tactics used in Islamic extremist violence have certainly helped to redress somewhat a degree of material imbalance in asymmetric warfare.

---

57 See UN Department of Public Education, 'Territories to which the Declaration on the Granting of Independence to Colonial Countries and Peoples continues to apply (as of 2007)', *The United Nations Today* (New York: A.S.D.F., 2008), pp. 298–304.
58 In accordance with UNGA Resolution 1541 (XV) of 14 December 1960, which defined the three 'legitimate' political status options as free association with an independent state, integration into an independent state, or independence.
59 UN Department of Public Education, supra note 57, p. 301.

In turn, the legal tools with which to fight unlawful forms of violence include the new ICC[60] and domestic criminal laws. Even then, one crucial difficulty remains: that of consistency in result. Specifically, while international criminal laws will be interpreted and applied by the ICC for purposes of genocide, war crimes, crimes against humanity and, ultimately, aggression, domestic anti-terror measures for use by governments are formulated to have a much broader and politicised scope and effect, which facilitates the inclusion of many more political opponents and liberation groups, as is now discussed.

60 The jurisdiction of which does not extend to acts of terrorism, per se. 1998 Rome Statute for an ICC Article 5.

# 6 Post-9/11 statutes and case law of the Security Council Permanent Members

## Introduction

States generally comply with international instruments in accordance with their express consent, yet when doing so, states will also be highly influenced by the examples set by the Permanent Member States of the UN Security Council within the latter's domestic legal systems. It is thus the purpose of this chapter to outline the principle domestic legal arrangements used to adopt anti-terrorism policies by the Permanent Members, inasmuch as it is within the probity of such legal arrangements that states are able to carry sufficient political weight at the international level to co-operate effectively and collectively. In turn, the sheer variety of issue areas contained within the international approach to terrorism since 9/11 is either foreshadowed by or predictive of the many existing domestic state arrangements to deter political opponents in general. Accordingly, not only do anti-terrorism mechanisms afford insights into how – if not why – states reflect policy in their laws, but further, that when acting purportedly in accordance with international policy to prevent *all* acts of non-state violence, states simultaneously afford each other the means to prevent revolution.

The contemporary over-emphasis on global security agendas to prevent non-state violence does not always, however, sit comfortably within other international mechanisms designed to maintain peace. With this in mind, after a brief overview of wider geopolitical events that unfolded after the late 1980s and the end of the Cold War, the main constitutional arrangements found within each of the Permanent Member States are outlined, inasmuch as those domestic arrangements enable individual states lawfully to utilise armed force against non-state violent actors. These codified domestic arrangements are surveyed inasmuch as they have been made available for publication to the UN on that organisation's dedicated anti-terrorism website, UNODC. As it is via such publication that the Permanent Member States are able to bring their influence to bear more widely, political and legal powers are also contrasted, inasmuch as the direction or content of the former tend not to be so transparently divulged.

In order to demonstrate the employment of collective international measures in the post-9/11 era in regard to terrorists and liberation fighters alike, a brief overview of recent events in the Balkan region is provided, inasmuch as the US, the UK, France and Russia have been intimately involved there. China remains a special case for various reasons, such as its preferences for more regional concerns and the safeguarding of its own economic interests. The other four Permanent Members, in contrast, are much more oriented towards the European theatre, and their individual ability and willingness to utilise armed force there against violent actors is highlighted in order to illustrate their differences in individual approach in the case of the breakaway Serbian province of Kosovo. Regarding the latter, a separatist armed conflict was waged throughout the 1990s, between the Albanian majority in the former Serbian province and Serbia itself. The fighting allegedly involved excessive exchanges of armed force between Serbian forces and the 'terrorist'/liberation group, the KLA.

In turn, whereas the international community might normally have stayed neutral regarding this dispute, the Security Council was finally forced to take action to end the violence. Peace negotiations between the Serbians and Albanian Kosovars proved fruitless and early in 2008 the Kosovo Albanians exercised their right of self-determination by issuing a Declaration of Independence from Serbia. The UN General Assembly subsequently requested an advisory opinion from the ICJ on the accordance of this declaration with international law, which opinion was handed down on 22 July 2010. Accordingly, the influence of the UN Security Council over the use of organised non-state violence is well illustrated in such cases as Kosovo, inasmuch as the latter provides a practical example of the difficulties encountered when states need to deal with non-state violent groups in their domestic legal systems. As different legal and political frameworks of analysis label 'terrorists' alternatively, it is thus in the use of lawful powers to determine authoritative terminology that the political rationales for the use of force are revealed or concealed, as is now discussed.

## Growing UN concern

The UN Security Council is responsible for the international peace and security on which mutual human survival depends, and peace and security necessitate certain fundamental rules of social behaviour. The content of the universal anti-terrorism instruments has already been discussed, but while all the Permanent Member States are party to the 1997 Bombing Convention and the 1999 Financing Convention, only two Permanent Members have joined the 2005 Nuclear Convention; the other three have merely signed it (China, France and the US), which lesser action obliges them only 'to refrain from acts which would defeat the object and purpose of [that] treaty'.[1] Permanent Member State unity is patchier still towards the 1998 Rome Statute for an ICC: only France and the UK are party. The Russian Federation signed the treaty on 13 September 2000, and the US signed it on 31 December 2000;[2] China has done nothing.

In turn, an undefined principle of self-determination poses an exceptional challenge to state control over uses of force. This makes it useful to recall the central role played by law. To illustrate the very different world in which self-determination struggles once were fought, a glance at a world map in the mid-1980s shows a rather different territorial alignment than the map today. Central government concerns were also different, among which were access to available resources and inter-ethnic peace. For example, southern and eastern Asia were not far behind Europe as the most densely populated areas.[3] Africa, where many wars for self-determination have been fought, was relatively lightly populated. Arable land, which is intimately connected with claims for self-determination, constituted only one-tenth of the earth's land surface, and was under increasing pressure. In turn, adherents of Islam dominated in Central and South Asia, the Malay Archipelago, the Middle East, northern and western Africa, and large populations inhabited eastern Africa, the Balkan Peninsula, Russia and China.

The Soviet Union generally supported wars of self-determination, while the other superpower – the US – opposed them. However, by the end of the Cold War, regional destabilisation and a resurgence of new types of self-determination struggle were readily apparent, as many new states, particularly in eastern Europe, emerged into independence. However, as Russia in the early 1990s was the largest oil producer in the world and second only to Saudi Arabia in oil exports, many states that had depended for generations on Russian fuel and raw materials found it impossible to source these supplies alternatively.[4] Other developing states were experiencing social stress of their own and found themselves at a difficult crossroads in terms of their economic development,[5] particularly as economic independence was as difficult to secure as political independence had been, due in large part to the sheer scale of western investment and exploitation.

Therefore, many new and existing states were 'hampered by weak currencies, rampant nationalism, and the legacy of 70 years of subsidies and industrial interdependence'[6] and the UN struggled to preserve international

---

1  1969 Vienna Convention on the Law of Treaties Article 18.
2  And, subsequently 'unsigned' it on 6 May 2002, stating 'the US has no legal obligations arising from its signature on December 31, 2000'.
3  The following statistics are drawn from *Philips' World Atlas* (London: George Philip & Son, 1984).
4  S. Whitebloom, 'Unbundling the USSR', *Observer Sunday*, 1 September 1991, p. 29.
5  See, e.g., G. Abraham, '"Lines upon Maps": Africa and the Sanctity of African Borders' [2007] 15(1) *A.J.I.C.L.* pp. 61, 82–4.
6  S. Whitebloom, 'Unbundling the USSR', *Observer Sunday*, 1 September 1991, p. 29.

peace and security and to alleviate economic and political hardship. Structural weaknesses were further exacerbated as younger generations sought to secure their place in the post-Cold War world order, yet opportunities to foster mayhem were on offer, particularly with the rise of the Al Qaeda phenomenon, as the latter promised new resistance ideologies and techniques, and offered alternative solutions to longstanding economic and political resentments, as is now discussed.

## From 'liberationist' to 'terrorist': the impact of Islamic fundamentalism

The relatively new phenomenon of Islamic extremism became noticeable with the pull-out of the Soviet Union from Afghanistan in the late 1980s, soon after which Security Council Resolutions 678 of 29 November 1990 and 687 in 3 April 1991 seemingly authorised the ongoing use of force against northern Iraq.[7] Once the Security Council handed a huge advantage to the Bosnian Serbs over their Muslim neighbours, in the blanket sanctions regime of Resolution 757 on 31 May 1992, the scope allegedly permitted for the US, the UK, and initially France as well, to use force, particularly in relation to Iraq, throughout the 1990s and early 2000s, spread widespread resentment in Muslim communities. After the Srebrenica massacre in July 1995, and as sanctions regimes hurt a local population as much, if not more, than a target government, many young Muslims, who had been radicalised by western uses of force or coercion in relation to Muslim states, were drawn to the Balkans, and subsequently far more widely, to assist in the struggles of their fellow adherents. These newly itinerant Muslim fighters not only solidified the ties of ethnic solidarity and resistance generally; they also gained experience and prestige in local conflicts for use later in 'global jihad'.

As noted by Stepanova earlier in the case of Chechnya,[8] the bending of certain liberation goals towards new and radical Islamic sponsors has nonetheless proven to be spectacularly counter-productive, as little else than violent Islamic extremism could have been more conducive to the integration of self-determination struggles into the global war on terror. Extremist actors not only have afforded to many governments the opportunity to criminalise an ever-broader array of acts; they have made even more theoretical any possibility of distinguishing between 'freedom fighters' and 'terrorists' in terms of law. For example, support for a liberation group in general might not engage the attention of the authorities, but support for a multifaceted group that has a 'terrorist' component certainly will, particularly if that group has not compartmentalised its operational arms in some way.

---

7 See S.S. Akermark, 'Storms, Foxes, and Nebulous Legal Arguments: Twelve Years of Force Against Iraq, 1991–2003' [2005] 54(1) *I.C.L.Q.* 221.
8 See Chapter 4.

Further, it has become nigh on impossible in certain states legally to defend a member of a prohibited group, even if that member is shown to have opposed particular group acts due to his own views on indiscriminate violence, for example. The variability in legal provision between different domestic legal systems means that, although regional legal *concepts* of international terrorism may vary, a concept is a separate issue to that of legal *definition*, and it is easy to leave conceptual gaps when drafting and applying a definition, e.g., as regards available defences. Accordingly, whereas the probity of admissible evidence might (or might not) depend on what a particular individual was doing when apprehended, ultimate guilt may (or may not) rest as easily on broader and/or circumstantial evidence as to the nature of any connection that may (or may not) exist between that group and that individual or, even, merely on what the group does or purports to do.

Moreover, in that a specific legal approach to terror acts is mandated under Geneva laws on armed force, what today is often missing is a legislative or judicial willingness to re-examine or reassess the contextual nature of an underlying fact pattern and to appreciate the difficulties encountered by those tasked with defending individual terrorist suspects, particularly should there be any attempt to carve out a self-determination defence capable of altering certain domestic criminal law arrangements.[9] For example, in a somewhat singular (and little reported) case on 'terrorism' in Italy,[10] a Milan magistrate in January 2005, acting as a court of first instance, acquitted three Moroccan and Tunisian nationals of violating the Italian Criminal Code, by recruiting and dispatching volunteers to Iraq and other war zones to train as Islamic fighters.[11] She felt that the public prosecutor had failed to carry the burden that the defendants intended to carry out actions against civilians; instead, she held that the men had been acting in support of legitimate guerrilla warfare directed against military personnel or military objectives.

The public prosecutor challenged these findings before the Court of Appeal of Milan,[12] which, in November 2005, confirmed the acquittals on the basis of international law and a new provision in the Criminal Code, which,

---

9 L. Aleni, 'Distinguishing Terrorism from Wars of National Liberation in the Light of International Law: A View from Italian Courts' [2008] 6 *J.Int.Crim.J.* 525.

10 *Bouyahia Maher Ben Abdelaziz, et al.* [20 September 2007] Supreme Court of Cassation (Italy), www.adh-geneva.ch/RULAX/pdf_state/Abdelaziz.pdf.

11 This provision introduced the crime of international terrorism into Italian criminal law.

12 *Abdelaziz, et al.,* supra note 10, paras F3–6. Para. F6 relies on the European Union Council Framework Decision on Combating Terrorism, 2002/475/JHA (in force 13 June 2002), Article 1 of which defines a terrorist act as: (1) an illegal act which could seriously cause damage to a state or an international organization, by spreading terror among the public; (2) directed against civilian targets or against military non-belligerent forces; and (3) based on an ideological or political objective and aimed at forcing the will of public authorities and international organizations, or at destroying their fundamental structures.

although not yet in force, had been introduced after the acquittals. This new provision added a requirement to assess terrorism by reference to 'other conduct defined as terrorist or with terrorist purposes by conventions and other rules of international law binding on Italy'. After first clarifying that a fundamentalist Islamic association could not automatically be equated with a terrorist group, the Court of Appeal went on to state that the new provision incorporated the existing distinction between terrorism and guerrilla warfare. In other words, an armed attack perpetrated against military targets might violate international humanitarian law, as would an armed attack directed solely against civilians, but mere harm to civilians would only constitute 'collateral damage'. In contrast, harming a civilian population in peacetime qualified as a possible terrorist act.[13]

The public prosecutor appealed the Court of Appeal's definition of international law before the Supreme Court of Cassation. He disputed the notion that acts by freedom fighters that harmed a civilian population were prohibited only if the latter were directly targeted. He considered instead that the liberation–terrorist distinction should be based on the rationale for the violence, rather than whether the liberation group attempted to maintain a combatant status. The Supreme Court first recognised that no global definition of terrorism exists because states disagree regarding the possibility of exempting persons from terrorist prosecution if they are engaged in a liberation or self-determination struggle. However, the Court held, the 1999 Financing Convention does contain a definition of international terrorism that applies at any time if the underlying intent is to spread terror. Accordingly, the Supreme Court held that, in order to prosecute a suspect for involvement in international terrorism, evidence is required of a political, ideological or religious/psychological motivation. Accordingly, the appeal panel should have investigated the defendants' motivation in utilising violence according to the nature of their inter-relationship, their awareness of their organisation's use of terrorism and whether connections existed between their organisation and other Islamic groups engaged in terrorist activities abroad. The appeal judgement was quashed and the matter was remanded to a different section of the Court of Appeal.

As can be seen, the judges on the Italian Supreme Court adopted a systematic approach in their decision.[14] However, by placing such importance, *inter alia*, on the 1999 Financing Convention, the Supreme Court arguably went too far when it made the following distinction, in pertinent part:

> An attack against a military target is to be considered a terrorist act when, . . . , the consequences would entail certain and inevitable harm to the life and physical wellbeing of civilians, resulting in the spread

---

13 *Abdelaziz, et al.*, supra note 10, paras F7–9.
14 L. Aleni, supra note 9, pp. 536–9.

of panic among the general public. An example of such a situation might be the bombing of a military tank in a crowded open-market. Armed attacks on combatants not actively engaged in hostilities, such as military personnel taking part in humanitarian activities, can also amount to terrorism.[15]

While the Italian Supreme Court was certainly correct in stating that the use of terror violence by a liberation group could be prosecuted either as a war crime or a crime against humanity,[16] more fundamental Geneva frameworks, such as the combatant–civilian distinction, are not so easily altered, particularly as they arise from the subjectivities of *military* necessity and proportionality, which are determined via conditions on the ground; related offences also differ according to their gravity, the status of the perpetrator and the underlying context.[17] Geneva laws generally prohibit only the perpetration of *indiscriminate* attacks during an armed conflict or while occupying enemy territory. Even Additional Protocol 1 of 1977 does not deal explicitly with the question of collateral damage occasioned by attacks on military objectives. Protocol 1 Article 51 only prohibits belligerent acts or threats of violence 'the *primary* purpose of which is to spread terror among the civilian population'.[18] Protocol 2 Article 13 is much to the same effect.

Further, Protocol 1 Article 52 provides that civilian objects 'shall not be the object of attack or of reprisals' *unless* they are deemed to constitute a military objective; military objectives are those objects that 'make an effective contribution to military action', and which 'offer a definite military advantage'. It is therefore arguable that the Court of Appeal's view was more accurate: an intention to terrorise or harm civilians is but one factor. As a final point, Geneva Convention IV Article 33 prohibits the punishment of 'protected persons' (e.g., civilians in occupied territory) 'for an offence he or she has not personally committed', while many peacetime anti-terrorism laws today criminalise mere membership.

It is noteworthy, too, that the Italian Supreme Court essentially agreed with the Court of Appeal that the inclusion of the defendants' names or their Islamic affiliations among those listed in such instruments as Security Council Resolution 1267 of 15 October 1999 is not alone conclusive of the facts. The purpose of such lists is to identify individuals and groups who have been targeted by UN sanctions. They thus have 'a merely

---

15 *Abdelaziz, et al.*, supra note 10, para. H4.
16 *Ibid.*, para. H3.
17 See, e.g., 'Report of the Preparatory Commission for the ICC, Addendum, 2000, Part II: Finalised draft text of the Elements of Crimes', pp. 18–37, www.un.org/law/icc/prepcomm/prepfra.htm.
18 Emphasis added.

administrative character'.[19] Nonetheless, inasmuch as terrorist watch lists of many descriptions have appeared in recent years, the risk is increased in domestic law that those lists will be used to incriminate individuals automatically. In other words, once proof of individual guilt requires only a plausible inference that a suspect is connected to Al Qaeda or an Al Qaeda affiliate, that individual is more likely to be tarred with collective guilt, as is now discussed.

### The proscription of Islamic fundamentalists and of others

Proscription is a means to publicise the fact that named persons, groups or organisations have been characterised as criminal. Proscription lists fix the automatic criminal liability of these persons from a specific point in time and are compiled for circulation to enforcing authorities. Proscription is especially useful in a law-and-order approach to crime generally and 'terror lists' have been maintained at state level for many years. However, the use of proscription at the international level has become much more frequent in the post-9/11 war on terror, which latter has its clearest origins as follows. Near the end of the Cold War, as the superpower rivalry was still in play, the US supported the fundamentalist Mujahideen in Afghanistan and helped the latter to fight the Soviet occupation of their country. The advantage for the US was as a means to counter Soviet influence in the Persian Gulf region generally.[20]

After the Soviet pull-out from Afghanistan, tribal warlords resumed their place, from whom the fundamentalist Islamic Taliban would emerge dominant. The Taliban afforded hospitality and protection to the Saudi bin Laden and his Al Qaeda extremist organisation. However, at that point the US would change its stance[21] and by the late 1990s, the UN Security Council had taken the opportunity to express frequent disapproval of many Taliban practices, such as widespread discrimination against women and girls, opium production, the use of its territory by terrorist groups, and the murder of foreign dignitaries and journalists.[22] A Sanctions Monitoring Committee was established by Security Council Resolution 1267 of

---

19 *Abdelaziz, et al.*, supra note 10, para. H5.
20 See, e.g., J. McCurry, 'Damage to Japanese Oil Tanker Caused by Terror Attack, say Investigators', *The Guardian*, 7 August 2010, p. 18 (militant group linked to Al Qaeda).
21 The 9/11 attacks were one result. Persons affiliated to Al Qaeda perpetrated an earlier attack on the World Trade Center in New York in late February 1993.
22 See, e.g., the following UNSC Resolutions in 1998: 1189 of 13 August, 1193 of 28 August, and 1214 of 8 December. See also UNSC Resolution 1267 of 15 October 1999, the fourth paragraph of which imposed a sanctions regime on the Taliban, while the sixth paragraph established a sanctions monitoring committee.

15 October 1999[23] and, after a US request for the surrender of bin Laden and his associates for trial for the August 1998 bombings of US embassies in Kenya and Tanzania was ignored, the Security Council in Resolution 1333 of 19 December 2000 extended the sanctions against the Taliban, including an arms embargo. The Sanctions Monitoring Committee was also requested, pursuant to paragraph 8(c) of Resolution 1333, 'to maintain an updated list, . . . , of the individuals and entities designated as being associated with Usama bin Laden, including those in the Al Qaeda organisation'.

This list was intended for an initial period of 12 months, renewable, unless the Taliban complied with Security Council demands, while in paragraph 12, the Security Council also decided that the Committee should:

> [M]aintain a list of approved organisations and governmental relief agencies which are providing humanitarian assistance to Afghanistan, . . . , that the Committee shall keep the list under regular review, adding new organisations and governmental relief agencies as appropriate and that the Committee shall remove organisations and governmental agencies from the list if it decides that they are operating, or are likely to operate, . . . for other than humanitarian purposes.

Pursuant to Security Council Resolution 1363 of 30 July 2001, a Monitoring Group was requested to oversee and report specifically on state co-operation in adopting anti-terrorist measures against the Taliban in Afghanistan and bin Laden. After the 9/11 attacks on New York, Washington, DC, and Pennsylvania on 11 September 2001, the Security Council adopted Resolution 1373 on 28 September 2001. This resolution, among other actions, established the Counter-Terrorism Committee to monitor its implementation. States were urged in paragraph 3(a) of Resolution 1373 to:

> Find ways of intensifying and accelerating the exchange of operational information, especially regarding actions or movements of terrorist persons or networks; forged or falsified travel documents; traffic in arms, explosives or sensitive materials; use of communications technologies by terrorist groups; and the threat posed by the possession of weapons of mass destruction by terrorist groups.[24]

---

23  See also 'The Consolidated List established and maintained by the 1267 Committee with respect to Al Qaeda, Osama bin Laden, the Taliban and other individuals, groups, undertakings and entities associated with them' (last updated 6 August 2010), www.un.org/sc/committees/1267/consolist.shtml.

24  See the CTC's 'Survey of the Implementation of Security Council Resolution 1373 (2001) by Member States', 3 December 2009, UN Doc. S/2009/620.

Among other Security Council initiatives adopted to counter international terrorism, Resolution 1540 of 28 April 2004 obligates states to prevent the proliferation of nuclear, chemical and biological weapons and related materials, and establishes the 1540 Committee to monitor progress. Interpol assists in these monitoring tasks and created a Fusion Task Force (FTF) in September 2002 to identify and maintain records on related criminals, criminal groups and organisations.[25] The FTF co-ordinates an extensive database from which information is provided to the international law enforcement community, and Interpol has nominated six regional task forces for areas considered particularly susceptible to terrorist violence.[26] Colour-coded 'notices' are issued regarding certain persons or organisations deemed to be dangerous or otherwise of interest,[27] and Interpol member states each maintain a National Central Interpol Bureau. The EU also shares its lists of terrorist names, and other activity includes the Council Common Position of 27 December 2001, which applies to certain longstanding liberation groups in Europe, as well as to persons, groups and entities identified by the Security Council; Council Regulation (EC) 881/2002 of 27 May 2002 provides measures dedicated for use against Al Qaeda and the Taliban.[28]

While they may be useful to a law-and-order approach by states to deter violent actors, 'terror lists' do little if anything to illuminate the underlying reasons for the use of illicit violence. The use of such lists in the context of liberation struggles is also contentious, as there is first an issue as to whether a relationship exists between a liberation group and a terrorist organisation. Second, lists containing the names of 'criminal' persons, etc., are highly incriminating, and too often prevent further inquiry. Prohibited organisations may indeed be funded through such criminal activities as drug trafficking, money laundering, armed robberies, kidnappings, revolutionary taxes, weapons trafficking and so on,[29] but legal variation in state implementation can further entrench any obstacles to defence rights for individual suspects. Inasmuch as international obligations

---

25 Interpol, ' "Best Practices" in Combating Terrorism, Executive Summary', Report submitted to the UNSC–C-TED, October 2006.
26 Project Pacific (Southeast Asia), Project Kalkan (Central Asia), Project Amazon (South America), Project Baobab (Africa), Project NEXUS (Europe) and Project Middle East.
27 E.g., a Red Notice denotes a person wanted for arrest and extradition. See 'Terror Suspects Linked to Al Qaeda "On the Run in Midlands"', 8 February 2009, Telegraph.co.uk.
28 Council Regulation 882/2002 also repeals Council Regulation (EC) No. 467/2001, which prohibited the export of certain goods and services to Afghanistan, etc. See also Commission Regulation (EU) No. 681/2010 of 29 July 2010, amending for the 132nd time Council Regulation (EC) No. 881/2002.
29 See, e.g., ICPO Interpol-General Assembly, Resolution No. AGN/53/RES/6 concerning violent crime commonly referred to as terrorism, 53rd session, Luxembourg, 4–11 September 2004 ('considering that: (a) in many countries there are organized groups engaging in violent criminal activities designed, by spreading terror or fear, to enable them to attain allegedly political objectives').

on states are made locally enforceable by domestic laws in which acts of 'terrorism' are also defined, domestic courts may or may not be afforded room for further discretion regarding the likely consequences of specific laws. Accordingly, a brief review now follows of the more influential anti-terrorist arrangements adopted individually by the Permanent Member States of the UN Security Council.

## The Permanent Five

The maintenance of a balance between official uses of armed force and individual rights entitlements can be precarious at the best of times, so when domestic law is used to authorise government force, underlying procedural requirements can reveal quite a lot about the differences between states, including such matters as whether any regard is had to peoples' *rights* to self-determination. Inasmuch as the Permanent Members of the Security Council in the contemporary era are by definition in the pre-eminent position to lead the rest of the world (and each other) by way of example, a brief overview now follows regarding the respective constitutional and legal arrangements made publicly available on the UNODC website, for purposes of authorising official uses of force to deter international terrorism.

### China

The People's Republic of China (PRC) authorises the use of armed force in its Constitution of 1982 (as amended), in pertinent part, as follows:

Article 28. The state maintains public order and suppresses treasonable and other counter-revolutionary activities; it penalises actions that endanger public security. . . .

Article 29. The armed forces of the PRC belong to the people. Their tasks are to strengthen national defence, resist aggression, defend the motherland. The state strengthens the revolutionisation, modernisation and regularisation of the armed forces in order to increase the national defence capability. . . .

Article 67. The Standing Committee of the National People's Congress exercises the following functions and powers: . . .

(18) To decide, when the National People's Congress is not in session, on the proclamation of a state of war in the event of an armed attack on the country or in fulfilment of international treaty obligations concerning common defence against aggression;

(19) To decide on general mobilization or partial mobilization;

(20) To decide on the enforcement of martial law throughout the country or in particular provinces, autonomous regions or municipalities directly under the Central Government [revised on 14 March 2004:

"... to decide on entering the state of emergency throughout the country or in particular provinces, autonomous regions, or municipalities directly under the Central Government"].

Article 80. The President of the PRC ... proclaims martial law; proclaims a state of war; and issues mobilization orders [revised on 14 March 2004: "... proclaims entering of the state of emergency"].

Article 89. The State Council exercises the following functions and powers:

(16) To decide on the enforcement of martial law in parts of provinces, autonomous regions and municipalities directly under the Central Government [revised on 14 March 2004: "to decide on the imposition of martial law in parts of provinces, autonomous regions and municipalities directly under the Central Government ..."].

The PRC does not appear to have a comprehensive anti-terrorism law, in the combined sense of defining the offence *and* authorising use of the armed forces to fight terrorists. Instead, PRC laws describe terrorism extremely broadly in the Criminal Code adopted on 1 July 1979, as subsequently amended on 14 March 1997 and 29 December 2001.[30] More general offences, such as threats to aviation and shipping, include forms of sabotage, hijacking and violence on board aircraft.[31] There is indicated a 1983 Decision Regarding the Severe Punishment of Criminals and the UNODC–PRC folder shows that the PRC has entered into a number of bilateral treaties in the past decade on arrangements for mutual legal and judicial assistance in criminal matters and extradition, most of which have yet to be translated into English for wider consumption. No PRC case law is listed.

## France

The French Constitution of 4 October 1958 (as amended) mentions the armed forces four times. It provides in Article 15 that 'the President of the Republic shall be Commander-in-Chief of the Armed Forces', in Article 20 that the armed forces are at the disposal of the government, which remains accountable to Parliament and, in Article 34, that statute determines the obligations imposed on citizens and their property for national defence purpose, the fundamental guarantees granted to members of the armed forces, and the basic principles for the self-government, powers and revenue of territorial communities. Article 35 provides that declarations of war are

---

30 E.g., Articles 112 (arms trade or theft), 114 (non-serious acts), 115 (serious acts), 120 (terrorist leadership), 120a (terrorist funding), 125 (possession, etc., of nuclear or biological substances), 127 (theft of firearms, and nuclear or biological substances), 191 (money laundering) and 291a (spread of terrorist hoaxes, empty threats or fabrications).

31 Articles 116, 117, and 119, Articles 121, 122 and 123, respectively.

authorized by Parliament, that the government shall inform Parliament of forceful interventions abroad within three days at the latest, and that either Parliament or the National Assembly must authorise forceful interventions lasting longer than four months.

The French Penal Code (updated 12/10/2005) provides specifically for terrorist offences in Articles 421 (substantive) and 422 (defences, mitigation, penalties). Article 421-1 criminalises the listed acts if perpetrated intentionally, in connection with an individual or collective undertaking, the purpose of which is seriously to disturb public order through intimidation or terror. The acts listed include wilful attack on persons or property, hijacking, theft, computer offences, firearms offences, the possession, etc., of biological or toxin-based weapons and chemical weapons, money laundering and insider trading activities. Damage to the environment is covered in Article 421-2 of the Penal Code and carries the same *mens rea* as that indicated in Article 421-1, as are participation in terrorist groups or associations, and financing terrorism. Article 421-3 provides for a terrorist motive to be an aggravating factor in sentencing. Rules against unlawful assembly or demonstration or membership of a 'combat group' are contained in Article 431. A 'combat group' is defined in Article 431-13 as 'any group of persons holding or having access to weapons, which has an organised hierarchy and is liable to breach the public peace'.[32] Abuses of authority directed against public administration are prohibited by Article 432.

Legislative activity after 2001 includes Law No. 2006-64 of 23 January 2006 concerning anti-terrorism measures for security and external border control, and Law No. 2008-1245 of 1 December 2008 to extend the application of Articles 3, 6 and 9 of Law No. 2006-64 beyond their original expiration date of 31 December 2008, to 2012. Article 3 concerns certain criminal procedural matters, Article 6, postal and telecommunications interceptions, and Article 9, police access to records of computerised data, *inter alia*, for driving records, national identity cards and passports and immigration. As for post-9/11 case law reports listed on the UNODC website, there are several, but they generally apply to persons suspected of participation, etc., in Islamic extremism.[33] Only one has a connection to

---

32  E.g., those disbanded by the Act of 10 January 1936 on Combat Groups and Private Militias.
33  No. 0313739016, *Ministere Public v Turk, et al.* [11 July 2007] Tribunal de Grande Instance (Paris) (criminal association and terrorist fundraising in support of Moroccan Islamic Jihad Group); No. 0205339019, *Ministere Public v Ben Mustapha, et al.* [19 December 2007] Tribunal de Grande Instance, 16th Chamber/1 (Paris) (extradition of alleged French terrorists from Guantanamo Bay to France); No. 272098, *Republique Francaise* [27 July 2005] Conseil D'Etat (Statuant au contentieux) (US extradition request for persons accused of fraud and money laundering; double criminality found; irrelevance of political offence exception); No. 0206300012, *Republique Francaise v Mbala Mbala* [11 July 2003] Tribunal de Grande Instance, 17th Chamber (Paris) (freedom of expression; no public 'apology' for terrorism); No. 03-84652, *Republique Francaise v Nizar, et al.* [4 January 2005] Cour de Cassation, Chambre criminelle (no jurisdiction to determine arbitrariness of arrests made in Afghanistan and Pakistan).

a 'traditional' liberationist group (ETA), but it concerns the application of the 1957 European Convention on Extradition.[34]

### Russian Federation

The entry for the Russian Federation indicates the 1993 Constitution of the Russian Federation, but the English webpage is unavailable. However, relevant legislation in English is indicated, as follows.

*Federal Law No. 35-FZ of 6 March 2006 on Counteraction Against Terrorism, adopted by the State Duma on 26 February 2006, endorsed by the Federation Council on 1 March 2006*

Federal Law No. 35-FZ establishes the fundamental principles on which counter-terrorist action may be adopted and applies to the use of the armed forces against terrorist groups. 'Terrorism' is defined in Article 3(1) quite broadly, to mean:

> [T]he ideology of violence and the practice of influencing the adoption of a decision by public authorities, local self-government bodies or international organizations connected with frightening the population and (or) other forms of unlawful violent actions.[35]

Article 3(2) provides that terrorist activity includes the establishment of an unlawful armed unit and the 'popularisation of terrorist ideas, dissemination of materials or information urging terrorist activities, substantiating or justifying the necessity of the exercise of such activity'. Article 3(5) authorises official anti-terrorist operations, which are defined as:

> [A] complex set of special, operational-combat and army measures accompanied by the use of military equipment, armaments and special facilities which are aimed at suppressing an act of terrorism, neutralising terrorists, ensuring security of natural persons, organizations and institutions, as well as at reducing to minimum the consequences of an act of terrorism.

Articles 6–10 indicate the type of actions in which subdivisions and military units of the armed forces may be utilised, including in the air, to ensure

---

34 No. 02-85233, *Republique Francaise v Juan Maria* [8 October 2002] Cour de Cassation, Chambre criminelle (ETA financing, membership, etc., of Gestoras Pro Amnistia [an organization defending imprisoned ETA activists]; extradition proceedings approved). Gestoras was banned in Spain in 2001. D.P.A., 'Mega-trial against ETA-linked Group begins in Spain', *Earth Times*, 21 April 2008, www.earthtimes.org.

35 This definition is certainly capable of manipulation for unrelated political and economic purposes in that it does not clearly distinguish between terrorism (in the extremist or political sense) and other forms of criminality or social disruption.

safe national maritime traffic in the inland waterways, the territorial sea, the seaways and industrial activities located on the Russian continental shelf, as well as Russian participation in anti-terrorist operations and to suppress international terrorist activities occurring extra-territorially. In regards to the latter, there is no application of international law other than treaties which the Russian Federation is a party (Article 10). Article 16 provides that terrorist political demands 'must not be considered' should negotiations be opened during an anti-terrorist operation. Articles 18–21 provide for compensation to victims for damage caused by terrorist operations. Article 22 allows broad parameters for the 'lawful infliction of damage', as follows:

> Depriving the person, who has committed an act of terrorism, of life, as well as causing damage to health and property of such person or to other legitimate interests of individuals, society or the state, while suppressing an act of terrorism or taking other measures pertaining to the struggle against terrorism by the actions, provided for or allowed by the legislation of the Russian Federation, shall be lawful.

No domestic cases are indicated on the UNODC–Russian folder, yet it should be recalled that, as the Russian Federation is a member of the Council of Europe, it is fully accountable for affording due respect to human rights guarantees in its domestic provision; the Russian Federation has, in fact, been challenged successfully on several occasions before the ECtHR in Strasbourg,[36] due to its use of disproportionate armed force against Chechen separatist insurgents, whom the Federation refers to as 'terrorists'. Moreover, the Federation has made no attempt to derogate from certain Convention articles, as permitted by Article 15(1) ECHR, once derogation measures are deemed necessary during a 'time of war or other public emergency threatening the life of the nation'.[37] Derogation is limited, however, 'to the extent strictly required by the exigencies of the situation' and cannot be 'inconsistent with its other obligations under international law', but in failing to take advantage of the Article 15 provision, the Federation is held to the stricter standards applicable in peacetime.

As a final point, the UNODC–Russian case law folder does list the 'Resolution Adopted by the Plenum of the Supreme Court of the Russian Federation No. 5, 10 October 2003, on "the application by courts of general jurisdiction of the commonly recognized principles and norms

---

36  See Chapter 4.
37  Article 15(1) of the ECHR does not permit derogation from Articles 2, 3, 4(1) and 7. Regarding Article 2, the 'right to life' can be disregarded, according to Article 15(2), 'in respect of deaths resulting from lawful acts of war'. The Secretary General of the Council of Europe must be informed of the measures taken, their reasoning and the date they cease to be in effect. Article 15(3).

of the international law and the international treaties of the Russian Federation" (excerpts)'. This Resolution is purely procedural and sets out the order of priority between international and national rules. Essentially, the resolution makes plain that as all elements of a crime should first be established in national law, international crimes should not be directly applied until the Criminal Code or other Federal law requires it, at which point international rules are to be given priority over domestic regulatory acts.

## United Kingdom

The UK has no written constitution, per se,[38] but the state is governed by the Executive in the name of the Crown, currently held by HM Queen Elizabeth II. The 'Royal Prerogative' contains the loosely defined, residual powers utilised, *inter alia*, for foreign policy and war powers, which are delegated generally to the government of the day by means of Orders in Council.[39] Accordingly, the members of the armed forces swear allegiance to the British monarch, who is their Commander-in-Chief, but the constitutional convention is that the Prime Minister of the day holds *de facto* authority over them. This means that the Executive has no legal obligation to take account of the monarch's opinion when utilising the armed forces. Therefore, pursuant to British constitutional law, the armed forces are subordinate to the Crown, but the British Army is the army of Parliament rather than of the monarch.[40] Further, Parliament must consent yearly to the continued existence of the armed forces during peacetime.

Prior to the negotiated end of the 'Troubles' in Northern Ireland, UK policy was generally to shy away from affording overly eager extradition assistance. Instead, the UK chose not to interfere with liberation struggles occurring in third states, as it hoped other states would not interfere in the situation in Northern Ireland. The UK preferred instead to rely on the specific, codified terms of the bilateral and multilateral extradition arrangements it had accepted. However, what had been temporary anti-terrorist provisions in UK law were made permanent in the Terrorism Act 2000 and, since 9/11, the UK has been extremely active in the 'war on terror', regarding which it has implemented authorisation for uses of armed force and many new laws, whether or not required by UN Security Council or EU Resolution

---

38 Constitutional documents are the Magna Carta (1215), the Petition of Right (1628), the *Habeas Corpus* Act 1679 and the Bill of Rights 1689. See, e.g., B. Robertson, 'Military Intervention in Civil Disturbance in Great Britain – What Is the Legal Basis?' [1990] 29(1–2) *Rev.Dr.Mil.Dr.G.* 307.

39 See, e.g., H. Barnett, *Constitutional and Administrative Law* (Abingdon: Routledge-Cavendish, 6th edn, 2006), pp. 115–49. Section 21 of the 1998 Human Rights Act categorises Orders in Council adopted under the Royal Prerogative as primary legislation.

40 As confirmed in the 1689 Bill of Rights.

or Regulation.[41] The UNODC–UK folder indicates 11 new pieces of legislation or explanatory memoranda, aimed generally against domestic or foreign Islamic extremism.[42]

A principle domestic criticism of new UK legislation is that its provisions are overly broad and rest on far too much political discretion for purposes of enforcement. Moreover, certain provisions are of potential application to non-Islamic terror events, such as the recent 'credit crunch'[43] or to civilian groups, e.g., those agitating for animal rights or the environment. However, the 'Troubles' in Northern Ireland provided the UK with experience in adopting anti-terror measures. In 2000, as noted earlier, surviving anti-terrorist measures were made permanent, and Schedule 2 of the Terrorism Act 2000 proscribed the following organisations:[44] the Irish Republican Army, Cumann na mBan, Fianna na hEireann, the Red Hand Commandos, Saor Eire, the Ulster Freedom Fighters, the Ulster Volunteer Force, the Irish National Liberation Army, the Irish People's Liberation Organisation, the Ulster Defence Association, the Loyalist Volunteer Force, the Continuity Army Council, the Orange Volunteers[45] and the Red Hand Defenders.[46]

Sections 11–13 of the 2000 Act based the grounds for proscription on membership, support and uniform. The last ground, in particular, is notable for its connection to 'legitimate' struggles for self-determination, in which Geneva laws require some form of distinguishing insignia during an armed attack for purposes of the combatant–civilian distinction. What is meant in the 2000 Act by the term 'uniform' is defined in s. 13(1) as follows:

41 E.g., provisions to prevent terrorist financing required by UNSC Resolution 1373 of 28 September 2001 and Regulation (EC) 2580/2001, OJ L 344 (28 December 2001), p. 70. On 27 December 2001 the European Council Common Position 2001/931/CFSP, pursuant to UNSC Resolution 1373, established a list of individuals and entities involved in terrorism for EU purposes. The list is published and updated by Council Decisions.

42 E.g., the Anti-terrorist, Crime and Security Act 2001 devotes large sections to religious hatred, communications data, police powers and weapons of mass destruction.

43 E.g., Anti-terrorism, Crime and Security Act 2001 section 4 empowers the Treasury to prevent funds being made available to or for the benefit of a foreign government or individuals. This power was utilised in The Landsbanki Freezing Order 2008, No. 2668.

44 Part 2 of the Act gave details of the proscription procedure and Schedule 3, of the 2000 Act provided for a Proscribed Organisations Appeal Commission.

45 'The Orange Volunteers' refers to the organisation that used that name to publish a press release on 14 October 1998.

46 Section 40(2) provides an interpretation of 'terrorist' that permits retrospective application, as follows: 'the reference in subsection (1)(b) to a person who has been concerned in the commission, preparation or instigation of acts of terrorism includes a reference to a person who has been, whether before or after the passing of this Act, concerned in the commission, preparation or instigation of acts of terrorism within the meaning given', *inter alia*, in sections 11 and 12.

A person in a public place commits an offence if he—
(a) wears an item of clothing, or
(b) wears, carries or displays an article,
in such a way or in such circumstances as to arouse reasonable suspicion that he is a member or supporter of a proscribed organisation.

Further, although previous UK practice applied anti-terror measures for domestic purposes only, the 2000 Act extended the UK's jurisdictional reach extra-territorially, in ss. 59–61 (incitement to commit abroad), 62 (bombing abroad) and 63 (financing terrorism abroad). Section 1 of the 2000 Act (as amended) defines 'terrorism' in terms of the classic triangular motive, as requiring the use or threat of action to influence the government or an international governmental organisation or to intimidate the public and to advance a political, religious or ideological cause. Prohibited acts include serious violence, etc., against persons or property and serious interference with or serious disruption to an electronic system. If the use or threat of prohibited action involves firearms or explosives, it also is considered terrorism. The terms 'action', 'person or property', 'public' and 'government' apply regardless of where located, and action taken for terrorist purposes includes action for the benefit of a proscribed organisation. The Terrorism Act 2006 compounds this broad approach and supplements the grounds for proscription by inserting new subsection 5A into s. 11 of the 2000 Act, which concerns a new offence of 'glorification' of terrorism. 'Glorification' includes those organisational activities that, a member of the public could reasonably infer, are meant to praise, celebrate, or associate that organisation with acts of terrorism as behaviour which should be emulated.

Various special intelligence and judicial procedures have long been utilised to incarcerate terror suspects prior to causing actual violence. In terms of relevant case law, the UK gained judicial expertise in dealing with terror suspects during the 'Troubles', e.g., in 'Diplock courts' (non-jury),[47] internment or similar practices for detaining suspects without charge, as well as regarding defence claims against confessions extracted under torture or similar practices. Certain of these measures, recommended in the 'Diplock Report' of late 1972,[48] marked the beginning of the UK's 'criminalisation' policy to remove any legal distinction between political violence and normal crime. The 'criminalisation' policy thus permitted paramilitary

---

47  Established by the government of Northern Ireland in August 1973 on the basis of the Northern Ireland (Emergency Provisions) Act 1973 s. 2. These courts were abolished in 2007 by the Justice and Security (Northern Ireland) Act 2007.

48  Report Presented to Parliament by the Commission to Consider Legal Procedures to Deal with Terrorist Activities in Northern Ireland, December 1972, Cmnd. 5185. The UK also decided to adapt certain aspects of the laws of war in 1972 for its interrogations of prisoners in Northern Ireland. A. Roberts and R. Guelff, *Documents on the Laws of War* (Oxford: Oxford University Press, 3d edn, 2000), pp. 25–6.

prisoners to be treated as common criminals at roughly the same time as negotiations opened in Geneva to extend the humanitarian rules for international warfare to 'wars of self-determination' in additional Protocol 1 Article 1(4).[49] In that the ECHR was not incorporated into British law until 1998, despite the UK being an original signatory of the convention in 1950, litigants were left with the additional expense and strict procedural formalities of final appeal before the ECtHR in Strasbourg.

UK incorporation of the ECHR finally occurred in 1998. Implementation in turn has meant that the UK is more directly obligated to comply with the treaty provisions and that English case law related to post-9/11 terrorism must reflect a far more delicate balance than previously in terms of the degree of political discretion allowed when weighing security concerns against individual rights entitlements. Nonetheless, the UK has, in fact, attempted to derogate from certain provisions, on the basis permitted by ECHR Article 15(1),[50] in the Derogation Order 2001, which was stated to be a temporary measure and subject to annual renewal. Certain practices for the detention, etc., of 'international suspected terrorists' had already been placed in Part IV of the Anti-terrorism, Crime and Safety Act 2001, but soon Part IV was declared incompatible with the Human Rights Act by the House of Lords in late 2004,[51] due to the discriminatory impact on 'foreign nationals' of Part IV measures. The subsequent provisions for 'non-derogating control orders' in s. 2(1) of the Prevention of Terrorism Act 2005 were intended to deal with this 2004 decision, but the orders were partially quashed again.[52]

Otherwise, the captions of what post-9/11 litigation is listed in the UNODC–UK folder generally identify suspects either by their non-English origin surnames or by anonymising letters of the alphabet; the cases tend for the most part to concern either administrative arrangements for dealing with those the legislature perceives as threats connected in some way with Al Qaeda or its affiliates, or they concern associated evidentiary difficulties when proving a person is so connected. A few cases consider evidence allegedly obtained under torture, as the UK is also a party to the

---

49 On 19 July 1995, the UK Geneva Conventions (Amendments) Act 1995, to implement Geneva Protocols 1 and 2, received the Royal Assent.
50 The Human Rights Act 1998 (Designated Derogation) Order 2001 was made on 11 November 2001, having been approved by both Houses of Parliament. Section 14(6) of the 1998 Human Rights Act permits such a derogation order to be made.
51 *A(FC) & Others v S.O.S. for the Home Department* [004] UKHL 56. The derogation clause in s. 30, Part IV of the Anti-terrorism, Crime and Security Act 2001, was repealed by the Human Rights Act 1998 (Amendment) Order 2005.
52 See Case No: T1/2006/9501, *S.O.S. for the Home Department v M.B.* [006] E.W.C.A. Civ. 1140; Case No: T1/2006/9502, *S.O.S. for the Home Department v J.J., et al.* [006] E.W.C.A. Civ. 1141. See also Case No. PTA 5/2005, *S.O.S. for the Home Department v E.* [007] E.W.H.C. 233 (Admin).

Torture Convention of 1984,[53] as both Article 2(2) of that convention and Article 3 of the ECHR make it quite clear that torture cannot be justified under any circumstances.[54]

## United States

The US has suffered relatively little from 'home-grown' terrorist violence, but what there has been in recent years is sourced generally in protest politics.[55] The main ethnic challenges have arisen from certain Native American tribes, the ongoing Civil Rights Movement and, more recently, Hispanic immigration. In contrast, the US has been at the forefront of international anti-terrorist efforts since the 1960s when aircraft hijackings and other violence began to endanger US investment and other interests, which illustrates the penetration of American power and influence pursued by the US since both world wars.[56] Moreover, many people world-wide are aware in the contemporary era of the general thrust of the US Constitution of 1787,[57] which is the supreme law of the land, as well as of many anti-terrorist initiatives devised recently by the US, as many of those initiatives have since been adopted or adapted by the UN.

In regard to the US Constitution, Article 1 Section 8 allocates legislative powers to Congress to declare and wage war, as well as to raise, regulate and support the armed forces for use in insurrections or to 'repel invasions'. Executive powers are vested in the Office of the US President, in accordance with Article 2 Section 2 of which provides 'the President shall be Commander in Chief of the Army and Navy of the US, and of the Militia of the several States, when called into the actual Service of the US'. Article 3 Section 3 defines treasons against the US as consisting 'only in levying War against them, or in adhering to their Enemies, giving them

53 The UN General Assembly adopted the convention on 10 December 1984.
54 See, e.g., *A(FC) & Others v S.O.S. for the Home Department* [004] UKHL 56; Appeal No. SC/15/2005, *Othman (a/k/a Abu Qatada) v S.O.S. for the Home Department* [26 February 2007] Special Immigration Appeals Commission; Appeal Nos: SC/1/2002, SC/6/2002, SC/7/2002, SC/9/2002, SC/10/2002, *Ajouaou & Others v S.O.S. for the Home Department* [29 October 2003] Special Immigration Appeals Commission.
55 A notable exception arose from the 'direct action' protests of the New Left movement of the 1960s and 1970s, factions of which included the Weather Underground Movement and the Symbionese Liberation Army. Other politically violent groups, such as the Animal Liberation Front, remain active and are listed by the US Department of Homeland Security as terrorist organisations.
56 *Pace* the US Monroe Doctrine of 1823, intended to deter European interference in the internal affairs of the American continents. R.H. Dana, Jr. (ed.), *H. Wheaten's Elements of International Law* (Oxford: Clarendon Press, 1936), p. 82 n. 36.
57 Which is just as well because the UNODC website, as of late August 2010, has published the UAE Constitution instead.

Aid and Comfort', and Article 4 Section 4 guarantees that the US 'shall protect each of them [the individual states] against Invasion; and on Application of the Legislature, or of the Executive (when the Legislature cannot be convened), against domestic Violence'. A Bill of Rights containing 10 amendments was added in 1789, to make 'further declaratory and restrictive clauses' and to extend 'the ground of public confidence in the Government'. Amendment 2 provides for the right to bear arms, as 'a well regulated Militia' is 'necessary to the security of a free State'; unreasonable search and seizure without probable cause are prohibited in Amendment 4, Amendments 5 and 6 protect criminal due process rights, and Amendment 8 states that 'Excessive bail shall not be required, nor excessive fines imposed, nor cruel and unusual punishments inflicted'.[58]

Despite these strict parameters, the US Presidency has gained increasing powers over the use of the armed forces.[59] After the 9/11 attacks, and Security Council Resolution 1368 of 12 September 2001 confirmed the right to use force in self-defence, Congress acted quickly to grant due authority to the President to use all 'necessary and appropriate force' against those whom he determined 'planned, authorised, committed or aided' the 9/11 attacks.[60] The invasion of Afghanistan in late 2001 was not controversial, but despite silence from the Security Council, Congress approved the Authorisation for Use of Military Force Against Iraq Resolution of 2002,[61] which again permitted the President to use the armed forces 'as he determines to be necessary and appropriate'. This resolution was voted against by a majority of Democratic Congressmen and it was subsequently challenged judicially, albeit unsuccessfully, at appeal level in early 2003.[62]

In terms of anti-terrorist legislation generally since 2001, the US has re-designated certain liberation groups as foreign terrorist organisations[63] and the UNODC website lists nine legislative acts or amendments covering specific security and weapons preparedness issues.[64] The best known of the post-9/11 Congressional initiatives is the USA Patriot Act of 26 October 2001 (as amended). This act has been described as a 'pendulum reaction

---

58  A further 17 amendments were added between 1789 and 1992.
59  See, e.g., the War Powers Joint Resolution (Pub.L. 93–148, H.J.Res. 542, enacted 7 November 1973).
60  Authorization for Use of Military Force Against Terrorists (Pub.L. 107–40, 115 Stat. 224, enacted 18 September 2001).
61  Pub.L. 107–243, 116 Stat. 1498, enacted 16 October 2002, H.J.Res. 114, was a joint Congressional resolution authorising the Iraq War, based on Constitutional and Congressional grounds for the President to fight anti-US terrorism; The Iraq Liberation Act of 1998, a Congressional statement of policy, had called for regime change in Iraq.
62  *Doe v Bush*, No. 03-1266 (1st Cir., 13 March 2003).
63  8 U.S.C. § 1189; Redesignation of Foreign Terrorist Organizations, 68 Fed. Reg. 56,860, 56,861 (2 Oct. 2003), section (a)(1) of which is provided in the Appendix.
64  One pre-2001 document is posted: the US Anti-terrorism and Effective Death Penalty Act of 24 April 1996.

to the events of 9/11'[65] and contains an extremely broad definition of terrorism, while affording highly intrusive executive powers, including government wiretaps, search warrants, trade sanctions and access to confidential information.[66] Title 3 deals with money laundering activities, terrorist fundraising and bank secrecy, Title 4 concerns border protections and immigration matters and Title 5, terrorist investigations. The Patriot Act section 802 amends the definition of 'domestic terrorism' found in Title 18 USCS section 2331.[67] 'International terrorism' is referred to 116 times in the Act, but is defined in the Patriot Act section 219 by cross-reference to section 2331 of Title 18 US Consolidated Statutes (2004).[68] Section 2331 provides in pertinent part as follows (emphasis added):

(1) the term 'international terrorism' means activities that—

    (A) involve violent acts or acts dangerous to human life that are a violation of the criminal laws of the US *or of any State*, or that would be a criminal violation if committed within the jurisdiction of the US *or of any State*;

    (B) appear to be intended—

        (i) to intimidate or coerce a civilian population;

        (ii) to influence the policy of a government by intimidation or coercion; or

        (iii) to affect the conduct of a government by mass destruction, assassination or kidnapping; and

    (C) occur *primarily outside* the territorial jurisdiction of the US, or *transcend national boundaries* in terms of the means by which they are accomplished, the persons they appear intended to intimidate or coerce, or the locale in which their perpetrators operate or seek asylum;

[. . .]

(3) the term 'person' means any individual or entity capable of holding a legal or beneficial interest in property;

---

65 Lord Carlile of Berriew, QC (Independent Reviewer of Terrorism Legislation), 'The Definition of Terrorism', Cm. 7052 [London: Her Majesty's Stationery Office, 15 March 2007], p. 15.

66 The full title is 'The Uniting and Strengthening America by Providing Appropriate Tools Required to Intercept and Obstruct Terrorism (USA Patriot Act) Act of 2001, To deter and punish terrorist acts in the US and around the world, to enhance law enforcement investigatory tools, and for other purposes', Public Law 107–56. The Legislative History of the Bill (H.R. 3162) is in Congressional Record, Vol. 147 (2001): on 23 and 24 October, the Bill was considered and passed by the House of Representatives, and considered and passed by the Senate on 25 October 2001. The US President's remarks can be found in the Weekly Compilation of Presidential Documents, Vol. 37 (26 October 2001).

67 Patriot Act section 802 is provided in the Appendix.

68 Title 18 USC is captioned 'Crimes and Criminal Procedure'.

(4) the term '*act of war*' means any act occurring in the course of—

(A) declared war;

(B) armed conflict, whether or not war has been declared, between two or more nations; or

(C) armed conflict between *military forces of any origin*; and

(5) the term '*domestic* terrorism' means activities that—

(A) involve acts dangerous to human life that are a violation of the *criminal laws* of the US *or of any State*;

(B) appear to be intended—

(i) to intimidate or coerce a civilian population;

(ii) to influence the policy of a government by intimidation or coercion; or

(iii) to affect the conduct of a government by mass destruction, assassination, or kidnapping; and

(C) occur primarily *within the territorial jurisdiction* of the US.

The interpretive notes and decisions accompanying section 2331 indicate that 'Funding, simpliciter, of foreign terrorist organization is not sufficient to constitute [the] act of terrorism . . . ; however, funding that meets the definition of aiding and abetting [an] act of terrorism creates liability . . .'.[69] Further, it is stated that:

> Even though [the terrorist] acts of September 11, 2001, clearly "occurred primarily" in the US, . . . they were acts of international terrorism since they were carried out by foreign nationals who apparently received their orders and funding and some training from foreign sources.[70]

Section 2332b is captioned 'Acts of terrorism transcending national boundaries'. Sections 444 and 508 of the Patriot Act cross-refer 'domestic terrorism' to the definition of 'Federal crime of terrorism' provided in section 2332b(g)(5)(B) of Title 18.[71] The interpretive notes and decisions accompanying section 2332b(g)(5) indicate that:

> [The] defendant need not have been convicted of [a] federal crime of terrorism as defined in 18 USCS section 2332b(g)(5) for [the] district court to find that he intended his substantive offence of conviction or his relevant conduct to promote such terrorism crime; however, in sentencing [the] defendant . . . , [the] district court must identify which

---

69  *Boim v Quranic Literacy Inst.* (2002) 291 F.3d 1000 (7th Cir.).

70  *Smith v Islamic Emirate of Afghanistan* (2003) 262 F.Supp.2d 217 (S.D.N.Y.).

71  Section 2332b(g)(5)(B) of Title 18 is provided in full in the Appendix.

enumerated "federal crime of terrorism" [the] defendant intended to promote, satisfy elements of section 2332b(g)(5)(A), and support its conclusions by [a] preponderance of evidence with facts from [the] record.[72]

As for relevant case law indicated in the UNODC–US folder, several are listed, including four Supreme Court cases[73] and five Appeal Court cases.[74]

## Kosovo and 'independence'

This small selection of new criminal and case law provides but a flavour of the many ways in which a broad law-and-order approach to terrorist violence, whether planned and/or perpetrated at home or abroad, can be activated and co-ordinated by the individual Permanent Member States for purposes of collective international action. Obviously, the documents published in the pertinent UNODC folders make little if any direct reference to the self-determination of peoples, which makes it possible to infer that any decision to regard a liberation group more favourably is a political one. For example, the US has supported an independent Kosovo for some time, while the Russian Federation has not. While the liberation struggle conducted by Kosovo's majority Albanian population against Serbia is well documented elsewhere,[75] for present purposes, more recent history is outlined in brief.

Kosovo has long been an integral part of Serbia and, until recently, was deemed to form a southern province in that state. As Kosovo has an

---

72  *US v Graham* (2001) 275 F.3d 490 (6th Cir.).
73  *Hamdi, et al. v Rumsfeld, et al.*, No. 03-6696 (S.Ct., 28 June 2004) (classification as enemy combatants); *Hamdan v Rumsfeld, et al.*, No. 05-184 (29 June 2006) (Geneva Conventions; unconstitutionality of Guantanamo Bay special military commissions); *Lakhdar Boumediene, et al. v Bush, et al.*, Nos 06-1195 and 06-1196 (2 April 2007) (*habeas corpus*); *Boumediene, et al. v Bush*, Nos 06-1195 and 06-1196 (12 June 2008) (*habeas corpus*).
74  *Efrat Ungar, et al. v The PLO, et al.*, No. 04-2079 (1st Cir., 31 March 2005) (no immunity from suit); *Padilla v Hanft (US Navy)*, No. 05-6396 (4th Cir. 9 September 2005) (designation as enemy combatant); *Boumediene, et al. v Bush, et al.*, No. 05-5062 (D.C. Cir., 20 February 2007); *El Masri v US (CIA)*, No. 06-1667 (D.C. Cir., 2 March 2007) (German citizen abducted by the CIA; state secrecy). *US v Fawaz Yunis*, No. 89-3208, 924 F.2d 1086 (D.C. Cir., 1991) (appeal from conviction for a 1985 hijacking) is also indicated.
75  See, e.g., J. Summers (ed.), *Kosovo: A Precedent? The Declaration of Independence, the Advisory Opinion and Implications for Statehood, Self-Determination and Minority Rights* (Leiden: Brill, [forthcoming] 2011); M. Weller, *Contested Statehood: Kosovo's Struggle for Independence* (Oxford: Oxford University Press, 2009); Report, Stevens, 'Filling the Vacuum: Ensuring Protection and Legal Remedies for Minorities in Kosovo', *M.R.G. International* (26 May 2009). For additional background, see also J. Friedrich, 'UNMIK in Kosovo: Struggling with Uncertainty' [2005] 9 *Max Planck U.N.Yb.* 225, at 244–8.

ethnically distinct majority Albanian population, it was granted the status of an autonomous province under the Yugoslav constitution of 1974, even though it desired equality with the other Yugoslav republics. In 1989 the Serb nationalist Slobodan Milošević engineered the revocation of Kosovo's minority rights and autonomy through amendments to Serbia's Constitution. Kosovo's Assembly was dissolved in 1990 and Serbian police were sent to suppress domestic agitation in the province. This autocratic treatment of Kosovo by Serbia ironically spooked the other Yugoslav republics, which proceeded to secede. As the state's dissolution wars raged throughout the 1990s, a Kosovo Albanian shadow government and Liberation Army arose, which from 1996 co-ordinated a violent struggle against Serbian sovereignty and authority. War crimes proliferated on all sides, as well as gross violations of human rights.

The UN Security Council imposed an arms embargo in Resolution 1160 of 31 March 1998, which Serbia ignored by commencing an ethnic cleansing campaign against Kosovo's Albanian population. With over 200,000 people displaced from their homes in just four months, the Security Council imposed Resolution 1199 on 23 September 1998, which demanded a ceasefire and the opening of negotiations. NATO threatened air strikes, despite opposition from Russia, yet civilian massacres continued to occur. International attempts by an international contact group in Rambouillet, France, and elsewhere, proved unsuccessful in negotiating a provisional agreement for an autonomous Kosovo under Yugoslav sovereignty. Serbian attacks on Kosovo continued and NATO was forced to launch an air campaign against Serbia lasting from 24 March to 8 June 1999. The Security Council imposed Resolution 1244 on 10 June 1999,[76] which temporarily suspended the exercise in Kosovo of Serbian sovereignty, and replaced it with an interim international presence pending a final settlement on 'substantial self-government for Kosovo', 'taking full account of . . . the demilitarization of the KLA'.

All members of the Security Council except China, which abstained throughout, had voted unanimously for these measures. As for the international civil and security presence authorised for Kosovo by Resolution 1244, it was intended to govern Kosovo by means of a Constitutional Framework adopted by the Secretary General's Special Representative on the basis of Security Council authority, and thus the authority of the UN Charter.[77] Both Security Council Resolution 1244 (1999) and the Constitutional Framework were still in force when the Kosovo Albanian representatives announced Kosovo's Unilateral Declaration of Independence from the Republic of Serbia

---

76 Resolution 1244 was expressly adopted on the basis of Chapter VII of the UN Charter and therefore clearly imposes international legal obligations.
77 The outcome of the final status process was left open in Resolution 1244.

on 17 February 2008.[78] As the Special Representative continues to wield considerable supervisory powers and international authority over the Provisional Institutions of Self-Government in Kosovo, the authors of the declaration acted on the basis of the inherent right of the Kosovo Albanian majority to exercise their self-determination, inasmuch as this right adheres to them alone, regardless of changes in their territorial administration. Accordingly, although the declaration expressly commits Kosovo to fulfil its international obligations, the management of Kosovo's external relations remains technically the prerogative of the Secretary General's Special Representative.

As it was entitled to do in accordance with UN Charter Article 96, the General Assembly, at the request of Serbia, referred the matter of the legality in international law of Kosovo's declaration to the ICJ on 8 October 2008. Written submissions were requested by 17 April 2009, and oral statements were scheduled for early December of the same year. The Court rendered its opinion on 22 July 2010. It first decided unanimously that the Court had jurisdiction over the legal question. However, in terms of the Court's discretion as to whether it should provide an opinion, the panel was divided, deciding by nine votes to five that it should comply with the request.[79] The Court then adopted a highly systematic approach to the central legal question in two stages: first, the compatibility of the declaration with general international law was considered, after which it examined the positive legal relevance of Security Council Resolution 1244, adopted on 10 June 1999. In conclusion, the Court held by a majority of ten votes to four that it 'is of the opinion that the declaration of independence of Kosovo adopted on 17 February 2008 did not violate international law'.[80]

The Court found, in relation to general international law, that there were numerous occasions during earlier centuries when declarations of independence were issued, while during the second half of the 20th century, the right of self-determination had prompted the emergence of many new states.[81] After noting that 'the scope of the principle of territorial integrity

---

78 The declaration was formulated at an extraordinary meeting of the Kosovo Assembly on 17 February which was boycotted by its Serb members. One hundred and nine Assembly members out of 120, including the province's President and Prime Minister, voted for the declaration. *Accordance with International Law of the Unilateral Declaration of Independence in Respect of Kosovo (Advisory Opinion)* [22 July 2010] ICJ, General List No. 141, para. 76.

79 Judges Buergenthal (USA), Greenwood (UK) and Abraham (France) were in the majority. The opposing states included Judge Skotnikov (Russian Federation). Judge Hanqin (China) was not present.

80 Again, Judges Buergenthal, Greenwood and Abraham voted with the majority. The opposing states included Judge Skotnikov.

81 *Kosovo (Advisory Opinion)*, supra note 78, para. 79. The Court nonetheless avoided the more general questions of a right to secede territorially, or a right of remedial self-determination. *Ibid.*, paras. 82–3.

is confined to the sphere of relations between States,[82] it pointed out that any condemnations by the Security Council in the past of declarations of independence had not stemmed from their unilateral character, but instead, from violations of international norms. Otherwise, there was no consistent state practice or *opinio juris* against declarations of independence in general and the Court concluded that 'the declaration of independence of 17 February 2008 did not violate general international law'.[83] The Court then turned to Security Council Resolution 1244 and the Constitutional Framework for Kosovo, the object and purpose of which were to establish a temporary, exceptional administration for Kosovo pending the development of meaningful self-government.

The Court first drew a distinction between general international law and Security Council resolutions, in that the latter must be drafted and voted on and can be binding on all member states. The Court noted that Resolution 1244 had been intended, for humanitarian purposes, to stabilise Kosovo and reconstruct a basic public order, but provided neither a permanent institutional framework for Kosovo, nor a termination timetable. Moreover, the Court did not find any specific prohibition on issuing a declaration of independence and it also noted that the Secretary General's Special Representative greeted the declaration with silence, even though he was under a duty to take action only against *ultra vires* acts 'of the Provisional Institutions of Self-Government designed to take effect within the legal order for the supervision of which he was responsible'.[84] Therefore, the Court concluded, the declaration:

> [W]as not issued by the Provisional Institutions of Self-Government, nor was it an act intended to take effect, or actually taking effect, within the legal order in which those Provisional Institutions operated. It follows that the authors of the declaration of independence were not bound by the framework of powers and responsibilities established to govern the conduct of the Provisional Institutions of Self-Government. Accordingly, the Court finds that the declaration of independence did not violate the Constitutional Framework.[85]

Among the four dissenting opinions on the merits was that of Judge Skotnikov (Russian Federation), whose disagreement with the majority rested both on the question of discretion, and the substantive issues. Judge Skotnikov felt it was inappropriate for the Court to attempt to interpret for legal purposes the action taken by the Security Council in its political

---

82  *Ibid.*, para. 80.
83  *Ibid.*, para. 84.
84  *Ibid.*, para. 108.
85  *Ibid.*, para. 121.

discretion, particularly as the latter 'itself has refrained from making a determination as to whether the [declaration] is in accordance with its Resolution 1244'.[86] He disagreed that Resolution 1244 did not impose obligations on the Kosovo Albanian leadership, as otherwise it made it appear the Security Council had created a 'giant loophole',[87] enabling the Kosovo Albanian majority to circumvent the Constitutional Framework by acting outside it. Judge Skotnikov considered the Court's interpretation of general international law to be misleading and potentially inflammatory. He preferred the view that such declarations should be considered in conjunction with claims for statehood,[88] regarding which latter the Court had refused to make any comment. He concluded by intimating that the political process in Kosovo had yet to run its course and receive endorsement by the Security Council.

In summary, what emerges from the majority's decision on Kosovo's independence, as just examined, is that a narrow and limited legal approach to acts that are not positively prohibited in general international law does not necessarily open the door to an inference that such acts are positively permitted. On the contrary, the ICJ majority refused to find a positive right of revolution, just as it avoided any consideration of the lawful parameters for exercises in self-determination by non-colonial groups, 'remedial' rights of self-determination, and/or rights of territorial secession.[89] This conclusion, in turn, conveys valuable information for purposes of assessing the wider reaches of autonomous state action generally and, in particular, those actions adopted against political opponents of many types. Accordingly, in that the international community's highest judicial authorities have thus recognised a broad and residual scope for state political discretion when tasked by or through law to exercise certain powers, alternative means must exist for holding those states accountable should those powers be abused. The majority on the ICJ bench may not have found a positive right of revolution, per se, but they did find that in certain circumstances there is no legal prohibition against revolution.

## Conclusion

As this brief survey of domestic anti-terrorist action illustrates, states align their compliance obligations in accordance with their self-interests. The Security Council is well placed to lead by example when requiring certain rules of international behaviour. Nonetheless, even though Security Council action may have legal consequences at both the international and domestic

---

86 *Kosovo (Advisory Opinion)*, Dissenting Opinion of Judge Skotnikov, para. 4.
87 *Ibid.*, para. 14.
88 *Ibid.*, para. 17.
89 *Kosovo (Advisory Opinion)*, supra note 78, paras 51–6.

state level, UN action is taken in a political environment that seeks to maintain international peace and security. This requires compromise, of foremost importance to which is the scope left for changes to be made to an existing map of states and territories. The fact of geopolitical change made in the post-Cold War world order is thus reflected in the ICJ majority's decision on Kosovo's bid for independence, inasmuch as many peoples have a right to determine for themselves the shape and direction of their future lives. There must thus remain room for the ancient revolutionary tradition of rejecting injustice.

Nonetheless, the indeterminate content of substantive rights in the principle of self-determination remains problematic in terms both of war and peacetime conditionality. The General Assembly's request to the ICJ for judicial guidance and advice on Kosovo's declaration of independence was thus particularly useful for gaining further insights into the central role played by lawful uses of force as opposed to mere violence, particularly as states have too often relied in the past on the principle of non-interference in each other's domestic affairs, yet, in acting as they please, states simply continue to sow the seeds of future difficulties. What thus remains of concern is the scope for broad levels of state discretion when authorising and using 'anti-terrorist' violence against political opponents of many descriptions. For example, even the Permanent Member States in the Security Council curtail individual rights of expression and association, and include groups struggling for national liberation in their broad definitions of terrorism.

Proscription lists, spearheaded initially by the UK for Northern Irish separatists, play a crucial role. France and the US have little 'home-grown' terrorist violence, but continue to seek means to prevent harm to their respective and extensive worldwide interests. The US permits the assassination anywhere of persons it deems to be terrorist enemies, as does the Russian Federation. Therefore, although the importance of certain legal human rights principles, such as people's rights to self-determination, has become such that states today should no longer be permitted to rely on Charter Article 2(7) to avoid external scrutiny, issues of statehood and independence generally are likely to remain of paramount concern, whether or not force has been used in contravention of peremptory norms of general international law. Accordingly, rights of self-determination may well be contested in international law, but revolution cannot be, inasmuch as more dangers to world peace today lurk in indeterminate states rights, than in those of self-determination.

# 7  Conclusions and final remarks

The use by states of the global anti-terror agenda to neutralise struggles for self-determination has characterised the post-9/11 era. The existence of international solidarity to prevent acts of international terrorism is, of course, a good thing, as non-state actors who inflict indiscriminate forms of harm and destruction to attain their own preferred political, ideological, religious, etc., life choices, cause everyone to suffer. Nonetheless, the serious politics of self-determination are at a dangerous crossroads, particularly as demands for self-determination are raised by people 'whom history has assaulted',[1] and there are many reasons which justify a renewed look at the principle.

But what, precisely is meant by self-determination? By the outbreak of the Second World War, a general concept of self-determination had certainly emerged, but that early concept was quickly overtaken by real world events, such that questions as to the relative importance of economic dependence, as distinct from *political* self-determination, soon lessened in importance. Instead, as the politics of self-determination were slowly transformed in the early UN era into tools of bipolar rivalry, 'internal' equal human rights of peoples would be viewed as far more important, at the expense of 'external' entitlements a people might demand, such as to secede territorially, or to control historic lands or natural resources, as is now summarised in conclusions and final remarks.

## Conclusions

The UN failed to hard-wire much clarity into the Charter principle of self-determination for a reason: this negligence has ensured a continuing circularity of 'rights' incorporations within the principle of self-determination. It thus is hardly surprising that the first Charter reference to self-determination is indirect, as found in the non-binding preamble: '[w]e the Peoples of the United Nations'. The post-1945 international order may have formalised the existence of a principle of self-determination, but that

---

1 S. Barry, 'Upfront', *The Observer Magazine*, 4 October 2009, p. 10.

principle has remained little more than the poor relation of an individually focused human rights paradigm. Of more concern, the right of self-determination is the first such 'right' to be edged to vanishing point in the modern anti-terrorist agenda.[2]

The innovative attempt made in the UN era to place an international rights agenda as central to that organisation's future contains one core weakness – the Charter paradigm requires a formal approach to equal state sovereignty that bears little relation to reality. The seeming paradox that results creates no enigma, however. Sovereign states are made responsible for incorporating their international obligations into domestic laws, which helps to square the power circle underpinning (un-)equal sovereignty. A Charter drafted by states for states was likely to change little on that score, and Charter Article 2(7) has generally been given an expansive meaning. Such issues were introduced in Chapters 1 and 2.

The advantages to states of favouring individual human rights over those of groups are thus fully reflected in the impact of the 'zero-tolerance' approach adopted by the UN towards individuals *and* groups deemed to be involved in acts of terrorism. 'Zero tolerance' represents a state-co-ordinated approach to non-state political opposition. Initially adopted by certain dominant states, it is the United Nations itself today that is utilised to pressure all states to proceed likewise. As certain legal obligations have been placed on states by Security Council action adopted pursuant to Charter VII of the Charter,[3] states are legally bound to comply. In turn, such Security Council requirements alone have caused a 'veritable surge of legal activity at the international, regional and national levels . . . of new norms and mechanisms designed to deal with terrorism'.[4]

It may well be 'widely accepted that state responses to terrorism should be proportionately compatible with the values of an open society',[5] but many governments have been so very active in creating broad forms of anti-terrorist legislation that they preside today over far less open 'societies' than they might otherwise have done. Most crucially, governments are enabled by post-9/11 *international* anti-terrorist obligations to bear down particularly harshly on their *domestic* struggles for self-determination. Accordingly, the operation of anti-terror domestic laws is less likely to have much in common with the far stronger international obligations relating to state uses of armed force, in that incorporation in domestic criminal peacetime laws will more closely reflect local power structures.

---

2  See, e.g., A. Asthana, *et al.*, 'Britain Scraps Report on Human Rights Abuses', *The Observer*, 22 August 2010, p. 1 (commercial interests prioritised over states' human rights records).

3  See, e.g., L.M.H. Martinez, 'The Legislative Role of the Security Council In Its Fight Against Terrorism: Legal, Political and Practical Limits' [2008] 57(2) *I.C.L.Q.* 333.

4  Book Review, Moeckli, 'Ben Saul, Defining Terrorism in International Law' [2007] 7 *H.R.L.R.* 643.

5  H. Davis, 'Lessons from Turkey: Anti-Terrorism Legislation and the Protection of Free Speech' [2005] 1 *E.H.R.L.R.* 75.

That is why the rise of extremist Islamic violence has only muddied the waters of self-determination as much as, if not more than, the prior state sponsorship utilised so frequently during the Cold War era. Traditional military contexts of 'necessity' and 'proportionality' are in danger of losing much of their value, inasmuch as governments prefer the more utilitarian frameworks of broad political discretion when taking forceful action against 'terrorists'. For example, laws of armed conflict cannot prohibit collateral harm to civilians or their objects if inflicted during pursuit of a genuine military objective. Peacetime human rights provisions, in contrast, require governments to show that conditions of absolute necessity exist before they resort to force.[6] If faced with an emergency situation that 'threatens the life of the nation', states may derogate from the right to life only 'to the extent strictly required by the exigencies of the situation',[7] as expanded on in Chapters 3 and 4.

The fact remains, however, that many riots or insurrections are fuelled by deep structural imbalances within societies, so no single definition of terrorism can command full international approval, which makes it difficult to see what the adoption of a global definition of terrorism at UN level could accomplish, particularly as such a definition would not be extended to forms of state terror. Neither has it been a concern generally in the early sectoral anti-terrorist instruments and later codifications to pay much attention to rights of self-determination. This means that what state-level support there may be for a lingering distinction between terrorists and freedom fighters is left to regional agreement, which is likely only to differentiate between the two in order to show ethnic or cultural solidarity elsewhere, even though by so doing, those codifications run the risk of being seen to interfere in the domestic affairs of other states as a matter of regional policy, as was discussed in Chapter 5.

In turn, the current judicial unwillingness to afford equal weight to laws of armed conflict when trying persons suspected of breaching more recent anti-terrorist provisions adopted in a 'zero-tolerance' approach to terrorism, as discussed in Chapter 6, is truly alarming. As different political systems create criminal laws peculiar to each,[8] Chapter 6 adopted a state-by-state overview of how the five Permanent Member States of the Security Council adopt forceful action against 'terrorists', in terms of their individual state constitutional arrangements. The review revealed deepening levels of state secrecy and surveillance powers, a greater involvement of private corporate interests, lengthening proscription 'terror lists', a tendency to impose criminal liability automatically and reduced access by a 'new class of outlaw' to ordinary rights of due process.[9]

---

6 See, e.g., Article 2 of the ECHR.
7 See, e.g., Article 15 ECHR.
8 See H. Kelsen, *The Communist Theory of Law* (New York: Frederick A. Praeger, Inc., 1955), p. 102.
9 Book Review, Sedley, 'Enemies of All Mankind', *L.R.B.*, 24 June 2010, p. 33.

The value of government restraint, civil liberties and human rights should not be forgotten so easily, however, particularly in relation to the administration of justice, inasmuch as terrorism raises aggravating factors of terms of criminality or when sentencing.[10] Even the International Military Tribunal held at Nuremberg after the Second World War required proof of personal involvement and culpability before it imposed individual criminal responsibility on the former Nazi leaders.[11] In contrast, as the traditional 'terrorist' requirement of an intentional act of violence perpetrated with a political, ideological and/or religious 'terrorist' motive is slowly loosened in order to extend criminal prohibitions to many others, a steady conflation of political, ideological and/or religious motivations with the separatist or other self-determining goals pursued by certain liberation groups – only some of whom may be sponsored through extremist Islamic networks – suffices.

This then permits a concluding inference – that the renewed drive to end self-determination by means of anti-terrorism can be located in the wider reaches of dominant state self-preservation in a less certain post-Cold War era. In other words, once *all* acts of non-state violence are prohibited, structural inequalities between states themselves can be more securely entrenched. For this purpose, the old notion of strategic pre-emption, as utilised in German policy in the early 20th century, has been revived in the 'war on terror'. In the military sense, pre-emption involves the destruction of the enemy's weapons before they can be used, while a pre-emptive 'war on terror' justifies a broad approach to state self-defence, in order 'to arrest a development that is not yet operational and hence is not yet directly threatening, but which, if permitted to mature, could be neutralised only at a high, possibly unacceptable, cost',[12] 'even where there is no reason to believe that an attack is planned'.[13] Not only do states continue to assault each other, albeit today in search of 'terrorists', but they simultaneously attempt to block any unfavourable shifts in the balance of power between them.[14]

---

10 See, e.g., M.S.-A. Wattad, 'Is Terrorism a Crime or an Aggravating Factor in Sentencing?' [2006] 4 *J.Int'l.Crim.J.* 1017.

11 This was particularly difficult in the context of the 'economic case'. See T. Taylor, *The Anatomy of the Nuremberg Trials* (London: Bloomsbury, 1993), p. 92, who queries 'why were contributions to the Nazi Party criminal any more than Vickers' contributions to the Conservative Party or Du Pont's to Republican or Democratic Party funds?'. See generally 'The I.M.T. (Nuremberg), Judgement and Sentences, 1 October 1946', reprinted at [1947] 41 *A.J.I.L.* 172.

12 N.A. Shah, 'Self-defence, Anticipatory Self-defence and Pre-emption: International Law's Response to Terrorism' [2007] 12 *J.Con.&Sec.L.* 95, at 112 (quoting Professor Reisman [2003]). Cf. the US National Security Strategy 2002, georgewbush-whitehouse.archives.gov/nsc/nss/2002/index.html.

13 N.A. Shah, supra note 12, p. 112 (citing Professor O'Connell [2002]).

14 *Ibid.*

# Final remarks

Throughout this book an attempt has been made to take a fresh look at contemporary debates surrounding the self-determination of peoples and their uses of force in the context of action adopted by states in the post-9/11 era against terrorism. It has been remarked at several points that many new powers afforded by international anti-terrorist action are being utilised in effect to neutralise various liberationist causes. The original promotion of self-determination in 1945, e.g., to restore former colonial lands, constituted just part of an agenda to rectify historical injustice, to restore inter-state friendly relations and for certain states, to liberate international trade. Subsequent events did not transpire so peacefully, and today's blanket condemnation of all non-state violent acts by overemphasising status and ignoring causation constitutes only a modern attempt to turn back the clock.

As many former limits on state powers to use force are diluted in order to re-impose and freeze an existing map of state units, the indeterminate content of substantive rights in the principle of self-determination remains problematic in terms both of war and of peace. Certain patterns in recent state practice signal only an intensifying mutuality to halt further progress towards human rights and humanitarian restraints. The recent General Assembly request to the ICJ for judicial guidance and advice on Kosovo's declaration of independence and exercise in self-determination, for example, has resulted in useful, if controversial, judicial insights into the politics of self-determination, revolution and territorial secession, but the preference of states so often in the past to rely on the principle of non-interference in one another's domestic affairs does not bode well for the future.

The principle of non-interference is thus the reason why the vagaries of self-determination today have become symptomatic of a Charter era in which international law is not adopted as a legal yardstick to decide international and domestic questions alike. It is instead a matter of interpretation for governments to integrate self-determination 'causes' into a global anti-terrorist agenda, in order strategically to pre-empt and silence political opponents, to treat different categories of citizens and groups unequally on grounds of 'security',[15] and to turn a non-interfering, blind eye to 'authorised' forms of state violence occurring elsewhere. To consider this damaging to the rule of law and the administration of justice generally is to state the obvious, but inasmuch as international 'peace' *and* 'security' are rather more complicated than their maintenance between states alone, the principle of non-interference also disregards a fundamental individual human right to protect oneself and to seek help when doing so.

Accordingly, the focus of this book might have been directed towards an attempt to highlight a steady increase in the strength of self-determination

---

15 See, e.g., N. Watt and H. Sherwood, 'David Cameron: Israeli Blockade has Turned Gaza Strip into a "Prison Camp"', *The Guardian*, 27 July 2010, guardian.co.uk.

in customary international law, but the post-9/11 era demonstrates instead that the provisions contained in the UN Charter to ensure international peace and security do not go nearly far enough. State responsibility at the macro level is needed, of course, but micro levels of autonomy are certainly more conducive to a generalised sense of peace *and* security. *Rights* to self-determination, and to struggle for it, are therefore likely to remain creatures of both circumstance and opportunity, as they were for the Permanent Members of the Security Council, which would not be the states they are today had they, too, not at some point undergone revolutionary change.[16] This indicates not only that every state should remain mindful of recurring patterns in human behaviour, but further, that 'terrorist' violence, worker strikes, peasant uprisings, inter-ethnic frictions, resource scarcity, etc., will continue to ensure that modern struggles for self-determination are easier to provoke than to manage.

16 E.g., in China, in 1911, 1913, 1926–7, 1946–50, and 1966–76; France, in 1789–99, 1848, and 1871; Russia, in 1905, 1917–21, and 1991; the UK, in 1640–60 and 1688 (disregarding Irish secession); the USA, in 1775–83, 1812 and 1861–5 (disregarding the African–American civil rights movement).

# Appendix: documents

## Chapter 1

### *Atlantic Charter of 14 August 1941*

[Department of State Executive Agreement, Series No. 236. The Atlantic Charter was formulated during the Atlantic Conference held at sea between US President Roosevelt and Prime Minister Churchill to discuss their war strategy against the Axis Powers. The Atlantic Charter would form the basis of the 1945 UN Charter.]

The President of the United States of America and the Prime Minister, Mr. Churchill, representing His Majesty's Government in the United Kingdom, being met together, deem it right to make known certain common principles in the national policies of their respective countries on which they base their hopes for a better future for the world.

First, their countries seek no aggrandizement, territorial or other;

Second, they desire to see no territorial changes that do not accord with the freely expressed wishes of the peoples concerned;

Third, they respect the right of all peoples to choose the form of government under which they will live; and they wish to see sovereign rights and self government restored to those who have been forcibly deprived of them;

Fourth, they will endeavour, with due respect for their existing obligations, to further the enjoyment by all States, great or small, victor or vanquished, of access, on equal terms, to the trade and to the raw materials of the world which are needed for their economic prosperity;

Fifth, they desire to bring about the fullest collaboration between all nations in the economic field with the object of securing, for all, improved labour standards, economic advancement and social security;

Sixth, after the final destruction of the Nazi tyranny, they hope to see established a peace which will afford to all nations the means of dwelling in safety within their own boundaries, and which will afford assurance that all the men in all the lands may live out their lives in freedom from fear and want;

Seventh, such a peace should enable all men to traverse the high seas and oceans without hindrance;

Eighth, they believe that all of the nations of the world, for realistic as well as spiritual reasons must come to the abandonment of the use of force. Since no future peace can be maintained if land, sea or air armaments continue to be employed by nations which threaten, or may threaten, aggression outside of their frontiers, they believe, pending the establishment of a wider and permanent system of general security, that the disarmament of such nations is essential. They will likewise aid and encourage all other practicable measures which will lighten for peace-loving peoples the crushing burden of armaments.

## Charter of the United Nations of 26 June 1945
### (pertinent provisions)

Article 2(7): Nothing contained in the present charter shall authorize the U.N. to intervene in matters which are essentially within the domestic jurisdiction of any state or shall require the Members to submit such matters to settlement under the present Charter; but this principle shall not prejudice the application of enforcement measures under Chapter VII.

Article 4(1): Membership in the UN is open to all [. . .] peace-loving states which accept the obligations contained in the present Charter and, in the judgement of the Organization, are able and willing to carry out these obligations.

Article 23(1): The Security Council shall consist of fifteen Members of the UN. . . .

Article 23(2): The non-permanent Members of the Security Council shall be elected for a term of two years. . . .

Article 24(1): In order to ensure prompt and effective action by the UN, its Members confer on the Security Council primary responsibility for the maintenance of international peace and security. . . .

Article 34: The Security Council may investigate any dispute, or any situation which might lead to international friction or give rise to a dispute, in order to determine whether the continuance of the dispute or situation is likely to endanger the maintenance of international peace and security.

Article 39: The Security Council shall determine the existence of any threat to the peace, breach of the peace, or act of aggression and shall make recommendations, or decide what measures shall be taken. . . .

Article 51: Nothing in the present Charter shall impair the inherent right of individual or collective self-defence if an armed attack occurs against a Member of the UN, until the Security Council has taken measures necessary to maintain international peace and security. Measures taken by Members in the exercise of this right of self-defence shall be immediately reported to the Security Council. . . .

Article 103: In the event of a conflict between the obligations of the Members of the UN under the present Charter and their obligations under any other international agreement, their obligations under the present Charter shall prevail.

# Chapter 2

## Covenant of the League of Nations of 28 June 1919 (pertinent provision)

Article 15(8): If the dispute between the parties is claimed by one of them, and is found by the Council, to arise out of a matter which by international law is solely within the domestic jurisdiction of that party, the Council shall so report, and shall make no recommendation as to its settlement.

## Charter of the United Nations of 26 June 1945 (pertinent provisions)

Preamble: We the Peoples of the United Nations Determined to save succeeding generations from the scourge of war, which twice in our lifetime has brought untold sorrow to mankind, and to reaffirm faith in fundamental human rights, in the dignity and worth of the human person, in the equal rights of men and women and of nations large and small, and to establish conditions under which justice and respect for the obligations arising from treaties and other sources of international law can be maintained, and to promote social progress and better standards of life in larger freedom,
[. . .].

## The Purposes of the UN are:

Article 1(1): To maintain international peace and security, and to that end: to take effective collective measures for the prevention and removal of threats to the peace, and for the suppression of acts of aggression or other breaches of the peace, and to bring about by peaceful means, and in conformity with the principles of justice and international law, adjustment or settlement of international disputes or situations which might lead to a breach of the peace [. . .].

Article 1(2): To develop friendly relations among nations based on respect for the principle of equal rights and self-determination of peoples, and to take other appropriate measures to strengthen universal peace; [...].

Article 2(1): The Organization is based on the principle of the sovereign equality of all its Members.

Article 2(3): All Members shall settle their international disputes by peaceful means in such a manner that international peace and security, and justice, are not endangered.

Article 2(4): All Members shall refrain in their international relations from the threat or use of force against the territorial integrity or political independence of any state, or in any other manner inconsistent with the Purposes of the United Nations.

Article 55: With a view to the creation of conditions of stability and well-being which are necessary for peaceful and friendly relations among nations based on respect for the principle of equal rights and self-determination of peoples, the United Nations shall promote:

a.  higher standards of living, full employment, and conditions of economic and social progress and development;
b.  solutions of international economic, social, health, and related problems; and international cultural and educational cooperation; and
c.  universal respect for, and observance of, human rights and fundamental freedoms for all without distinction as to race, sex, language, or religion.

[...].

## The Economic and Social Council

Article 62(2): It may make recommendations for the purpose of promoting respect for, and observance of, human rights and fundamental freedoms for all.

Article 73: Members of the United Nations which have or assume responsibilities for the administration of territories whose peoples have not yet attained a full measure of self-government recognize the principle that the interests of the inhabitants of these territories are paramount, and accept as a sacred trust the obligation to promote to the utmost, within the system of international peace and security established by the present Charter, the well-being of the inhabitants of these territories, and, to this end:

a.  to ensure, with due respect for the culture of the peoples concerned, their political, economic, social, and educational advancement, their just treatment, and their protection against abuses;

b.  to develop self-government, to take due account of the political aspirations of the peoples, and to assist them in the progressive development of their free political institutions, according to the particular circumstances of each territory and its peoples and their varying stages of advancement;
c.  to further international peace and security;
d.  to promote constructive measures of development, to encourage research, and to co-operate with one another and, when and where appropriate, with specialized international bodies with a view to the practical achievement of the social, economic, and scientific purposes set forth in this Article; and
e.  to transmit regularly to the Secretary-General for information purposes, subject to such limitation as security and constitutional considerations may require, statistical and other information of a technical nature relating to economic, social, and educational conditions in the territories for which they are respectively responsible other than those territories to which Chapters XII and XIII apply.

[. . .].

Article 76: The basic objectives of the trusteeship system, in accordance with the Purposes of the United Nations laid down in Article 1 of the present Charter, shall be:

a.  to further international peace and security;
b.  to promote the political, economic, social, and educational advancement of the inhabitants of the trust territories, and their progressive development towards self-government or independence as may be appropriate to the particular circumstances of each territory and its peoples and the freely expressed wishes of the peoples concerned, and as may be provided by the terms of each trusteeship agreement;
c.  to encourage respect for human rights and for fundamental freedoms for all without distinction as to race, sex, language, or religion, and to encourage recognition of the interdependence of the peoples of the world; and
d.  to ensure equal treatment in social, economic, and commercial matters for all Members of the United Nations and their nationals, and also equal treatment for the latter in the administration of justice, without prejudice to the attainment of the foregoing objectives and subject to the provisions of Article 80.

Article 83(1): All functions of the United Nations relating to strategic areas, including the approval of the terms of the trusteeship agreements and of their alteration or amendment shall be exercised by the Security Council.

Article 84: It shall be the duty of the administering authority to ensure that the trust territory shall play its part in the maintenance of international peace and security. To this end the administering authority may make use of volunteer forces, facilities, and assistance from the trust territory in carrying out the obligations towards the Security Council undertaken in this regard by the administering authority, as well as for local defence and the maintenance of law and order within the trust territory.

## Chapter 3

### Preamble to the 1899 Hague Convention II [Preamble to the 1907 Hague Convention IV] (the 'de Martens' clause)

Until a more complete code of the laws of war is [has been] issued, the High Contracting Parties think it right [deem it expedient] to declare that in cases not included in the Regulations adopted by them, populations [the inhabitants] and belligerents remain under the protection and empire [the rule] of the principles of international law [the law of nations], as they result from the usages established between/among civilized nations, from the laws of humanity and the requirements [dictates] of the public conscience.

### Article 23 of the Regulations annexed to the 1907 Hague Convention IV (in pertinent part)

In addition to the prohibitions provided by special Conventions, it is especially forbidden—

(a) to employ poison or poisoned weapons;
(b) to kill or wound treacherously individuals belonging to the hostile nation or army;
(c) to kill or wound an enemy who, having laid down his arms, or having no longer means of defence, has surrendered at discretion;
(d) to declare that no quarter will be given;
(e) to employ arms, projectiles, or material calculated to cause unnecessary suffering.
[. . .].

### Common Article 2 of the four Geneva Conventions of 1949

[The territorial 'link' required for international responsibility.]

In addition to the provisions which shall be implemented in peacetime, the present Convention shall apply to all cases of declared war or of any other armed conflict which may arise between two or more of the High Contracting Parties, even if the state of war is not recognized by one of them.

The Convention shall also apply to all cases of partial or total occupation of the territory of a High Contracting Party, even if the said occupation meets with no armed resistance.

Although one of the Powers in conflict may not be a party to the present Convention, the Powers who are parties thereto shall remain bound by it in their mutual relations. They shall furthermore be bound by the Convention in relation to the said Power, if the latter accepts and applies the provisions thereof.

### 1977 Additional Protocol 1 to the four Geneva Conventions of 1949 (pertinent provisions)

Article 1(2): In cases not covered by this Protocol or by other international agreements, civilians and combatants remain under the protection and authority of the principles of international law derived from established custom, from the principles of humanity and from the dictates of public conscience.

Article 1(3): This Protocol, which supplements the Geneva Conventions of 12 August 1949 for the protection of war victims, shall apply in the situations referred to in Article 2 common to those Conventions.

Article 35:
1. In any armed conflict, the right of the Parties to the conflict to choose methods or means of warfare is not unlimited.
2. It is prohibited to employ weapons, projectiles and material and methods of warfare of a nature to cause superfluous injury or unnecessary suffering.
3. It is prohibited to employ methods or means of warfare which are intended, or may be expected, to cause widespread, long-term and severe damage to the natural environment.

Article 51(6): Attacks against the civilian population or civilians by way of reprisals are prohibited.

### Rome Statute of the International Criminal Court of 1998 (pertinent provisions)

Article 5(1): The jurisdiction of the Court shall be limited to the most serious crimes of concern to the international community as a whole. The Court has jurisdiction in accordance with this Statute with respect to the following crimes:

(a) the crime of genocide;
(b) crimes against humanity;
(c) war crimes;
(d) the crime of aggression.

Article 12: Preconditions to the exercise of jurisdiction:

1.  A State which becomes a Party to this Statute thereby accepts the jurisdiction of the Court with respect to the crimes referred to in Article 5.
2.  In the case of Article 13(a) or (c) [concerning the exercise of jurisdiction], the Court may exercise its jurisdiction if one or more of the following States are Parties to this Statute or have accepted the jurisdiction of the Court in accordance with paragraph 3:

    (a) the State on the territory of which the conduct in question occurred or, if the crime was committed on board a vessel or aircraft, the State of registration of that vessel or aircraft;
    (b) the State of which the person accused of the crime is a national.

3.  If the acceptance of a State which is not a Party to this Statute is required under paragraph 2, that State may, by declaration lodged with the Registrar, accept the exercise of jurisdiction by the Court with respect to the crime in question. The accepting State shall cooperate with the Court without any delay or exception in accordance with Part 9.

## Chapter 6

### US Constitution of 1787 (as amended)
### (pertinent provision)

Article 1 Section 8: [the legislative powers of the US Congress include] To regulate Commerce with foreign Nations, and among the several States, and with the Indian Tribes; . . . To define and punish Piracies and Felonies committed on the high Seas, and Offences against the Law of Nations; To declare War, grant Letters of Marque and Reprisal, and make Rules concerning Captures on Land and Water; To raise and support Armies, but no Appropriation of Money to that Use shall be for a longer Term than two Years; To provide and maintain a Navy; To make Rules for the Government and Regulation of the land and naval Forces; To provide for calling forth the Militia to execute the Laws of the Union, suppress Insurrections and repel Invasions; To provide for organizing, arming, and disciplining, the Militia, and for governing such Part of them as may be employed in the Service of the US, reserving to the States respectively, the Appointment of the Officers, and the Authority of training the Militia according to the discipline prescribed by Congress.

### US Patriot Act of 2001 Section 802

(a) Domestic Terrorism Defined – Section 2331 of title 18, US Code, is amended—

(1) in paragraph (1)(B)(iii), by striking 'by assassination or kidnapping' and inserting 'by mass destruction, assassination, or kidnapping';
(2) in paragraph (3), by striking 'and';
(3) in paragraph (4), by striking the period at the end and inserting; 'and'; and
(4) by adding at the end the following:

'(5)  the term "domestic terrorism" means activities that
'(A)  involve acts dangerous to human life that are a violation of the criminal laws of the US or of any State;
'(B)  appear to be intended—

'(i)  to intimidate or coerce a civilian population;
'(ii)  to influence the policy of a government by intimidation or coercion; or
'(iii)  to affect the conduct of a government by mass destruction, assassination, or kidnapping; and

"(C)  occur primarily within the territorial jurisdiction of the US.'

(b) Conforming Amendment—Section 3077(1) of title 18, US Code, is amended to read as follows:
'(1)  "act of terrorism" means an act of domestic or international terrorism as defined in section 2331'.

### Title 18 US Code (2004) Section 2332b(g)(5)(B)

[Subcaptions have been shortened.]

(g) Definitions. As used in this section—
(5) the term 'Federal crime of terrorism' means an offence that—
(B) is a violation of—

(i) sections 32 (destruction of aircraft or aircraft facilities), 37 (violence at international airports), 81 (arson within special maritime and territorial jurisdiction), 175 or 175b (biological weapons), 229 (chemical weapons), subsection (a), (b), (c), or (d) of section 351 (congressional, cabinet, and Supreme Court assassination and kidnapping), 831 (nuclear materials), 842(m) or (n) (plastic explosives), 844(f)(2) or (3) (arson and bombing of Government property risking or causing death), 844(i) (arson and bombing of property used in interstate commerce), 930(c) (killing or attempt during attack on a Federal facility with a dangerous weapon), 956(a)(1) (conspiracy to murder, kidnap, or maim persons abroad), 1030(a)(1) (computer protection), 1030(a)(5)(A)(i) (computer protection), 1114 (killing or attempt of US officers and employees), 1116 (murder or manslaughter of foreign officials, etc.), 1203 (hostage taking),

1362 (destruction of communication lines, etc.), 1363 (injury to buildings or property in special maritime and territorial US jurisdiction), 1366(a) (destruction of an energy facility), 1751(a), (b), (c), or (d) (Presidential and staff assassination and kidnapping), 1992 (wrecking trains), 1993 (terrorist attacks and violence against mass transport), 2155 (destruction of national defense materials, etc.), 2280 (violence against maritime navigation), 2281 (maritime fixed platforms), 2332 (homicides and violence against US nationals outside the US), 2332a (use of WMD), 2332b (acts of terrorism transcending national boundaries), 2332f (bombing of public places, etc.), 2339 (harboring terrorists), 2339A (providing material support to terrorists), 2339B (providing material support to terrorist organizations), 2339C (financing of terrorism), or 2340A (torture) of this title;

(ii) sections 92 (prohibitions governing atomic weapons) or 236 (sabotage of nuclear facilities or fuel) of the Atomic Energy Act of 1954 (42 U.S.C. 2284); or

(iii) section 46502 (aircraft piracy), the second sentence of section 46504 (assault on a flight crew with a dangerous weapon), section 46505(b)(3) or (c) (explosive or incendiary devices, or endangerment of human life by means of weapons, on aircraft), section 46506 if homicide or attempted homicide is involved (application of certain criminal laws to acts on aircraft), or section 60123(b) (destruction of interstate gas or hazardous liquid pipeline facility) of title 49; or

(iv) section 1010A of the Controlled Substances Import and Export Act (relating to narco-terrorism).

## 8 US Code (2003) Section 1189

Designation of foreign terrorist organizations
(a) Designation
(1) In general
The Secretary is authorized to designate an organization as a foreign terrorist organization in accordance with this subsection if the Secretary finds that—

(A) the organization is a foreign organization;
(B) the organization engages in terrorist activity (as defined in section 1182(a)(3)(B) of this title or terrorism (as defined in section 2656f(d)(2) of title 22), or retains the capability and intent to engage in terrorist activity or terrorism); and
(C) the terrorist activity or terrorism of the organization threatens the security of US nationals or the national security of the US.

# Index

For Product Safety Concerns and Information please contact our EU
representative GPSR@taylorandfrancis.com
Taylor & Francis Verlag GmbH, Kaufingerstraße 24, 80331 München, Germany

www.ingramcontent.com/pod-product-compliance
Lightning Source LLC
Chambersburg PA
CBHW050514280326
41932CB00014B/2316